# Food Security Policies In The SADCC Region

Citation:
Mandivamba Rukuni, Godfrey Mudimu and Thomas S. Jayne, eds. 1990. *Food Security Policies in the SADCC Region*. Proceedings of the Fifth Annual Conference on Food Security Research in Southern Africa, October 16-18, 1989. University of Zimbabwe/Michigan State University Food Security Research in Southern Africa Project, Department of Agricultural Economics and Extension, University of Zimbabwe, Harare.

# Food Security Policies In The SADCC Region

Edited by
Mandivamba Rukuni
Godfrey Mudimu
Thomas S. Jayne

Published by:

UZ/MSU Food Security Research in Southern Africa Project
Department of Agricultural Economics and Extension
University of Zimbabwe
1989

Published by:

UZ/MSU Food Security Research in Southern Africa Project
Department of Agricultural Economics and Extension
University of Zimbabwe
P.O. Box MP 167
Mount Pleasant, Harare, Zimbabwe
Telex 26580 UNIVZ ZW
Fax 263-4-303292
Telephone 303211 Ext.1516

ISBN Number 0-908307-13-6
UNIVERSITY OF ZIMBABWE 1990

Typesetting and page layout:
Daphne Chanakira and Murie Hutchison

Printed by:
Sebri Printers (Pvt) Ltd., P.O. Box AY2, Amby, Harare

# TABLE OF CONTENTS

v

# Preface

The Fifth Conference on Food Security Research in Southern Africa was held in the tradition of previous annual conferences. Researchers reported on their ongoing research while SADCC's food security civil servants reported on national efforts to improve the food security situation. Debate on national policies and the implications of research findings has improved considerably over the years.

At the genesis of SADCC in 1980, government officials accorded high priority to the need to promote food security in the region. Policy statements during this period suggest an overwhelming emphasis on accelerated food production -- the supply side of the food security equation. A highlight of the Fifth Annual Conference was Session II where national sector coordinators reported on the evolving perceptions of food security and strategies to attain it among SADCC states. This session is reported in Section II of this volume, entitled: *Perspectives on Food Security Policy Options in the SADCC Region: Country Experiences*. It is striking to note from these presentations the evolution to a more balanced view of supply- and demand-side components of food security, such as food access, demand, and nutrition. These national strategy statements, along with a comprehensive regional perspective by SADCC Food Security Unit Sector Coordinator K.J.M. Dhliwayo, are contained in Section II of this volume. This volume has been entitled *Food Security Policies in the SADCC Region* in recognition of the evolutionary nature of the national policies.

Section III of this volume presents an assessment of recent and ongoing reforms in the grain markets of Tanzania, Kenya, Zimbabwe, Mozambique, and Mali. The frequent and often radical policy vacillations described in several papers, often at the behest of foreign donors, underscores the need for timely, policy-relevant research on which viable and stabilising market polices may be based.

The papers in Section IV explore the intricate linkages between technology, marketing, trade, and household food security. Several papers shed light on the degree to which many rural farming households are unable to produce enough food to meet their own consumption requirements, due to various production and marketing constraints. Such findings carry important implications regarding the ability of price policy alone to stimulate broad based increases in food production. Other papers addressed the problems experienced in promoting small grains -- sorghum and millet -- in the region, despite their apparent agronomic suitability as food security crops in low-rainfall areas.

Sections V and VI focus on the food access side of the food security equation. Section V contains a selection of papers that widen the field of view from grains to other important contributors to food security, such as livestock and cashcropping. Forthcoming conferences will continue to report ongoing research results on the potential synergies and trade-offs between cash crop and food production. Section VI specifically focusses on constraints to food access in Malawi and Mozambique, two areas keenly affected by political and natural calamities in recent years. In Malawi, L.A.H. Msukwa argues that food insecurity is a symptom of poverty, thus requiring solutions that move the analysis far beyond agricultural development issues.

# Acknowledgements

These proceedings have been successfully published through the efforts of a number of individuals. The Editors would like to acknowledge the work done by these people. Carl Eicher carried out the first technical edit of the conference papers. The typesetting and page-layout was done by Daphne Chanakira and Murie Hutchison. Beverley Rusike helped with the typing. Lovemore Nyabako and Maxwell Chiwashira provided the computer support for the type-setters. We also appreciate the assistance of the Ministry of Information for providing the photographs for the cover.

The success of the Fifth Conference can be attributed to both the Food Security Research Project office and the back-up from Michigan State University. Mike Weber, Jim Shaffer, Rick Bernsten, Josue Dione and Carl Eicher and Janet Munn provided support from MSU for this Conference. Thembi Sibanda, assisted by Murie Hutchison, organised the Conference. Logistical support was provided by Pete Hopkins, Andrew Barnes, George Nyamatemba, Ronnie Sagwete and Darlington Sibanda.

The Conference is simply one activity of the overall project. This project has enjoyed unqualified support from Sam Muchena, John Dhliwayo and Tobias Takavarasha in the Ministry of Lands, Agriculture and Rural Resettlement. The project is funded by USAID (Southern Africa Regional Programme). Our particular appreciation to Allison Herrick, Doug Pickett and Joshua Mushauri.

The working relationships between the University of Zimbabwe and MSU is greatly strengthened by the collaboration with other universities in SADCC: University of Dar es Salaam, University of Malawi, University of Swaziland, University of Botswana and the University of Zambia. We appreciate the ongoing research being carried out by Haidari Amani, Nguyupa Lipumba, Steve Kapunda, Ben Kandoole, Ben Kaluwa, Louis Msukwa, Vincent Sithole and Jan Testerink.

Mandivamba Rukuni
Godfrey Mudimu
Thomas Jayne

# I

# Officiàl Opening

# 1

# Building African Scientific And Managerial Capacity: A Voice From Africa[1]

*Professor W.J. Kamba*[2]

## INTRODUCTION

It gives me great pleasure to join in the celebration of the Fifth Annual Conference on Food Security Research in Southern Africa. This conference has followed the tradition of the previous four conferences; it is organised and developed jointly by the SADCC Food Security Administrative and Technical Unit and the Department of Agricultural Economics and Extension of the University of Zimbabwe. Researchers, representatives of SADCC member states, donor and international agencies are assembled to distill the results of ongoing research, to identify new problems and to agree on a research agenda that is to be followed to generate information for policy makers on improving household, national and regional food security.

Over the past five years I have observed a widening and deepening of the food security research agenda to reflect the growing understanding that we must go beyond simple slogans such as "food self-sufficiency" and "food self-reliance", and address the central policy question:

> *What is the most cost effective mix of domestic food production, storage, trade, and food access programmes to meet household, national and regional food security objectives?*

## A SALUTE TO BOTSWANA

Before turning to the topic I have chosen for today's address, I would like to congratulate Botswana for its extraordinary success in combating drought from 1983 to 1987 and in preventing drought from turning into famine. Two months ago an international jury announced that His Excellency, President Quett K.J. Masire of Botswana, was the co-winner of the 1989 Africa Hunger prize of US$50 000. Under President Masire's leadership, Botswana developed a permanent institutional capacity to respond to drought. The Inter-Ministerial Drought Committee includes

[1] Address given on behalf of the Vice-Chancellor by Dr. P. Makhurane, Pro-Vice Chancellor of the University of Zimbabwe.

[2] Vice-Chancellor, University of Zimbabwe.

representatives of six ministries under the assumption that a single ministry does not have the capacity to respond to drought.

It is also instructive to note that Botswana's 1983-1987 famine prevention programmes concentrated on both sides of the food security equation -- food availability and access to food. Botswana expanded programmes to increase food availability, such as the drilling of wells, grants to crop farmers for replanting and the preparation of feasibility studies for a major intensification of irrigation. Botswana increased food access through supplementary feeding and rural income and employment generation projects.

In 1987, the supplementary feeding programme assisted some 600 000 beneficiaries or about 60 percent of Botswana's total population; employment generation programmes provided 45 000 jobs; the agricultural relief programme assisted 20 000 farmers with a subsidy on animal traction and 120 000 farmers received free seed to plant up to three hectares of food crops. I assume that representatives of SADCC member states, after careful analysis, will be in a position to determine whether they should borrow components of Botswana's model and introduce them in their own national food security programmes.

But Botswana's success is not restricted to breaking the famine cycle. Botswana actually improved household food security during a period of adversity. For example, as a result of carefully planned school feeding programmes and child nutrition clinics, the incidence of underweight children has been reduced to 15 percent in 1987, down from 25 percent in 1980. Botswana's success story reinforces the basic point that African nations have much to learn from each other. This is one of the objectives of the UZ/MSU Food Security Research Project: to bring together researchers and policy makers to exchange ideas and share experiences on food security problems.

## BUILDING AFRICAN SCIENTIFIC AND MANAGERIAL CAPACITY

Today, it gives me great pleasure to discuss "Building African Scientific Capacity: A Voice from Africa". This is a topic close to my heart. It is also a topic of great interest to SADCC in light of the current deliberations by SACCAR to map out a programme of regional cooperation to strengthen facilities of agriculture, forestry and veterinary medicine in the region. This is also a topic of great interest to Vice-Chancellors, Presidents and Rectors of institutions for higher education in Southern and Eastern Africa. In fact, conferences at Mbabane (1985), Harare (1987) and Harare (May, 1989) provide proof of this region's commitment to improving the quality, relevance and cost effectiveness of higher education in the region.

Although the current annual output of university graduates in Africa has been increased to around 70 000 as compared with 1 300 in 1960, Sub-Saharan Africa is facing some complex human capital problems. The following raw facts speak for themselves:

  o    About one-third of all university undergraduates are being educated outside Africa.

o   20 percent of Africa's Ph.D.s are earned in overseas universities.

o   Africa has roughly one-fourth the number of trained scientists and engineers per million people as Asian countries.

o   The cost of higher education in many African universities is as high or higher than in overseas universities.The brain drain is enormous in many countries.  UNESCO reports that 330 000 Sudanese are working abroad. This includes 60 percent of Sudan's skilled workers, 40 percent of its professional workers and 30 percent of its medical doctors.  There are an estimated 10 000 trained Nigerians now working in the United States. These sobering figures illustrate the basic point that expanding the supply of trained people is not the automatic answer to Africa's human capacity problem.

o   Most students in African universities are reading books that are written by scholars living in industrial countries.  Very few textbooks used in the universities in SADCC countries are written by local authors and illustrated with local examples of the ecology, environment and political realities of Southern Africa.

o   Africa is on the receiving end of an estimated 80 000 to 100 000 long term resident expatriates at an annual cost of US$4 billion of official development assistance.  Without question, Africa is the continent of technical assistance *par excellence*!

But these problems are part of a broader crisis, including Africa's debt problem and the economic crisis of the 1980s where the average real *per capita* income in 1989 is around 20 percent lower than it was when the Lagos Plan of Action was launched in 1980.

We must address the problems of human resource development in the SADCC region with humility and an acceptance of past shortcomings.  In developing solutions to these problems, I would like to draw on my recent address entitled "Toward Academic and Professional Excellence in Higher Education".  In that address I noted that:

> We are emerging from the ivory towers of the past and are
> collaborating with society and ourselves instead of observing the real
> world from a detached distance.

I also reported that we must pursue a collective sub-regional approach to developing an efficient division of labour between individual universities within SADCC.  We cannot afford to pursue a *laissez-faire* policy, for our purpose in higher education is to provide the high level manpower for our respective countries and our national programmes for development.

In endorsing the need for a sub-regional approach to strengthening human capacity in the region, I am, of course, indirectly applauding the yeoman work of the Southern Africa Centre for Cooperation in Agricultural Research (SACCAR).

## Some Capacity Building Puzzles

Despite the progress being made in developing a collective vision on how to strengthen institutions of higher learning and research in the SADCC region, there are some important human capacity puzzles that require further analysis and debate within the region and with our international partners.

Let me set the stage by noting that the World Bank is preparing an African Capacity Building Initiative (ACBI) in policy analysis and economic managements in Sub-Saharan Africa. The preliminary thinking emerging from this initiative has been quietly debated in meetings of key Africans, and potential partners, including the African Development Bank and the UNDP.

Although much staff work remains to be done, there is encouraging evidence that additional donor resources might be forthcoming for this initiative. For example, at the annual meeting of the World Bank in Washington just two weeks ago, the Minister of Finance of Japan announced a voluntary gift of US$300 million to the World Bank over a three year period for the establishment of a special fund for policy and human resource development. The purpose of the special fund is to initiate technical cooperation for the developing countries and to develop human resources for formulating and implementing development policy. Japan's contribution to a world-wide initiative is a vote of confidence in the Bank's renewed emphasis on human capacity building.

But, before the World Bank, African Development Bank and the UNDP pass the hat for additional funding for Africa for capacity building in the area of economic policy analysis, there is one curious "puzzle" that needs to be addressed.

The puzzle is why should the World Bank request donors to contribute additional funds to an African Capacity Building Initiative (ACBI) when human resources have historically received such low priority in the World Bank's Africa portfolio; for example, in fiscal year 1984, the World Bank approved two education projects in all of Sub-Saharan Africa, representing 3,6 percent of its world-wide education portfolio. Five years later, the World Bank's Annual Report for 1989 shows that the World Bank approved only four education loans covering primary, secondary and tertiary education in Africa in fiscal year 1989 for a total of US$88 million: Chad (US$22 million), Mali (US$26 million), Mauritania (US$18,2 million), and Uganda (US$22 million). Three observations flow from the World Bank's modest support to education in Africa in fiscal year 1989:

o    First, no education loans were extended to any SADCC state for education at any level (primary, secondary or tertiary) in fiscal year 1989.

o    Second, the four education projects for Chad, Mali, Mauritania and Uganda totalled US$88 million or about 3 percent of the US$4 billion of official development assistance extended by the World Bank to Africa in fiscal year 1989.

o    Third, the US$88 million for the four projects is less than the annual average of US$102 million that the bank allocated to education in Africa for 1980-84.

From these three observations, let me make some humble suggestions:

The World Bank's international appeal for donor funds for an African Capacity Building Initiative (ACBI) is laudable given that the Bank itself has accorded low priority to human resources in Africa throughout the 1980s.

f .y second observation is that the scope of the Bank's proposed ACBI in training ,olicy analysts and economic managers seems to be narrow. It seems as if the Bank's determination is to help speed structural adjustment lending. If this is the case, then the Bank is functioning as a Bank rather than the world's premier development institution. In my judgement, the Bank's Capacity Building Initiative should be broadened to include support to strengthen Africa's capacity in science, technology, and bio-technology as well as policy analysis and macro-economic management. To restrict a capacity building initiative to introducing Brookings-type institutions in Africa or expanding the number of MBA programmes would represent a narrow response to African needs. Africa currently requires assistance in developing strong faculties of agriculture, engineering and science as well as strong faculties of commerce, mahagement and economics.

I am well aware that some will argue that the international agricultural research centres such as CIMMYT, IITA and ICRISAT can assist in strengthening the capacity of faculties of science, engineering and agriculture. But the primary mission of the international centres is to develop improved food crop technology. Although we appreciate the focused approach of the centres to strengthen local capacity in their specific programme of work, there is need for greater direct donor support to national agriculture research systems and faculties of agriculture, science and engineering.

The third suggestion relates to the time frame for a Capacity Building Initiative. Most donors are locked into a conservative time frame of 3 to 5 year projects. Because of the accretionary nature of Human Capacity Building I urge the co-sponsors of the ACBI initiative to develop a long term assistance mode for institution-building, including support for 10 year initiatives.

We all know that great universities are built through decades and centuries of effort, and we have learned that money is a poor substitute for time. Africa would be ill served if the capacity building exercise turns out to be "old wine in new bottles" -- that is -- more three to five year projects. The ACBI should be cast in the time frame of a 20 to 30 year effort, including the possibility of responding to requests from African governments and universities for 10 year institutional building projects, including the possibility of renewal.

The fourth suggestion relates to technical assistance. I am pleased to note that donors are starting to question the US$4 billion that is spent each year on some 80 000 to 100 000 expatriates in Africa. The challenge is developing an orderly process of reducing overseas training while strengthening post graduate training and research in SADCC universities in an evolutionary fashion. Currently the technical assistance issue has two interlocking components. First how can the quality of technical assistance be improved at the same time that the number of technical experts is reduced in line with local staff development programmes. The second component of the issue is the blend of short and long term technical advisors.

Already there are signs that donors are substituting short term advisors for resident advisors and researchers on two year contracts.

In the world of science, technology and postgraduate training, Africa would be ill served if the number of short term advisors and consultants were increased. Most countries are flooded with short term consultants. African universities will require some high quality long term scientists to serve as teachers and researchers for years to come.

The goal of donors in the coming decade is to improve the quality and reduce the number of long term experts. I propose that US$1 billion of the US$4 billion of funds spent each year on technical assistance be reallocated to invest in African capacity to train scientists and managers. This is a feasible goal if donors are serious about strengthening Africa's institutional capacity to train scientists and managers in the 1990s.

Fifthly, I turn to the apparent silent role of foundations in African Capacity Building. We know the foundations played a leadership role in education in Africa in the 1960s. But the 1970s were a period of retrenchment followed by a cautious period of rediscovery of the strategic role of human capacity in national development in the 1980s. Without doubt, foundations operating in the SADCC region are offering much appreciated scholarships, support for staff development programmes and funds for the purchase of books, buildings, and equipment, but I have observed that few foundations are willing to come forward with ten year commitments to help open up new areas of research and post graduate training in fields such as bio-technology, natural resources and research on AIDS.

In wrapping up my analysis of suggestions for capacity building, it seems legitimate to ask why were foundations so much more forward-looking in the 1960s? Why are foundations not providing intellectual leadership in shaping the debate on capacity building in Africa in 1989?

## THREE EXAMPLES OF REGIONAL COOPERATION

Let me close on a positive note by citing three examples of institutional innovations to promote regional cooperation in training, research and policy analysis.

**SACCAR** (the Southern Africa Centre for Cooperation in Agricultural Research). The decision by SADCC to establish SACCAR in 1984 has proven to be a wise stroke because it is already providing a valuable voice from Southern Africa in helping shape a sub-regional strategy for human capital improvement. SACCAR's "voice", in practice, is a collective voice of directors of national agricultural research systems and deans of faculties of agriculture. It is gratifying to note that CORAF, an institution modeled after SACCAR, has recently been inaugurated in Francophone West Africa. SACCAR's experience reinforces my conviction that the preparation of an African strategy of strengthening agricultural research and post graduate training in agriculture would be a utopian exercise. Sub-regional approaches such as those being pioneered by SACCAR are the feasible approaches of the future.

**The African Economic Research Consortium** is a successful example of a regional capacity building programme that grew out of a 1984 initiative by the IDRC of Canada. The consortium has recently broadened its geographical scope with support from numerous organisations, including IDRC, Rockefeller and Ford Foundations. It is directed by Professor Benno Ndulu of Tanzania and Jeffrey Fine of IDRC.

**The UZ/MSU Food Security Research Project** was launched five years ago by the University of Zimbabwe in cooperation with Michigan State University and funding from USAID. The UZ/MSU Food Security network is working cooperatively with SADCC's Food Security Technical and Administrative Unit and researchers in various SADCC universities in furthering policy analysis and developing Africa research capacity.

I trust that these examples of institutional innovations will be factored into the deliberations of the task force that is preparing the World Bank's African Capacity Building Initiative. It goes without saying that the programme of work of the ACBI should be built upon a firm understanding of African dreams, African initiatives and the political and economic realities of Africa.

Mr. Chairman, it is my sincere hope that your deliberations in this Conference will be as fruitful as the four previous Conferences. Ladies and gentlemen, today 16th October, is World Food Day. Your Conference is therefore starting not only on a significant but a commemorative day. It is on this note that I have the pleasure and honour to declare this Conference officially open.

# II

# Perspectives On Food Security Policy Options In The SADCC Region: Country Experiences

# II

# National Food Security Policies And Challenges: SADCC Countries' Experiences

*K.J.M. Dhliwayo*[1]

## INTRODUCTION

Most of the SADCC member States depend heavily on agriculture to provide food and incomes for the majority of their population. As such, agriculture, and in particular, food security are among those sectors that have been accorded a high priority in the SADCC Programme of Action. In recent years, most SADCC member States have reviewed or/and reformulated their policies to stimulate agricultural production and rural development in general. As a result of these reviews, a number of important policy adjustments have been undertaken. Projects and programmes to achieve these policy objectives are being developed and implemented throughout the region. The successful implementation of these programmes hold some promise of increasing agricultural production and reducing poverty throughout the SADCC region.

Two of the major elements of the Regional Food Security Strategy have been the establishment of a mechanism for exchange of technical information and experiences and the reinforcement of national food production capacities. The implementation of these strategies has been pursued through conducting policy seminars and workshops, short-term training courses and the mobilisation of resources for the implementation of national and regional agricultural projects and programmes.

The workshops, seminars and exchange visits provide a forum for discussing not only regional but also national food and agricultural strategies and policies. In addition to these technical meetings, there are also regular meetings of senior officials from Ministries of Agriculture and Natural Resources, Ministers of Agriculture and Natural Resources and the Council of Ministers. At all these levels, progress reports on programme activities are reviewed, new project proposals are discussed and policy guidelines for the implementation of the programme are provided. The meetings, whether technical or political form an essential part of the programme development and planning. They contribute towards the improvement of effective decision-making in SADCC and its institutions and the coordination and administration of the programme.

[1]Sector Coordinator. Food Security Technical and Administrative Unit. Ministry of Lands. Agriculture and Rural Resettlement. Zimbabwe.

The formulation and execution of regional development plans require not only that national policies and strategies of member States are clearly understood and taken into consideration but also that all the relevant planning and executing agencies in member States are involved in the process. National policies and strategies of member States provide an essential input into the development and implementation of regional programmes while national institutions become part of the planning and executing machinery for the regional programmes.

Most of the components of regional programmes are implemented at the national level and become part of national development plans. In order to achieve the desired results, therefore activities must be properly coordinated at both regional and national levels. Through this process it is intended that regional programmes will have a direct positive influence on national programmes and that their further development will be influenced by national policies and development strategies.

Through the collective analysis of the problem of food insecurity, SADCC member states have continued to sharpen and clearly define their concept of food security. Some earlier misconceptions on food security *vis-a-vis* food self sufficiency have been removed from the minds of many of the SADCC planners and policy makers. There is now a clear understanding by SADCC of the differences between the concept of food security and national self-sufficiency on the one hand and between food security and collective self-reliance on the other. This is demonstrated by the distinct but complementary policies and interventions that are being pursued by member States to address the issues of food security, on one hand, and self-reliance on the other. SADCC member States accept that the objective of national food self-sufficiency, though ideal, cannot be pursued and achieved at any cost. There is a growing appreciation by member States that this noble objective can only be achieved through cost-effective means.

This paper, however, is not intended to provide a comparative analysis of the problems relating to the concepts of food security and food self-sufficiency, notwithstanding the importance of such an analysis. Indeed, a detailed analysis of the constraints to, and opportunities for improved food security and food self-sufficiency is very important. It will certainly constitute the essential starting point from which practical programmes can be developed and implemented to address the issues of food seeurity in the region.

The paper is confined to the presentation of a summary of some of the food security policies and interventions being pursued by most SADCC member States. The paper serves as a summary of documents which have been prepared by members of the Technical Sub-Committee for Food Security in which food security policies and interventions of individual Governments are presented.

SADCC firmly believes that food security is achieved (nationally and/or regionally) only when a country/region can guarantee all its citizens both physical and economic access to adequate food of an appropriate nutritional standard all year round. As such, food security can only be achieved through both adequate availability of food and affordability at the household level.

## FOOD SECURITY IN THE REGION

In almost all the SADCC countries, the problems of food insecurity, particularly at the household level, are experienced in some rural areas and among the urban poor and unemployed. Both the magnitude and the nature of the problem of food insecurity differ from country to country and from one season to another. In some SADCC countries the problem of food insecurity is transitory while in others it has been chronic.

Transitory food insecurity is mainly caused by a fall in agricultural production or instability in food supplies resulting from drought, crop diseases, or floods. The poor capacities of the marketing and transport systems to purchase and collect agricultural products from widely dispersed rural producers and to distribute essential agricultural inputs on time, also contribute to the fall in production in some years.

Poverty, arising from a lack of access to sufficient land and capital, unemployment and, political instability resulting from the economic destabilisation activities by the South African Government have resulted in chronic food insecurity being experienced in some of the SADCC countries. Other factors that contribute to both transitory and chronic food insecurity in the region are indicated in the next section of this paper.

It should be pointed out, however, that food self-sufficiency cannot be achieved at national and regional levels without achieving access to food by all the members of society.

Considering the region as a whole, SADCC achieved 98 percent and 108 percent self-sufficiency in its major staple foods (maize, sorghum and cassava) during the 1988-89 and 1989-90 marketing years, respectively. The Regional Early Warning Unit's latest assessment of the food security situation for the 1989-90 marketing year, based on information submitted by member States to the end of May 1989, indicates that the domestic availability of the commodities being monitored by the project (maize, sorghum/millet, cassava, wheat and rice) is expected to be 16,90 million tonnes of maize equivalent (ME). This is an increase of 1,29 million tonnes over the 1988-89 marketing year. During the same year (1989-90) the region's total gross domestic requirement is expected to be 15,70 million tonnes ME resulting in a net surplus amounting to an impressive 1,20 million tonnes ME in the 1989-90 marketing year. These estimates take into account the anticipated net deficit of 0,56 million tonnes of wheat, and 0,2 million tonnes of rice.

While the foregoing describes an improved regional food availability in 1988-89 and an impressive overall regional prospect for 1989-90, it should be pointed out that the majority of the SADCC countries continue to experience food insecurity at both national and household levels. At a national level, five SADCC member States are facing an overall food deficit situation and none of the nine countries are fully self-sufficient in every commodity being monitored by the Regional Early Warning project. Even in those countries with a net surplus, problems of food insecurity are being experienced at a household level among certain vulnerable groups.

The food consumption patterns in most of the SADCC countries are not the same as the food production patterns. During the 1989-90 marketing year, all of the nine countries will have wheat deficits while four countries will have surpluses of maize, five of sorghum, three of millet and two of the other staple foods (rice, beans, *etc.*)

The analysis of the 1988-89 regional food situation reveals that while the issue of adequate availability, at regional level (*i.e.*, collective self-sufficiency), has been more or less achieved, the goal of access was not successfully accomplished. In 1988-89 six deficit countries intended to import 1,5 million tonnes of cereals but were able to import only 1,0 million tonnes. In contrast, three member States had a surplus of 1,2 million tonnes but were able to export only 0,4 million tonnes, some of which went outside the SADCC region. It is evident therefore that while some opportunities for reducing SADCC's dependence on sources of food outside the region are bright, opportunities for enhancing demand for regional production and increasing the flow of commodities from surplus to deficit areas within the region are not being sufficiently explored and exploited.

## CAUSES OF FOOD INSECURITY

Several reasons have been advanced to explain why the region was not more successful in exploiting its regional/collective self sufficiency gains and achieving its objective of food security at both national and household levels. An attempt is made in this paper to group these factors in accordance with the level of food insecurity on which they have the most direct impact.

### Regional Food Insecurity

As pointed out above, SADCC failed to exploit the handsome regional self-sufficiency position it attained in the 1988-89 marketing year. Some of the reasons for this situation include:

a)     The likelihood that national authorities were not aware, in time, of the size of the ultimate deficit or surplus in order to make advance import and export plans. In order to minimise this problem in the future, there is need to improve the quality, content, presentational clarity and timeliness of the food security early warning reporting at both national and regional levels. It may also be very important to establish and formalise a regional steering committee of senior officials to review these food situation reports and use the information therein to determine appropriate plans for improving regional food security. In particular, mention needs to be made of the need for accurate production estimates and realistic assessment of domestic needs.

b)     The likelihood that financial constraints, particularly inadequate foreign currency, forced importing countries to rely on food aid programmes to secure a large proportion of their food needs. This is a condition arising from the generally poor performance of their economies and their technological, financial and market dependence on external economies which, as a result, expose them to the vicissitudes of the world markets over which they have very limited control. To overcome this constraint every effort needs to be made to give greater attention to the general development strategies of SADCC economies. This would include continued attention to reforming macro-economic and trade policies, financing basic infrastructure, creating new employment opportunities, developing and financing formal and informal industrial sectors and creating an economic environment that is attractive to local, regional and international investors.

c)     It is also possible that delays in negotiating marketing and delivery contracts between member States, delays in delivery, quality problems and uncompetitive prices may have also played an important part in restricting intra-regional trade in staple food commodities.

d)     The inadequate capacities of the road and railway transport systems may have caused delays or/and non-delivery of contracts.

e)     Lack of a clear policy on the size of the national carry-over stock requirements.

f)     Uncertainties about the size of the next year's harvest force some member states to hold more stocks than otherwise necessary.

To overcome these problems in the future there is need first to recognise their scale and then to practise forward planning by all parties involved in dealing with the problem of regional food insecurity.

## National Food Insecurity

Both transitory and chronic food insecurity problems have continued to be experienced in the SADCC region, resulting from fluctuations and instabilities in food production and supply. Fluctuations in food production have been caused largely by droughts particularly during the 1986-87, 1987-88, and 1988-89 production seasons. In the 1988-89 production seasons for example, rains came fairly early in November after most farmers have started planting. After a short period, the rains disappeared until mid-January when a heavy downpour occurred leading to flooding, forcing farmers to replant in some parts of the region. It is possible that most small and poor farmers were seriously affected as they could not afford to mobilise the necessary inputs (seeds and fertilizers) for a second planting programme.

Other factors that contribute to low production and inadequate food supply in most member States include:

o     poor road conditions that hamper the collection of produce, and inadequate storage infrastructure;

o     lack of sufficient numbers of skilled manpower to implement government policies efficiently;

o     banditry activities supported by South Africa;

o     declining land/man ratios resulting from a high population growth rate;

o    a generally low level of investment in agriculture;

o    lack of adequate procurement programmes.

## Household Food Insecurity

The basic factor that contributes to household food insecurity is poverty. The level of poverty is determined by a number of factors namely; lack of access to the basic agricultural resources -- land and livestock; lack of access to employment opportunities; and lack of access to a reasonable and regular income. For those with access to land, the level of income they can derive from that land is also determined by the size of the land *vis-a-vis* the size of the household, the availability of labour to operate the land, access to basic agricultural inputs such as fertilizer, improved seeds and credit, access to training and extension services and the capacity of the farmer to transport and market his/her produce. All these present the issue of affordability.

## GOVERNMENT FOOD SECURITY INTERVENTIONS

There are various well-meaning programmes and projects that are being undertaken by SADCC member states to address the issue of food security. SADCC member States have recognised that improving food security is a multi-faceted issue and that no single Ministry can, on its own, adequately address the problem of food insecurity. As such, all programmes and measures that will promote economic and social activities to enable all the people, particularly the poor, to lead a healthy and active life, contribute to food security.

Recognizing the multi-dimensional nature of the food security issue, most SADCC member States have established some inter-ministerial committees to coordinate projects and programmes needed to address both the supply and demand sides of the food security issue.

Some of the policies and programmes that are pursued by member States to promote agricultural production and to ensure people's access to food are summarised below.

### Supply Side

SADCC Governments' interventions which are aimed at ensuring the availability of food through either local production, storage and/or commercial imports are:

o    Establishment of favourable and guaranteed producer prices aimed at inducing increased production by farmers.

o    Resettlement programmes aimed at improving access to land by the poor and the unemployed. Zimbabwe and Mozambique are engaged in such resettlement programmes. In Mozambique the resettlement programmes are also designed to benefit the workers who are returning from South Africa.

o   Special credit facilities with affordable conditions have been designed and established specifically to assist small-scale rural farmers. In some countries, these programmes are designed and implemented as a package to include improved training and extension services, adaptive research on both traditional and modern crops, and the provision of crop packs to some target groups particularly in areas where drought would have seriously hit the farmers. Such crop packs would include essential inputs such as hybrid seeds, fertilizers and other inputs.

o   Improving the condition of rural feeder roads and establishing seasonal storage/cereal collection points within easy reach of farmers in order to encourage them to produce marketable surplus.

o   Establishing irrigation schemes and providing water for domestic and livestock use, particularly in rainfall deficit areas.

o   Establishing Government tractor-hire schemes in areas where farmers are unable to afford their own tractors and do not have adequate draught power.

o   Establishment of strategic stocks which are also used for supply stabilisation purposes.

o   Soliciting food aid.

o   Arrangement for commercial imports.

## Access To Food

As indicated earlier in this paper, the main factor that contributes to the problem of food insecurity at household level is poverty. Poverty is a function of a number of factors which, among other things include: lack of the basic agricultural resources (land and livestock), lack of regular incomes and unemployment.

Among the programmes aimed at reducing the social impact of poverty are school feeding and emergency relief programmes. As part of a general development strategy aimed at benefiting the whole population, particularly the food insecure, most SADCC governments are giving increasing   attention to the following programmes:

o   Developing and implementing nutrition programmes.

o   Building and maintaining rural roads, constructing small-scale rural dams, schools, clinics and other basic rural infrastructures through food-for-work programmes. These programmes have both economic and psychological advantages. People that are involved in the programmes do not feel they are destitute since they are offered an opportunity to contribute towards the betterment of the environment in which they live.

o    Raising the purchasing power of the poor through a deliberate policy on minimum wages. Most SADCC governments have established minimum wages in conjunction with control of the prices of the basic food and other items. In some of the SADCC countries, this policy is also complemented by the subsidisation of the basic food items. This is intended to maintain prices within reach of the majority of the poor urban and rural people. However, because of the high financial costs involved and the inability of such schemes to benefit only the intended target groups, most SADCC member States are gradually phasing out food subsidies.

o    Child spacing programmes aimed at reducing the current high population growth rate commensurate with the level of economic growth.

All these programmes are designed to generate employment and incomes for the poor and to contribute towards the overall economic development strategy of the countries.

## CHALLENGES FOR THE 1990S

Against the background of high population growth rates, and generally low economic growth and development, the challenges that most SADCC member States will continue to face in the 1990s include, among others:

o    How to generate sufficient foreign and local currency to support the economies of their countries by providing credit facilities to local industrial and agricultural producers and by increasing investment in agriculture particularly in such complementary areas as roads, storage, water, transport, seeds, fertilizer, training, research and extension.

o    How to generate more employment opportunities for a larger number of school leavers who enter the employment market every year. Due to lack of formal employment opportunities in some countries, migrant employment to neighbouring countries has caused serious adverse effects on agricultural development and food production.

o    How to combat the effect of drought and other natural catastrophes such as outbreaks of crop-diseases and migrant pests.

o    The need to draw up, finance and implement action programmes that can successfully reinforce both economic growth and food security. In order to enhance food security through economic growth, there is a need, firstly, to identify the food insecure, and secondly to assess their condition and then determine the factors that cause their food insecurity. This information must then be used to design, develop and implement sustainable high-return or/and labour-intensive programmes that generate real incomes for food insecure people.

o    How to develop and promote adequate, appropriate and affordable technologies needed to increase land and labour productivity.

o    The need to establish an effective machinery to coordinate agricultural programmes and strategies that promote both agricultural growth and food security.

o    How to increase intra-regional trade better to exploit the potential of regional self-sufficiency. This will enable member States to gain from comparative advantage in the production of different products and to reduce barriers to trade. This will also require member States to improve the intra-regional transport network and the marketing infrastructure.

## CONCLUSION

In conclusion, food security policies have been clearly defined. What remains is to systematically and painstakingly translate these policies into the desired actions. This requires real commitment, particularly financial, and the courage to sacrifice today's transitory comfort for tomorrow's lasting security. Perhaps this could be achieved by promoting thrift among the population and mobilising internal savings for national development programmes.

# 3

# Lesotho : Food Security Issues And Challenges For The 1990s

*Mookho Moeketsi*

## INTRODUCTION

### Background

Lesotho is a small, food-deficit, land-locked country of 1,6 million people and a total area of about 30 000 square kilometres. It often has to cope with unique circumstances and problems which arise primarily from its geographic position, being completely surrounded by the Republic of South Africa. Lesotho, a mountainous country, often referred to very fondly by its inhabitants as "Kingdom in the Sky", has only about 10 percent of its land area as suitable for crop cultivation. The country's badly eroded land base condition can be attributed mainly to its growing population pressure, poor grazing practices and poor land management practices. Lesotho, like other Southern African countries suffers from cyclical drought. In addition, the country suffers from other natural catastrophes such as severe hail-storms which occasionally cause damage, particularly to the crops. Early frost in winter has posed a great risk to crop farming in particular. The country's livestock has occasionally also suffered from heavy hail- and snow-storms.

It comes as no big surprise then that, Lesotho, given her geographic position and being an agricultural country in a situation where agriculture is a declining sector, depends on her powerful and only neighbour, the Republic of South Africa for essential aspects of her national livelihood. More than 90 percent of Lesotho's foodstuffs is imported, mainly from the Republic of South Africa. The unhealthy economic condition of the country has not gone unnoticed by the Government. For example, the Government has introduced grazing regulations to combat overgrazing. There are also a number of projects which are aimed at increasing food production and the attainment of food self-sufficiency. The ultimate goal of the Government of Lesotho is national food security.

### Definition of National Food Security

Food security is the availability and accessibility of food supplies in adequate quantities to meet the nation's food needs. The food does not only have to be physically accessible, but people should be able to purchase it.

The concept of food security takes a number of factors into account. There are food policies and action programmes aimed at attaining sufficient, nutritionally balanced quantities of food. In order for the non-farming households or those families who do not produce enough to be in a position to purchase food they must first of all earn income. There is, therefore, a need for employment opportunities either on or off the farm. There is also a need for efficient marketing systems which will involve the storage, distribution and processing of food.

The major food security issues on the national agenda in Lesotho are the availability of food in sufficient amount to meet at least the minimum nutritional requirements for the Basotho nation, and the availability of food supplies to insure against natural calamities and poor harvests.

The Government of Lesotho has launched some programmes to attain food self-sufficiency, but these are only part of a national strategy to achieve food security. Although Government has experienced costly food self-sufficiency programmes such as the maize programme that was launched in 1979, the Government of Lesotho will not strive to achieve food self-sufficiency at any cost.

The objectives and strategies of the Government of Lesotho to alleviate food insecurity are contained in the country's Five-Year Development Plans, the current plan being the fourth, covering the years 1986-87 to 1990-91.

## CURRENT STATUS OF FOOD INSECURITY IN LESOTHO

Lesotho, like other countries, has experienced years of good and poor harvests. For example, 1976-77 and 1977-78 were marked by favourable rainfall during the growing season and by high fertilizer use. In these two years, for example, the country's harvest of staple grains was very good. Looking at maize, in 1976-77, 125 932 tonnes were produced and in 1977-78, 143 168 tonnes were produced. In 1987-88, 159 726 tonnes were produced. Even in these years of exceptionally good harvest, the country does not produce enough to feed its people; production falls short of basic food requirements by about 30 percent.

**Table 1**
**Crop production in Lesotho, 1973-74 to 1987-88**

| Year | Maize | Sorghum | Wheat | Pulses |
|------|-------|---------|-------|--------|
| 1973/74 | 122,500 | 84,000 | 57,000 | 14,700 |
| 1974/75 | 70,292 | 37,443 | 45,337 | 19,172 |
| 1975/76 | 48,928 | 24,540 | 44,640 | 14,413 |
| 1976/77 | 125,932 | 62,313 | 61,381 | 27,897 |
| 1977/78 | 143,168 | 85,775 | 57,906 | 15,210 |
| 1978/79 | 124,856 | 68,952 | 33,629 | 15,206 |
| 1979/80 | 105,619 | 59,286 | 28,194 | 8,147 |
| 1980/81 | 105,674 | 47,729 | 17,293 | 6,715 |
| 1981/82 | 83,028 | 26,158 | 14,462 | 9,423 |
| 1982/83 | 76,200 | 30,687 | 14,810 | 4,991 |
| 1983/84 | 79,384 | 33,768 | 17,127 | 4,977 |
| 1984/85 | 92,350 | 54,823 | 18,434 | 5,75? |
| 1985/86 | 86,488 | 33,458 | 11,009 | 5,281 |
| 1986/87 | 94,912 | 31,232 | 18,520 | 4,811 |
| 1987/88 | 159,726 | 53,447 | 19,237 | 9,981 |

Source: Bureau of Statistics, Agricultural Situation Report, 1989 Edition

On the other hand, during the drought years of 1975-76, domestic production of cereal was 48 928 tonnes which was less than 40 percent of the basic national food requirements. From 1981-82 through 1986-1987 maize production was low.

As already indicated, the country has not been able to produce enough cereal to feed its entire population. It has always been necessary to supplement domestic produce by imported foodstuffs either through food aid or commercial imports. Food unavailability in Lesotho can therefore be said to be chronic because it recurs over the years.

Lesotho is divided into three ecological zones:

1)    Mountains which are suitable for livestock rearing;
2)    the foothills; and
3)    the lowlands consisting of a narrow strip along the western side of the country, which are more suitable for the cultivation of crops.

Although the lowlands and the foothills of Lesotho have land suitable for crop production, not all the households in these parts of the country have access to land. It has been established in the 1986-87 Household Budget Survey that only 47 percent of the households in Lesotho own both land and livestock while 25 percent of the households do not have access to either land or livestock. The fact that a household has access to a piece of land is no guarantee that such land will be fully utilised. The 1979 Agricultural Census revealed that 55 percent of the households who had the potential to reach food self-sufficiency under-utilised the land and/or livestock at their disposal. It follows, therefore, that while the resource poor households are regarded as the most critical, there are at the same time households at risk due to under-utilisation of resources.

The growing season in the mountains is short. This, coupled with the heavy snow and early frost, poses a disadvantage as far as crop production is concerned. The unfavourable growing season and hostile weather conditions team up with low productivity in the mountainous parts of the country to expose the households living in the mountain district of Lesotho to higher risks of food insecurity.

The above discussion serves to show that while it is important to have cash in order to have access to food supplies, accessibility to food is not governed by the power to purchase alone. There are also some socio-geographical factors. The ruggedness of the country and the remoteness of some villages limit access to food, particularly during the harsh winters.

## CURRENT STATUS OF FOOD SECURITY POLICIES, PROGRAMMES AND PROJECTS

The Government of Lesotho has set up strategies that are directed at increasing production of crops and livestock for both domestic consumption and export. The document: Agricultural Development - A Blueprint for Action, states that Government's objective of increased production *will continue to have high priority until such time as Lesotho has obtained that degree of self-sufficiency which will guarantee its security in food and its freedom from dependence upon its neighbour.*

Although this document was drawn up during the Third Five-Year Plan period, this objective still remains valid.

The government policy is to attain self-sufficiency in production of basic staple crops, high-valued fruit and vegetables, livestock and forest products consistent with the nation's natural resource base. The Government is also expanding trading links with other nations to enable Basotho to improve overall living standards and attain levels of nutritional well-being. Attention in this regard is also extended to the improvement of storage and food preservation at the household level. While the principles of government policy do aim at addressing the food problem, the circumstances within which these policies have been put into practice have not been particularly supportive. It should therefore be borne in mind, when looking at the achievements of these policies, that these were implemented under constraints. Some of the constraints that can be mentioned are limited financial and manpower resources. These constraints will become even more limiting when viewed in light of the IMF Structural Adjustment Programme.

The Government's key strategy areas which address the issue of food insecurity, as far as increasing food availability, have been clearly laid out in the Fourth Five-Year Development Plan. These strategies are aimed at implementing policy through programmes and projects. Policy in turn derives from government objectives and strives to achieve those objectives. The key strategy areas in the Ministry of Agriculture, Cooperatives and Marketing are:

### Crops

a)    Dryland farming which emphasises the contractor/sublease arrangements as outlined in the Land Act of 1979. Land which is currently being inefficiently cropped will be utilised by the landless, male-headed households who will adopt intensive/commercial approaches to crop production.

b)    Horticulture which emphasises promotion of irrigated crop production, provision of specialised marketing assistance to small farmers and the possibility of reducing input prices, thereby increasing profit margins and improving the competitive position of small Basotho farmers relative to the RSA producers.

Some of the projects in this area include the Food Self-Sufficiency Programme (Lesotho Government/UNCDF), Strengthening Food Production (Japan), Irrigated Crop Production (BAUER) and Small-Scale Irrigated Vegetable Production (EEC), to mention just a few.

### Livestock

a)    The intensive livestock programme aims at utilising the limited land area available in the lowlands to produce livestock under a commercialised/ intensive production system that makes the best use of the limited resources available and reduces pressure on overgrazed rangelands. The strategy will involve the stall feeding of cattle; and the production of dairy, poultry, pig, rabbit, fish and duck. The key linkages related to this strategy are the availability of sufficient feed/fodder and the provision of market outlets.

b)    The extensive livestock programme aims at improving the quality of overstocked rangelands and livestock herds.

The projects aimed at achieving these strategies include Lesotho Dairy Development (CIDA), Integrated Fish-cum-Duck (FAO), Pullet Rearing (FAO), Livestock Improvements Centres and Woolsheds (ODA), Thaba-Tseka Veterinary Clinic (ODA), and Lesotho Agricultural Policy Support Programme (USAID).

## FORESTRY AND CONSERVATION

The Conservation and Watershed Management strategy places emphasis on conservation methods that integrate conservation and production. This programme has rural households as its target group. There is also an aim to provide an integrated approach to land use planning towards increased production and rational utilisation of land relative to the available natural resources within specific catchment areas.

The projects in this area include Land Conservation and Range Management (USAID), Soil and Water Conservation and Agroforestry Programme (IFAD) and Farm Improvement with Soil Conservation (SIDA).

Apart from the food stuffs that are commercially imported, grain is imported as food aid. The FMU serves as a Central Coordination Point for all food assistance projects and programmes and is responsible for receiving and storing food supplies and transporting them to district stores.

As a means to improve access to available food stuffs by vulnerable groups, there are some programmes that Government entered into with assistance from such organisations as the WFP. These programmes involve the provision of food aid for institutional feeding, primary school feeding, and mothers and pre-school children feeding. The primary schools were not just being provided with food, but garden tools in order to encourage involvement in production activities.

Government has engaged in activities to improve the road network throughout the country. While large contractors were engaged in the building of major roads, the access roads, particularly in the rural areas, were built using labour under the food-for-work programmes. The primary school feeding programme is, however, being phased out in favour of self-sufficiency at school level.

In the past, workers in food-for-work programmes were paid in food. This had to be stopped and redirected because of the negative impact it had on production. People neglected producing for themselves because they were guaranteed to have something to eat at the end of the day.

## ORGANISATIONAL STRUCTURE FOR MANAGING FOOD SECURITY

The concept of food security does not specifically belong to a single ministry. It cuts across a number of government ministries and departments. Among those government ministries that are involved with the implementation of food security include the Ministry of Planning and Economic Affairs; Ministry of Agriculture,

Cooperatives and Marketing; Ministry of Water, Energy and Mining; Ministry of Health; and the Ministry of Interior. The Ministry of Planning is the overall controller and coordinator of government policy.

The Ministry of Planning is the chief participant in the realisation of food production objectives. The Ministry mainly provides assistance and technical advice to the farmers. This Ministry also monitors the country's food security situation through the National Early Warning Unit in close collaboration with the Department of Meteorology in the Ministry of Water, Energy and Mining, and the Bureau of Statistics in the Ministry of Planning.

The Ministry of Agriculture has its parastatals such as Co-op Lesotho, which provides farmers with agricultural inputs. The basic inputs, fertilizer and seed, that Co-op Lesotho sells to the farmers are those which have been recommended by the Ministry's Division of Research. There is also the Lesotho Flour Mills, which is the Ministry's strategic enterprise for the production of flour. It has silos which are used as reserves for grain. The farmers either sell directly to the mills or sell their grain through Co-op Lesotho.

It is not the responsibility of Government alone to resolve the problem of national food insecurity. It is indeed up to all citizens, either individually or collectively to engage in measures geared towards food security. There are some traders and millers who buy the farmers' produce to either redistribute it in the same form or process it and then sell the processed product.

The Food Management Unit, which is under the Office of the Government Secretary, is responsible for the management of donated food stuffs. The food that the FMU receives may be put into a number of different uses. The foodstuffs may either be used for social benefits or on the other hand it may be used for development purposes. The food is sometimes monetised and the money is used to finance some developmental projects. Again, it may be used in school feeding programmes or in food for work programmes. The FMU is the only institution in the country that has strategic stores in the mountain disaster prone areas.

The Food and Nutrition Coordination Office (FNCO) is an office within the Ministry of Agriculture whose major mandate is to monitor the country's nutrition status. This office works in close collaboration with the Rural Health Department of the Ministry of Health. The Ministry of Health collects information on nutritional status from its rural health clinics and other clinics.

The role of land allocation that is played by the Ministry of Interior is of primary importance. In order for a farmer to produce and increase his production, he must first of all have a piece of land to cultivate. The Ministry of Interior does not just give away land and forget about it. It also has the responsibility to see to it that land is put to proper use. If land is not being put to use, the Ministry has the authority through the Chief to withdraw it and reallocate it.

All these ministries, through their respective offices, and the private enterprises, may appear interested in achieving their individual goals. In reality they work together towards a common goal - that of food security.

There are committees in the country which deal with the management or handling of food. The National Disaster Relief Committee was formed in 1987. One of its main duties is to make plans to respond to food shortages. Temporary sub-committees may be formed by this Committee to look into specific disaster issues.

There is also a Government/Donor Food Aid Coordinating Committee composed of officials of the Government of Lesotho and representatives from all donor missions resident in Maseru. This Committee meets every other month to review the country's food security situation and aid requirements, and make recommendations to Government.

## ANTICIPATED PROBLEMS

As far as Lesotho is concerned, food insecurity may not necessarily be caused by new problems during the early 1990s. The present problem will most likely continue well into the 1990s if not beyond. Food insecurity will largely be caused by insufficient food production.

### Land Degradation and Soil Erosion

Because of the steepness of the terrain, overgrazing and poor land use practices, Lesotho suffers from massive soil erosion. Although government developmental efforts have taken this erosion into consideration and are raising public awareness, soil erosion damage cannot be repaired in the short-run. Soil erosion and land degradation will continue until such time that awareness has been effected at grassroots level. This will have a considerably negative impact in Lesotho's ability to achieve security in food production. As a result, Government considers soil and land conservation measures as the number one priority for sustained food production.

### Population Growth

Population growth has resulted in encroachment on the already small land base. This problem is common in the lowlands, where the industries and the big border towns are located. This is the part of the country where the cropland lies. Government has imposed restrictions on allocation of new sites, but still, allocation continues unabated on the black market as people migrate to towns to seek employment.

### Migrant Employment in South Africa

This is a historical event which has been documented in numerous publications. It will be mentioned here insofar as it affects production and productivity. With the men gone searching for employment in the mines, leaving agricultural activity in the hands of the elderly people, women and children, there is a limited extent to which this work can be properly and efficiently done. This is mainly because decision-making often remains in the hands of heads of families in the RSA.

Under these circumstances, the decision-making process is unable to take advantage of cheap prices, weather conditions and other time-limited benefits. These factors, together with stiff competition from the RSA, have often meant that agriculture is a part-time occupation with little scope for income generation. The threat of repatriation of these miners is constantly hanging over Lesotho. If this becomes a reality, a further strain will be made on the resources (including food resources), contributing to further food insecurity.

## Lack of Credit Facilities

In Lesotho, women are largely considered as minors. As a result, women have to obtain permission from their husbands before they can commit the family by borrowing. Small farmers also face problems of lack of credit. This is because these farmers are considered to be a bigger risk than their larger counterparts. The lending institutions will require collateral, which in most cases the small farmers cannot afford. The lack of credit, therefore, still continues to limit agricultural production.

## Marketing and Distribution

Food security does not only require that food be produced, but that people should have access to such food. This is where marketing and distribution come in. In the past, distribution of food has been severely hampered by lack of infrastructure. Although Lesotho has had easy access to food imports from South Africa, the interior of the country, which is rugged, has suffered because of the poor road system. The road network will be redressed by the Highland Water Scheme road network by the early 1990s.

It is, however, lack of market infrastructure and market systems which is worrisome. This alone has contributed more to the decline in production than any other factor. There are several known instances where produce has rotted in the field because of the lack of marketing structures. Overgrazing continues to be a problem because there are inadequate market outlets for live animals.

## SADCC INITIATIVES

The establishment of the SADCC Food Security Unit is indication enough of the fact that the region is aware of the food insecurity problem. The work that the Unit has undertaken since it establishment in the form of projects is commendable. More effort remains to be directed towards the strengthening of the food security projects that exist. For instance, the Regional Early Warning Project is a good project whose function is to disseminate information pertaining to the deficit/surplus situation within individual member states.

The Unit has to work very closely with other SADCC sectors such as the Industry sector. Perhaps a mechanism could be worked out between the Unit and the Industry sector and other sectors on how to facilitate regional trade. There are some organisations outside the region which are involved in some cases relevant to the regions's own food problems. It is important for the Unit to get in touch with such organisations and obtain whatever information that could be put to use for the benefit of SADCC.

## RESEARCH REQUIRED

Researchers have done commendable work as far as finding ways and means to improve food production. For instance, it is through research that today there are broilers which reach maturity in a shorter time than it takes a normal chick. Researchers have also come up with farming systems methods. What remains to be done is to carry out research in appropriate technologies, especially those which reduce dependence on the outside world. Such technologies should be harmonious with the environment and ecology.

# 4

# Malawi : Food Security Issues And Challenges For The 1990s

*M.J.K. Mughogho*[1]

## INTRODUCTION

Malawi's economy depends primarily on agriculture and the rural economy which provides income for 85 percent of the population of 8,5 million. There are two broad groups of producers: smallholders who cultivate on customary land and estates which cultivate leasehold and freehold land. Maize is the most important food crop with an annual production of about 1,4 million tonnes per year.

Malawi currently faces a number of food security issues. Poor weather conditions and crop disease have exacerbated the declining *per capita* production and there have been significant shortfalls in domestic food production in recent years. Even in good harvest years, domestic production barely meets domestic requirements. There is also an increasing incidence of chronic food insecurity and malnutrition as a result of increasing land pressure, rising agricultural input prices and limited access to food within food-deficit households.

As in other countries, in Malawi food security is defined as access by all people at all times to sufficient food for an active, healthy life. The essential prerequisites are the availability of food and ability to acquire it.

Malawi's food security objective is self-sufficiency in the dominant food crop, maize (Malawi, 1987). While self-sufficiency at the national level is readily obtainable via price incentives and the maintenance of a strategic grain reserve, a major challenge is to ensure that food-deficit households do not suffer as a result of the commercialisation of staple food production.

## MAJOR FOOD SECURITY ISSUES IN MALAWI

The household food insecurity problem in Malawi needs to be broken down into two components: rural and urban food insecurity.

### Household Food Insecurity: Rural Areas

As a result of small farm sizes, chronic shortages of and labour constraints, the overall productivity of a number of farms (especially those below 1,0 ha) is inadequate to meet the basic needs of many rural families. Production is largely

[1]Planning Division, Ministry of Agriculture, Lilongwe, Malawi.

confined to food for family use, and, for a number of families, the farm does not supply its caloric requirements. This problem is illustrated in Liwonde and Blantyre Agricultural Development Divisions (ADDs) where over 60 percent of farmers have a mean holdings size of 0,55 ha. On a farm of 0,55 ha about 75 percent is allocated to local maize (0,41 ha). Average yields of unfertilized local maize under these conditions are about 800 kg/ha so that total field production would be 328 kilograms. Allowing for seed saved and losses in storage and pounding, this would produce only 268 kilograms of edible maize. For a typical farm family consisting of four to five people, this amount of maize would satisfy only 38 percent of their caloric requirements. This situation is typical of small farmers throughout the country. Table 1 shows the percentage of farmers in each Agricultural Development Division (ADD) who are unable to meet their family food requirements from their own holdings. This shows that the problem is more serious in the Southern Region (where Liwonde, Blantyre and Ngabu ADDs are located). As a result, a number of smallholders are net purchasers of food staples.

**Table 1**
**Percentage of households meeting consumption requirements from
own farm production by holding size and calorie requirements**

| | Holding size (Hectares) | | | | | |
|---|---|---|---|---|---|---|
| | <0,5 | 0,5-1,0 | 1,0-1,5 | <0,5 | 0,5-1,0 | 1,0-1,5 |
| ADD | % of Households | | | % of Cal. Requirement | | |
| Karonga | 35 | 37 | 14 | 31 | 71 | 110 |
| Mzuzu | 14 | 29 | 29 | 40 | 86 | 153 |
| Kasungu | 12 | 20 | 21 | 39 | 104 | 142 |
| Lilongwe | 20 | 8 | 23 | 25 | 61 | 105 |
| Salima | 26 | 34 | 19 | 31 | 59 | 84 |
| Liwonde | 32 | 34 | 21 | 20 | 51 | 86 |
| Blantyre | 47 | 32 | 12 | 35 | 74 | 107 |
| Ngabu | 40 | 32 | 17 | 19 | 37 | 55 |

Source: World Bank (1989)

The food deficit at the household level is further reflected in the national figures for maize availability. Since 1980-81 the amount of maize produced and consumed has fluctuated between 136 and 198 kilograms per head as shown in Table 2. From 1981-82 to 1985-86 the national deficit was met by maize imports. Moreover, because of the lack of purchasing power, many households are unable to meet their food needs even though there are unsold stocks at ADMARC sales outlets.

**Table 2**
**Estimated maize production, ADMARC transactions,**
**trade and per capita consumption**

| Production year | Estimated production ('000t) | Market year ('000t) | ADMARC purchases ('000t) | ADMARC sales ('000t) | Exports (imports) ('000t) | Popul-ation ('000t) | Kgs per capita |
|---|---|---|---|---|---|---|---|
| 1980-81 | 1 237 | 1981-82 | 137 | 63 | -56 | 6 522 | 186 |
| 1981-82 | 1 244 | 1982-83 | 246 | 73 | -1 | 6 765 | 158 |
| 1982-83 | 1 369 | 1983-84 | 245 | 190 | 76 | 7 009 | 198 |
| 1983-84 | 1 398 | 1984-85 | 297 | 86 | 180 | 7 252 | 189 |
| 1984-85 | 1 355 | 1985-86 | 272 | 164 | 46 | 7 496 | 173 |
| 1985-86 | 1 295 | 1986-87 | 111 | 286 | 32 | 7 739 | 194 |
| 1986-87 | 1 211 | 1987-88 | 113 | 130 | -140 | 7 983 | 136 |

Source: World Bank (1989)

From the above, it would appear that a large number of Malawian farmers do not produce adequate food for their basic requirements and are required to undertake other income generating activities or rely on remittances to provide supplementary food.

As a result of small farm size and low cash incomes, which in turn limit access to improved technology and access to food, many poorer adults suffer from seasonal under-nutrition. Almost 50 percent of Malawi's rural children are chronically malnourished.

### Household Food Insecurity: Urban Areas

Food insecurity is not just a problem of rural families; it is also a significant problem for a large number of urban households. At present, knowledge about the characteristics and distribution of this vulnerable group is limited. What is known, however, is that their food security is steadily declining as market prices of maize increase. Maize prices have risen due to a combination of factors, principally the result of a supply shortfall which coincided with the introduction of the private sector to maize and other crop marketing. As a result of higher free market prices, the marketing corporation purchased only small quantities of maize and thus were not in a position to defend a ceiling price with limited stocks. Maize was in short supply, free market prices rose and the small consumer subsidy on maize was eliminated. However, higher maize prices stimulated an increase in marketed maize both this season and last with prices stabilising at levels higher than those when the marketing corporation was the sole trader, but lower than when maize was in short supply during 1987.

Families on fixed income, especially those receiving the minimum wage, have experienced a gradual erosion of their purchasing power as a result of increasing maize costs and inflation. In recent months, this has been offset to some degree by a near doubling in minimum wage rates.

## CURRENT STATUS OF FOOD SECURITY POLICIES, PROGRAMMES AND PROJECTS

The Government is addressing national food insecurity by encouraging increased productivity in the smallholder and estate sectors. Since the end of the 1970s, the Government's National Rural Development Programme (NRDP) has provided a wide range of services to the smallholder sub-sector. By 1984, 80 percent of the smallholder sub-sector was under NRDP. The NRDP has been designed to increase smallholder productivity through the provision of agricultural inputs and farm services and to increase the scope and efficiency of extension, marketing and credit services. Cultivation of new areas of land has been discouraged in favour of increasing the productivity of areas already cultivated. Attention is given to soil conservation, watershed management and afforestation.

In addition to the promotion of food production, Malawi has constructed a strategic grain reserve (SGR) with a capacity of 180 000 tonnes to be available when production shortfalls occur. The role of the strategic grain reserve is to provide some measure of protection against fluctuations in output to reduce the economic losses incurred through unprofitable grain exports and to ensure relatively stable prices of maize both to the consumer and producer through the accumulation or release of stocks during periods of domestic surplus or shortfall.

### Increasing Access to Food

Since the majority of the population earns their living as smallholders, the Government's strategy to promote access to food entails increasing productivity on smallholdings. This is intended to improve on-farm consumption, raise rural incomes and increase the marketable surplus of maize. For the urban households, especially those on the minimum wage, the priority is to ensure that they have access to food. To meet this objective, the Government periodically reviews the minimum wage to take into account the cost of living, especially the food component.

In addition to the above measures, the Government through the Ministry of Health has a feeding programme for children suffering from malnutrition in under-five clinics. The Government also distributes free food through its emergency relief programme to people who have been affected by natural disasters such as drought, floods and crop diseases.

### Organisational Structure for Managing Food Security

Food security and early warning activities are presently carried out at two levels. With the assistance of the World Bank, a Food Security and Nutrition Unit (FSNU) was established in 1987 in the Office of the President and Cabinet (OPC). In addition, early warning activities undertaken by the SADCC/FAO/DANIDA Project have been assigned to the Ministry of Agriculture.

The major responsibilities of the FSNU are: to maintain an overview of existing policies and activities related to food security and nutrition; to undertake analyses of existing data and collect new data where necessary to assess the impact of existing and proposed Government policies and programmes on food security and nutrition of vulnerable population groups; and to develop a comprehensive strategy for identifying and addressing Malawi's food security and nutritional needs including early warning surveillance systems, strategic grain reserve management and possible project interventions to address hunger and malnutrition problems.

## Anticipated Problems

As far as transitory food insecurity is concerned, the biggest challenge of the 1990s will be to produce sufficient food domestically to feed the population. Given the long and expensive routes from nearby ports at Durban and Dar-es-Salaam and the unreliability of supplies on regional markets, national food self-sufficiency remains a central objective of economic policy. Tackling supply constraints through improvements in maize output and agricultural productivity is a primary government policy. Production incentives, via both official and free market prices can serve to increase the marketed surplus in line with demand while at the same time maintaining prices at a level which will allow most households to buy the balance of their requirements. Intervention in the market during food shortage or surplus periods can take place using working stocks held by the marketing corporation and in the last resort, the strategic grain reserve. In addition, through its child-spacing programme, Government is addressing and attempting to reduce the current high levels of population growth.

Addressing the problem of chronic food insecurity is more difficult. The aim is to improve the nutritional status of poor households with insufficient cash income to purchase the maize they need and currently cannot grow. This can rarely be achieved or afforded in developing countries in the form of broad sectoral policies. The requirement to first identify individual vulnerable households and then target appropriate assistance has been recognised in Malawi as an almost overwhelming constraint to the rapid solution of the problems facing chronic food deficit households. By virtue of these difficulties, many of the approaches under discussion are "self-targeting" -- these include food and/or fertilizer-for-work schemes; small credit packages, cheap (possibly subsidised) maize substitutes and intervention/assistance at clinics, hospitals, *etc.*, where the undernourished and/or malnourished may present themselves. While many of these schemes are still in their infancy, the Government is encouraged that such a targeted approach will prove a less costly and more effective means of directing assistance to the very poor than the blanket subsidisation of all sectors of the population.

## SADCC Initiatives

One of the critical issues in the production of food in Malawi is the availability of fertilizer on a timely basis and at a reasonable price. Rising world prices for fertilizer and high external transport costs mean that the resources available to the Smallholder Farmers' Fertilizer Revolving Fund (SFFRF) are not sufficient to procure adequate quantities of fertilizer to maintain food self-sufficiency. The Government has outlined a target fertilizer programme for the next five years and is seeking longer term pledges of grant-aided fertilizer from donors.

# REFERENCES

Eicher, Carl K. and John M. Staatz. 1985. *Food Security Policy in Sub-Saharan Africa*. Invited paper prepared for the XIXth Conference of the International Association of Agricultural Economists. Malaga. Spain. August 22 - September 5. 1985.

FAO. 1989. *SADCC Project Proposal: Early Warning.System for Food Security, Phase II*. Rome. July 1989.

Malawi Government. 1987. *Statement of Development Policies 1987-1996*.

Malawi Government Food Security and Nutrition Unit. 1989. *Food Security and Nutrition Bulletin*. Vol.1. No.1. April 3, 1989.

Mtawali, K.M. 1988. *Malnutrition in Malawi - An Overview*. Preliminary paper prepared under the Kellogg International Program in Food Systems (KIFP/FS). July 1988.

Mtawali, K.M. *Agricultural Prices, Production and Distribution: What Must be Done to Relieve and Prevent Famine* [Incomplete]

World Bank. 1985. *Malawi: Agricultural Extension and Planning Support Project*. Staff Appraisal Report.

World Bank. 1988. *Malawi: Agricultural Marketing and Estate Development Project*. Staff Appraisal Report.

World Bank. 1989. *Malawi: National Rural Development Programme*. (NRDP) Technical Issues Review.

# 5

# Swaziland : Food Security Issues And Challenges For The 1990s[1]

*Samkele S. Hlophe*[2]

## INTRODUCTION

It is important to understand the agricultural policy framework within which Food Security should be considered in Swaziland. This policy is laid down in the Five Year National Development Strategy of 1986 and consists of the following major objectives:

1) Achievement of basic food self-sufficiency.
2) Improving nutritional levels.
3) Increasing agricultural exports.
4) Boosting rural incomes and employment.

The strategy was further refined in 1987 and 1988 with the aim of concentrating policy on the alleviation of major constraints to agricultural development such as poor use of land and water resources, low livestock off-take, and an inadequate marketing and crop storage infrastructure. The strategy emphasises the intensification of production rather than extensification, transfer of technology to small farmers through the traditional system and conservation of the natural resource base.

It is within this context that food security programmes and projects are implemented in Swaziland.

## FOOD SECURITY

Food Security can be defined as ensuring that all members of a society have access to enough food throughout the year to lead an active and healthy life. The essential elements of food security are availability of food through domestic production, storage and/or trade, and access to food through home production, purchase in the market or food transfer.

---

[1]The views expressed in this paper are the sole responsibility of the author and may not always represent the policy of the Swaziland Government.

[2]Senior Agricultural Economist, Ministry of Agriculture and Cooperatives, Department of Research and Planning, Mbabane, Swaziland.

The objectives of food security are:

o    To satisfy the basic needs of the population of the country and progressively to improve food supplies to all the people, irrespective of their positions in the society.

o    To achieve national self-sufficiency in food supply to the maximum extent possible in order to reduce the national dependence on external sources of food aid.

o    To eliminate periodic food crises which affect some areas of the country

Swaziland is a net importer of its staple food, namely maize. However, it is believed that in 1985-86 Swaziland was very near the level of self-sufficiency. Again in 1988 a good harvest was realised in the country and had it not been for the unfavourable weather conditions between 1986 and 1988 national requirements would have been met. Imports have assumed a downward trend over the past six years. To illustrate this, last year, following a severe drought imports were approximately 37 000 metric tonnes whereas in the late 1970s and early 1980s approximately 50 000 metric tonnes had to be imported following bad weather. In general, maize production has approximately doubled since independence.

The inability to produce sufficient maize for internal consumption can be attributed to a number of factors such as the following:

o    the reliance on rainfall;

o    inadequate draft power at crucial planting periods;

o    access to credit (to acquire inputs);

o    inadequate markets and related infrastructure in the country side;

o    low prices which meant that it was not profitable to produce maize above subsistence level;

o    inadequate on-farm and off-farm storage.

These factors may directly or indirectly result in food insecurity.

The Swaziland government, through the Ministry of Agriculture and Cooperatives (MOAC) and the cooperation of the private sector is pursuing a food security policy -- aimed at ensuring that adequate supplies of food are always available for all members of the society. The policy is based on continuous monitoring of food production and availability both within and from external sources. Present policy places more emphasis on small farmer production -- shifting from subsistence to semi-commercial and commercial farming while not ignoring large-scale production on Title Deed Land (TDL).

Furthermore, the government is giving priority to:

o    the newly established Early Warning Unit (EWU) to provide forecasts
     on changes which are occurring in production, prices and availability off
     supplies;

o    preparing an economically sound food reserve programme for reasons
     of social, economic and political stability and;

o    determining the financial costs of holding various strategic stocks and
     means by which these costs can be met.

## CURRENT STATUS OF FOOD INSECURITY

### Food Security Situation in the Country

Food security in Swaziland largely depends on the production of maize, the staple
food crop and the availability of incomes to buy food, particularly among the rural
population. Maize production is constrained by a number of factors as mentioned
above. Food insecurity is at the moment less chronic than transient in nature and
the government is giving this long-term remedial considerations to improve the food
security situation.

To combat the effects of insufficient rainfall, a major consideration is the
development of the water resources. New irrigation schemes have been established
and those rendered unserviceable through the cyclone Domino (1984) are being
rehabilitated. These are small irrigation schemes (which largely cater to small
vegetable production) compared to larger areas under maize at present. Larger
schemes have been identified in repurchased farms through extensive feasibility
studies, especially in the dry drought-prone areas of the Lowveld. In these schemes
farmers will grow a surplus in maize, cotton and vegetables for the market, according
to land suitability.

Inadequacy of draft power at the peak of the ploughing season is, as mentioned, a
constraint on increased production. One means to address this problem was
Government's tractor leasing facility that was set up on an experimental basis --
where the government guaranteed a loan for purchase of a tractor plus a complete
set of implements to individuals or groups of proven capability in farming.
Government has rehabilitated the Tractor Hire Pool (THP) to increase the number
of tractors because of the acceptability of the programme.

Lack of access to credit (another constraint of increasing production) to acquire
inputs is also being addressed by the government. Through the Smallholder Credit
and Marketing (IFAD) project, the farmers in the irrigation schemes are able to
obtain loans for the purchase of inputs. Government has initiated a maize block
credit programme whereby farmers are supplied with inputs on loan with the
collateral being the farmer's capability and capacity to produce. The loan is
recovered from the sale at harvest.

In the past there were no price incentives for farmers to produce more maize. In
the course of time Government, introduced a guaranteed minimum price of maize

and a ready market through the cooperatives and the National Maize Corporation (NMC). Initially the minimum price was based on import parity. Price fixing is now no longer based on import parity but on the costs of production, to ensure economic prices. Another incentive is early price announcements (before planting).

The Central Cooperatives Union (CCU) assists farmers in the procurement of maize from rural areas to the NMC and uses temporary storage at transit sheds to facilitate marketing.

A number of silos (total present capacity 16 000 metric tonnes) have been constructed at strategic locations of the country to provide grain storage for food security purposes. The Grain Storage Section of the Ministry of Agriculture and Cooperatives provides extension education through the promotion of the construction of rural structures to reduce post-harvest losses in the rural areas.

In ensuring that the programme on preparing an economically sound food reserve system is implemented, the government has considered increasing the number of silos to meet not only the present but future production levels of the country. Government will ensure that the existing strategically located silos are operational. This will also facilitate distribution of the maize from surplus producing areas to deficit areas.

Although previous reports have indicated that Swaziland is one of the best fed among the SADCC states, undernutrition in some communities, particularly in the Lowveld is still persistent. National food aid programmes provide about 5 500 tonnes of cereal products (every year) under regular programmes to vulnerable groups. The latter have increased due to the refugee influx from neighbouring countries.

## Food Security Situation for the 1987-88 to 1989-90 Marketing Year

The Ministry of Agriculture and Cooperatives through the Early Warning Unit monitors food crop conditions during the crop growing season as well as the general food situation (surplus/deficit) in the country.

In this 1988-89 analysis the EWU covered three cereal crops, namely maize, wheat and rice. While maize is the staple food, the latter two are mostly consumed by the urban population. As such the demand for these during the year was met largely through imports at reasonable prices. In view of this no serious food insecurity problem was anticipated in these commodities.

Maize plays a very vital role in the food security situation of the country. Wheat and rice also deserve due attention because they constitute a sizeable magnitude of the total cereal consumption and they also serve as partial substitutes for maize.

In the absence of relevant data, the total requirements of wheat and rice could not be estimated. Since market forces function efficiently to bring a balance in the supply and demand at reasonable price levels, total availability was taken as total requirements. The requirements of wheat and rice during the marketing year were estimated at 20 000 and 2 000 metric tonnes respectively.

The total production of maize was estimated at 110 700 metric tonnes by the Central Statistical Office (CSO). Adding the opening stock with the National Maize Corporation (NMC) as of May 1, 1988, total maize availability reached 112 300 metric tonnes. Against this the total maize requirement was estimated to be 148 800 metric tonnes leaving a 36 500 metric tonnes gap. This gap was further widened with unplanned exports of about 6 000 metric tonnes. At the closure of the marketing year 1988-89, the total gap of 42 500 metric tonnes had almost been covered by planned imports of 38 900 metric tonnes comprising commercial imports (36 700 metric tonnes) and food aid (2 200 metric tonnes). The NMC's contribution was about 90 percent of the commercial imports.

The existence of an uncovered gap of 3 600 metric tonnes did not pose any serous problems during the marketing year under review.

### Food Security Trends : 1987-88 to 1989-90

Based on the water requirement satisfaction indices and the overall crop conditions reported by the field staff, the forecast of maize production during the 1988-89 crop season was placed at 135 000 metric tonnes.

The 1983 Agricultural Census (CSO) results revealed that about 65 percent of homesteads growing maize did not produce enough maize to meet their home consumption requirements. The limited disposable income renders this category of homestead unable to satisfy their total demand for food in the market and as a corollary to this, the free play of market forces cannot effectively safeguard their interest. Food requirements of the vulnerable section of the population have to be taken care of through appropriate measures under the national food security system.

### Table 1
### Food security situation for the period 1987-88 to 1989-90
('000 tonnes)

| Item | Maize 1987-88 | Maize 1988-89 | Maize 1989-90 |
|---|---|---|---|
| Opening stocks | 1,6 | 1,6 | 2,0 |
| Domestic production | 85,7 | 110,7 | 135,0 |
| Total availability | 87,3 | 112,3 | 137,0 |
| Estimated consumption[a] | 143,5 | 146,8 | 151,5 |
| Carryover requirements | 2,0 | 2,0 | 2,0 |
| Total requirements | 145,5 | 148,8 | 153,5 |
| Surplus (+)/Deficit (-) | -29,5 | -36,5 | -16,5 |
| Exports (unofficial) | 6,0 | 6,0 | 6,0 |
| Import requirements | 35,5 | 42,5 | 16,5 |
| Stocks | - | 2,3 | - |
| Forecast closing stock | 2,0 | 2,0 | - |
| Population (estimate) | 712 013 | 733 373 | 755 374 |

[a] Includes requirements for seed, feed, and human consumption; consumption is based on per cap/p.a/187,5kg consumption (gross) of maize of mid-year population.
Source: Ministry of Agriculture, Government of Swaziland. Early Warning Unit, Quarterly Bulletins (1980-1989)

In the three year period domestic production of maize has increased steadily. The percentage increases were 30 percent and 22 percent for 1988-89 and 1989-90. There was an increase of two percent in 1988-89 and a three percent increase is expected in the 1989-90 marketing year.

### Table 2
### Maize imports and exports for the period 1987-88 to 1989-90
('000 tonnes)

| Item | 1987-88 | 1988-89 | 1989-90 |
|------|--------|--------|--------|
| Import requirements | 35,5 | 42,5 | 42,5 |
| Imports planned | 5,5 | 32,8 | 38,9 |
| Commercial imports received | - | 20,2 | 36,7 |
| Commercial imports to be received | 5,5 | 10,4 | 0,0[a] |
| Food aid received | - | 2,2 | 2,2 |
| Food aid but not received | - | - | - |
| Uncovered import gap | - | 9,7 | 3,6 |
| Surplus | - | - | - |
| Exports | - | 6,0 | 6,0 |

[a] Figures not available
Source: Ministry of Agriculture, Government of Swaziland, Early Warning Unit, Quarterly Bulletins (1988-1989)

## CURRENT STATUS OF
## FOOD SECURITY POLICIES, PROGRAMMES AND PROJECTS

In addition to the establishment of an Early Warning System to provide insights on changes which are occurring in production, prices and availability of supplies, government, through the Ministry of Agriculture and Cooperatives and with the cooperation of the private sector, will give priority to: preparing an economically sound Food Reserve programme for reasons of social, economic and political stability; and determining the financial costs of holding various strategic stocks and the means by which these can be met.

### Increasing Food Availability

With the implementation of the Rural Development Areas Programme (RDAP) which was initiated in the early seventies, maize production has more than doubled on Swazi Nation Land (SNL). Current maize yields range from one to four metric tonnes per hectare on SNL.

As an initiative to increase maize production, the Government has adopted a policy of announcing the price of maize before the planting season. Farmers are also encouraged to grow suitable crops in each ecological zone based on research results.

Surveys carried out in the early eighties indicate that post harvest losses of maize are estimated at 23 percent. However, further investigative work needs to be done on the causes of these losses as they relate to the availability of marketing outlets and other incentives.

The Government imports maize from the Republics of Kenya, South Africa and SADCC region to meet commercial demand, particularly in the urban areas. In rural grain-deficit areas the demand is met through informal sales or bartering.

## Increasing Access to Food

Farmers on SNL are progressively becoming commercialised and most of them grow a maize surplus to sell to cooperatives who act as an agent of the National Maize Corporation (NMC), the main commercial marketing outlet for maize. In areas where maize is not a suitable crop, cotton, tobacco and beans are grown, sold and the proceeds are used to buy food.

Under Phase II of the EWS project there is a provision for a nutrition component to complement work already being done by the Home Economics Section of Ministry of Agriculture and Co-operatives (MOAC), the Ministry of Health and other non-governmental organisation (NGO).

## ORGANISATIONAL STRUCTURE FOR MANAGING FOOD SECURITY

Food security planning has not been integrated among the various ministries in the government organisational structure. The reason for this is that food security is still a new concept in Swaziland. There are instead, policies through the different ministries aimed at finding a solution to the problem of food insecurity both at national and at household level. Hence, the considerations being given to the vulnerable groups mentioned earlier.

### Roles of the Various Institutions Involved in Planning and Administration

The Food Aid Assistance Section in the ministry of Agriculture and Cooperatives works together with the Ministries of Health, Education and Interior and Immigration to distribute food aid donated by the World Food Programme (WFP). The section aims at improving the nutritional status of designated vulnerable groups (Table 3). These consist of expectant and nursing mothers, pre-school children (between ages 6 month and 5 years). This ensures regular attendance of mothers and children at health centres and enables them to receive more adequate health care and educate mothers in better child feeding practices. Refugees and those in areas hit by natural disasters also receive food aid assistance.

The Food Assistance programme also aims at increasing the effectiveness of schools and training centres by providing nutritious daily meals throughout the country, thus improving the nutritional status of school children.

The number of institutions and beneficiaries participating in the feeding schemes is increased with the assistance of the Ministries of Education and Health. There is also some collaboration with some non-governmental organisations *eg.* Save the Children Fund.

Through the Ministry of Interior and Immigration, the government distributes food aid to refugees. The food aid comes from the WFP as well as the United Nations High Commission for Refugees in Swaziland (UNHCR).

## Table 3
## Objectives of the Food Assistance Section

|  | Present | End of Period |
|---|---|---|
| Primary schools (No.) | 243 | 300 |
| Children feeding No.) | 82 988 | 10 000 |
| Day sec. schools (No.) | 59 | 70 |
| Feeding (No.) | 13 295 | 15 000 |
| Nursery schools (No.) | 164 | 184 |
| Feeding (No.) | 7 200 | 7 600 |
| Boarding schools (No.) | 19 | 21 |
| Feeding (No.) | 2 883 | 3 200 |
| Training centres (No.) | 5 | 12 |
| Feeding (No.) | 702 | 1 200 |
| Clinics (No.) | 107 | 117 |
| Feeding No.) | 48 339 | 50 000 |

Source : Food Aid Assistance Annual Report (1988)

## Table 4
## World Food Programme food distribution for the months of May, June and July 1988

| Month | Distribution Centre | No. Of Refugees | Maize (90kg) | Beans (50kg) | C.Oil (20kg) | Fish |
|---|---|---|---|---|---|---|
| May | 1. Lomahasha/Shewula | 2 440 | 494 | 98 | 138 | 102 |
|  | 2. Ndzevane | 4 987 | 492 | 17 | 160 | - |
|  | 3. Malindza | 2 091 | 266 | 65 | 354 | - |
|  | Total | 9 518 | 1 252 | 180 | 652 | 102 |
| June | 1. Lomahasha/Shewula | 4 208 | 514 | 137 | 188 | - |
|  | 2. Ndzevane | 5 213 | 645 | - | 89 | - |
|  | 3. Malindza | 2 133 | 268 | 77 | 454 | - |
|  | Total | 11 284 | 1 427 | 214 | 731 | - |
| July | 1. Lomahasha/Shewula | 4 865 | 619 | 107,5 | 243 | 132 |
|  | 2. Ndzevane | 5 137 | 662 | 129 | - | - |
|  | 3. Malindza | 2 376 | 345 | 85 | 528 | - |
|  | Total | 12 378 | 1 626 | 321,5 | 771 | 132 |

Source: WFP Food Distribution Report for May, June and July 1988

The Ministries involved, among others include the Ministry of Agriculture and Cooperatives, Ministry of Education, Ministry of Health, and Ministry of Interior and Immigration

As mentioned before, within the Ministry of Agriculture and Cooperatives (MOAC), there is the Early Warning Unit which is responsible for the monitoring of food crop conditions during the crop growing season. It also monitors the general food situation in the country.

The activities of the Early Warning System for food security will be coordinated by a committee tasked with the responsibility to facilitate the planning and implementation of such a programme (food security).

A Coordination Committee for the Early Warning System is to be formed. This will consist of representatives from the different ministries and departments involved in the collection of agricultural data relevant to the monitoring of the food security situation in the country. The Coordination Committee will consist of representatives from the following units:

o   From the Ministry of Agriculture and Cooperatives:
    Early Warning Unit, Marketing Advisory Unit, Monitoring and Evaluation Unit, Home Economics, Information Section, Research Station.

o   Department of Economics Planning Section in the Prime Minister's office.

o   Ministry of Natural Resources (Meteorology Section).

Data will be provided by the Central Cooperatives Union, National Maize Corporation, Chinese Agricultural Mission, World Food Programme, UNDP (Project Officer) and Swaziland United Bakeries.

The formation of such a committee is expected to lay a foundation for the expansion of the early warning programme in the future.

## ANTICIPATED PROBLEMS

a)   Food production is likely to fall short of the rapidly rising population, and rural-urban migration may have adverse effects on food security due to a less attractive rural agricultural sector.

b)   If the political problems in South Africa and Mozambique are not resolved, the refugee influx into Swaziland will intensify and food insecurity will be exacerbated.

c)   Severe variations in food production due to drought, other weather problems as well as natural hazards.

## SADCC INITIATIVES

The SADCC's Food Security Unit can assist in providing Technical Assistance (TA) to conduct Food Security Research. It can also assist in implementing the SADCC Food Reserve Project with the new focus as agreed in the Mbabane meeting of

Standing Officials on June 7 to 9, 1989. SADCC can seek Technical Assistance to complete Phase I of the national component of the Regional Early Warning System Project and implement Phase II of this project. Technical Assistance to Phase I of this project was terminated on August 31, 1989 instead of June 1990, the completion date, according to the implementation plan in the project document. Possible food security areas for future research include:

o    food security surveys at the household levels;

o    access to food and food preferences and trends in the consumption patterns;

o    investigation of national seed stocks and sources of supply for both farmer saved and commercially produced seed.

## REFERENCES

Ministry of Agriculture, Government of Swaziland. (various issues). *National Early Warning Unit Bulletins.* Government of Swaziland. Mbabane.

Food Aid Assistance Annual Report. 1988.

World Food Programme Food Distribution Report. 1988. Various monthly issues.

# 6

# Tanzania: Food Security Issues And Challenges For The 1990s

*D Biseko*[1]

## INTRODUCTION

The government of Tanzania's conception of food security is contained in the Agricultural Policy of 1983. The policy goals with regard to food security are achieving national self-sufficiency and raising the nutritional standards of living of all Tanzanians; earning foreign exchange for the nation apart from meeting its own sectoral needs; and developing an integrated agricultural sector, using methods of scientific husbandry and technology appropriate to the respective crops, size of operation and national resources.

The targets set forth in the 1983 policy are *inter alia*:

o    to increase output, variety and marketing of food which is adequate in quantity and quality for all Tanzanians, and thereafter to raise output growth at least as fast as population growth;

o    setting up of a properly managed National Strategic Grain Reserve;

o    improved efficiency in the production, marketing and processing of agricultural commodities;

o    increased investment in the agricultural sector.

Based on the Agricultural Policy, the Government launched a National Food Strategy (NFS) in 1984 which elaborated upon the options for attaining food security. The extended and deep-seated crisis in the Tanzanian economy, however, led the Government to devise more short-term measures which were aimed at removing the bottlenecks to smooth operation of the economy.

[1]SADCC Food Security Liaison Officer, Ministry of Agriculture and Livestock Development, Tanzania.

Acknowledgements: I am heavily indebted to colleagues at the Ministry of Agriculture and Livestock Development (MALD) for assisting with information, and giving suggestions and comments. Moreso to Mrs J. Lwakatare for the typing and Word Processing, any errors remaining are solely mine. The views expressed in this paper do not necessarily represent the position of the Government of the United Republic of Tanzania of which the author is an employee.

The Economic Recovery Programme (ERP), 1986-1988, a successor to two previous programmes to revive the economy (Structural Adjustment Programme (SAP) and National Economic Survival Programme (NESP)) brought remarkable achievements. By emphasising institutional changes with regard to marketing and distribution which had been overlooked by the previous two programmes, together with price incentives, the ERP has been able to restore production particularly of major agricultural commodities to pre-crisis level, reduce Government deficits, increase exports and reduce inflation. This has paved the way for long term planning of the economy as evidenced by the launching of the Second Union Five Year Development Plan (FYDP) (1988-93).

Both the Agricultural Policy (1983) and the NFS (1984) form the pillars of the FYDP in the Agricultural Sector. The 1989-90 Annual Plan, drawn-up within the framework of the FYDP, sets out the following priority areas for implementation: increasing support to smallholder farmers by improving extension services, farm service centres, crop and livestock research, pests and disease control, land conservation and proper land use together with promotion of modern inputs, equipment, agro-chemicals, veterinary drugs and improved seeds.

## FOOD SECURITY STATUS

During the past three years, 1986-87 to 1988-89, Tanzania has experienced a favourable food situation as shown in Table 1 despite food deficit pockets in some parts of the country due to transitory drought or flood conditions. An occasional paper on the food situation published in May 1988 by the Food Strategy Unit of the Ministry of Agriculture and Livestock Development (MALD) includes a national food balance sheet which reveals *per capita* consumption of 2 882 calories, 63,4 grams of protein and 37,3 grams of fat per day; these figures indicate adequate consumption, particularly for calories, relative to the FAO/WHO standard of 2 300 calories for Tanzania.

### Table 1
### Tanzania mainland production estimate 1983-84 to 1988-89
('000 metric tonnes)

|                  | 1983-84 | 1984-85    | 1985-86    | 1986-87    | 1987-88    | 1988-89* |
|------------------|---------|------------|------------|------------|------------|------------|
| Maize            | 1 939   | 2 093      | 2 210      | 2 359      | 2 339      | 3 125      |
| Millet           | 760     | 1 024      | 943        | 954        | 700        | 804        |
| Paddy            | 356     | 427        | 547        | 664        | 629        | 720        |
| Beans            | 540     | 441        | 321        | 425        | 386        | 503        |
| Wheat            | 74      | 83         | 72         | 72         | 76         | 97         |
| Bananas          | -       | 774        | 777        | 792        | 813        | 743        |
| Cassava          | -       | 2 052      | 2 031      | 1 709      | 1 744      | 1 948      |
| Sweet Potatoes   | -       | 308        | 291        | 352        | 246        | 267        |
| Total Grains     | -       | 4 068      | 4 093      | 4 473      | 4 130      | 5 249      |
| Roots & Bananas  | -       | 3 134      | 3 099      | 2 854      | 2 803      | 2 959      |
| Total Production | -       | 7 202      | 7 192      | 7 327      | 6 933      | 8 208      |
| Population       | -       | 21 290 478 | 21 886 612 | 22 499 437 | 23 129 421 | 23 129 431 |
| Consumption      | -       | 5 440      | 5 592      | 5 749      | 5 626      | 5 926      |
| Surplus/Deficit  | -       | 1 762      | 1 600      | 1 579      | 2 131      | 2 282      |

Source: United Republic of Tanzania, (1989).

Climatic factors still contribute greatly to food insecurity in Tanzania. This is largely due to the fragile nature of smallholder peasant agriculture. In 1988 drought conditions necessitated famine relief in parts of Lindi and Kilimanjaro regions and floods have affected one fourth of the regions in mainland Tanzania. An estimated 18 327 hectares were waterlogged as a result of the floods, necessitating 6 875 tonnes of maize for famine relief.

Crop pests and diseases are significant causes of food insecurity in Tanzania. The emergence of the larger grain borer in three maize growing regions has posed a threat to grains stored on-farm. The cassava mealy bug, is reported in seven regions representing approximately one third of mainland Tanzania, and the banana weevil are also important crop pests. Recently, the banana disease, Black Sigatoka, has been reported in two coastal regions adding to the causes of food insecurity in the country. Rodents, quelea and armyworms remain a chronic threat to farmers' crops.

Socio-economic factors also contribute to food insecurity, particularly for the non-agricultural population such as those living in urban areas. The severity of the problem in Tanzania, however, is not well known, as it is difficult to estimate urban incomes. Amani *et al.* (1988, 1989) report food expenditures exceeding official incomes in most households in Dar es Salaam. It is understood that many people perform other income earning activities outside their official jobs. But it is not known whether this applies to all income groups. In some regions which experience frequent drought, low income has also been a major cause of food insecurity. This has often led to failure in the market operation and institution of food transfer programmes.

Infrastructural bottlenecks have currently emerged as critical problems in alleviating food insecurity, though not a cause of food insecurity. In the South Western regions, where transport and storage facilities are inadequate, surplus grain is stored in the open where it can easily be spoilt by rain and pests. Such bottlenecks have been a serious constraint on efficient operation of the food market and have in many cases led to localised food shortages.

## CURRENT STATUS OF FOOD SECURITY
## POLICIES, PROGRAMMES AND PROJECTS

### Increasing Food Availability

The 1988 paper by Amani *et al.* examined the macro-economic policies which affected food supply between 1984 and 1986, namely currency devaluation, increase in producer prices, removal of input subsidies and reduction of internal trade barriers, removal of consumer subsidies, partial import liberalisation, exchange rate adjustment, increase of producer prices and reduction of price controls.

Since the implementation of the NFS in 1984, Government has established a Food Strategy Unit (FSU) in the Ministry of Agriculture and Livestock Development (MALD), which has been charged with the duty of formulating food policy and programmes, monitoring their implementation and reviewing them when necessary.

The FSU has already prepared a Drought Resistant Cereals Strategy which focuses on Sorghum and Millet, a Cassava Development Strategy and a Rice Development Programme and a Village Level Storage Programme.

A review of the 1989-90 Annual Plan offers a clear perspective of the on-going programmes and projects aimed at improving the food situation at the national level. The plan provides for continued implementation of seven irrigation projects which when completed will increase irrigated land by an estimated 17 000 hectares. All these projects are intended to grow paddy as the major crop.

Under the State-owned National Agricultural and Food Corporation (NAFCO), the government aims at improving and expanding the production of maize and wheat in state farms.    The target is to improve maize productivity and expand wheat cultivation by 8 000 hectares.

The Government also aims to improve smallholder production through implementation of four projects, viz: a fertilizer programme which has the objective of promoting the proper use of fertilizer to attain high yields; a Southern Highlands Crop Improvement programme which seeks to utilise the potential of the major maize growing regions in the south (Ruvuma, Mbeya, Rukwa and Iringa Regions); a Food Security Programme which aims at providing support services to farmer, to enable farmers to increase their yields of food crops; and a pilot project on extension research linkages in food crop production which aims to involve peasants in crop research and adoption of research results.

The 1989-90 Annual Plan includes research projects in paddy, maize, sorghum, millet, banana, roots and tubers together with beans.    There are five ongoing projects on plant pest and disease control which are in the Plan.    These cover rodents, banana weevils, cassava mealy bug, armyworms and the larger grain borer.

The Government aims to continue implementing a grain storage and milling project with the objective of rehabilitating existing milling machines and expanding milling and storage capacity.

Although under favourable climatic conditions, Tanzania is self-reliant in maize, this is not the case with the other preferred staples, rice and wheat.    There has been a substantial reliance on imports of these items as evidenced in Table 2.

The Food Security Unit estimates import requirements of 30 000 tons of rice and the same amount of wheat for 1989-90 consumption.

### Increasing Access to Food

Major interventions by the Government in increasing access to food have been through: the price mechanism, reorganisation and rationalisation of the marketing and distribution system, nutrition programmes and food relief.

Following the launching of the 1983 Agricultural Policy, government has relied more heavily on the price mechanism to induce increased production rather than direct intervention in agriculture as shown in Table 3.    Price policy reforms in the agricultural sector have helped increase incomes in rural communities.    In 1986, the

Government committed itself to increase producer prices by 5 percent annually in real terms, or setting them equivalent to 60-70 per cent of F.O.B. prices, whichever is higher. Amani, *et al.* (1988) confirm that there has been an increase in real incomes among the rural population which is largely explained by the increase in agricultural producer prices.

### Table 2
### Commercial food imports and food aid 1982-83 to 1988-89
('000 Metric.Tonnes)

|  | 1982-83 | 1983-84 | 1984-85 | 1985-86 | 1986-87 | 1987-88 | 1988-89 |
|---|---|---|---|---|---|---|---|
| **Maize:** | | | | | | | |
| Commercial | 17,0 | 125,1 | 111,1 | 22,6 | 85,4 | - | - |
| Aid | 106,4 | 69,2 | 26,5 | 3,0 | 8,8 | - | - |
| Total | 123,4 | 194,3 | 137,6 | 25,6 | 94,2 | - | - |
| **Rice:** | | | | | | | |
| Commercial | - | 30,4 | 20,5 | 19,5 | 56,0 | 31,0 | 12,2 |
| Aid | 45,2 | 26,7 | 26,1 | 22,2 | 37,5 | 21,3 | 7,3 |
| Total | 45,2 | 57,1 | 46,6 | 41,7 | 93,5 | 52,3 | 19,5 |
| **Wheat:** | | | | | | | |
| Commercial | 9,4 | - | - | - | - | 20,0 | - |
| Aid | 2,0 | 46,3 | 33,5 | 21,7 | 26,6 | 13,7 | 28,9 |
| Total | 11,4 | 46,3 | 33,5 | 21,7 | 26,6 | 33,7 | 28,9 |

Source: United Republic of Tanzania, (1989)

### Table 3
### Commercial producer prices
(Shs/Kg)

| Crop | 1986-87 | 1987-88 | 1988-89 | 1989-90 |
|---|---|---|---|---|
| Maize | 6 | 8 | 9 | 11 |
| Rice | 10 | 14 | 17 | 19 |
| Wheat | 7 | 9 | 10 | 13 |
| Cassava | 4 | 5 | 5 | 5 |
| Sorghum/Millet | 5 | 6 | 7 | 7 |
| Beans | 14 | 22 | 25 | 27 |

Source: United Republic of Tanzania, (1989).

Liberalisation of the market has also improved accessibility to food. By removing the monopoly of the National Milling Corporation (NMC) on food trade and reducing internal trade barriers, open market consumer prices for maize declined thus increasing the real purchasing power of consumers.

Nutrition interventions are planned by the Food and Nutrition unit of the MALD. This unit was reorganised in 1985 and charged with the tasks of working closely with other ministries and institutions in improving food and nutrition, developing food and nutrition programmes, and improving and developing skills and capabilities of agricultural nutrition workers. The unit and UNICEF are currently implementing a Household Food Security Nutrition and Child Survival Programme. The programme covers two districts of mainland Tanzania, Masasi and Shinyanga Rural Districts, and two regions in Zanzibar. Priority areas to improve household food security for those most at risk, are:

- o    production of cassava and other drought resistant crops;

- o    reduction of the workloads of women; and

- o    nutrition education and child care.

The geographical regions chosen are among those which have been identified as having high rainfall variability and experience frequent drought conditions.

The Household Food Security and Child Survival Programme are drawing on the experience of the pilot WHO/UNICEF Joint Nutrition Support Programme which was successfully implemented in Iringa Region between 1983 and 1988. The objectives of the Iringa Nutrition Programme were to:

- o    reduce infant and young child mortality and morbidity;

- o    increase child growth and development; and

- o    improve maternal nutrition.

The project was able to achieve these goals due largely to the methods adopted in mobilising the people. Known as the 'campaign approach' the people were mobilised by party, government and village leaders to participate in the project. Thus they came to identify themselves with the project.

## ORGANISATIONAL STRUCTURE FOR FOOD SECURITY

The present structure for managing food security is a result of an FAO food security mission's review of the country's food situation in 1986, which recommended the establishment of a Food Security Unit under the Ministry of Agriculture and Livestock Development (MALD).

The Food Security Unit (FSU) is charged with:

- o    providing Government with information on the nation's overall food security situation;

- o    responsibility for the management of the Strategic Grain Reserve (SGR); and

- o    liaising with other organisations and agencies, as well as coordinating the work of Regional Food Security officers.

In 1988 the Government issued orders to set up a Board of Trustees to exercise "final control" over the Strategic Grain Reserve (SGR) and the Food Security Unit. The Board of Trustees is composed of representatives from the Prime Minister and First Vice-President's Office (PMO), Ministry of Finance, Ministry of Local Government, Community Development, Cooperatives and Marketing and the Ministry of Agriculture and Livestock Development, which is responsible for food production.

The SGR is owned by the Government and is not part of the working stock of the National Milling Corporation (NMC). NMC is an agent for managing the stocks on behalf of the Government. Its role is that of a warehouseman, *i.e.* maintaining the SGR stocks according to proper warehousing practices, including recycling and rotation of stocks and fumigation.

Within this framework, the Early Warning and Crop Monitoring Unit, incorporated under the Food Security Unit, (FSU) submits periodic reports to the Food Security Officer. In the event of an emergency, the Board of Trustees of the FSU will notify the NMC and the PMO and provide specific instructions to the Food Security Unit to release SGR stocks.

## Anticipated Problems

Tanzanian agriculture during the early 1990s will continue to be dominated by smallholder rainfed agriculture, which will be highly susceptible to variations in rainfall. Hence climatic factors will play a major role in determining food availability in the country. Given scarce foreign exchange resources, the level of investment in irrigated agriculture is not expected to change significantly.

Socio-economic factors are crucial in determining accessibility of the people to various foodstuffs. Greater efficiency in food marketing can play a major role in enhancing accessibility. The marketing system has hitherto been inefficient in performing its tasks, largely due to infrastructural problems of inadequate storage capacity and the poor state of road and transport facilities. Due to the high investment requirements of such facilities, this problem is likely to continue in the early 1990s, given the economic situation of Tanzania. As such, transportation costs form a significant proportion of the price of foodstuffs in urban food markets.

Plant pests and diseases will be a continuing problem but the scale of the problem will not be as large as the aforementioned ones since it is generally under control.

## SADCC Initiatives

Tanzania's food security programme, as discussed above, has yet to achieve its goal due to a number of constraints such as climatic factors, socio-economic factors and plant pests and diseases. It is indeed in these areas that the SADCC Food Security Unit could offer its assistance.

Climatic problems in Tanzania require the development of skills in water management and in the design and execution of irrigation projects. To improve decision-making in food security, more reliable information, particularly on food access, needs to be generated and incorporated within the Early Warning System. Furthermore, future growth in food production has to be based on the use of improved seed varieties. Tanzanian farmers still depend largely on traditional seed varieties. Thus, efforts are needed in breeding, production, promotion and distribution of improved seeds to the farmers.

The alleviation of food insecurity in the region, apart from dealing with the direct causes, must involve improved capacity in Food and Agriculture Policy Analysis (FAPA) within the region.

In this respect, the Food Security Unit could organise regional training workshops for operational staff involved in FAPA related activities. At the national level, the Food Security Unit can assist member countries by supporting in-service training together with post-graduate training in FAPA.

## Research Required

While in the Tanzanian case the price mechanism has been used to raise rural incomes, it is not clear whether this instrument has generated changes in investment in the agricultural sector, largely dominated (more than 80 percent) by smallholder farmers. There is a need to understand investment trends on the farms so as to predict output, incomes and productivity in future years. This information is useful in determining food security in the medium term.

Furthermore, more information is needed on urban incomes in Tanzania. Formal wages are far less than expenditures on food by households. Whereas it can be assumed that people earn extra incomes from other activities outside formal employment, this may not be the case for the whole urban population. There is need therefore to study different income groups in urban areas so as to understand their accessibility to food.

## CONCLUSION

Tanzania's food situation has improved over the past three years in response to favourable climate, agricultural prices and marketing policy together with the farmers' positive response to this conducive environment.

However, greater effort is required to ensure that this level of production is sustained and increased. Furthermore, to balance the food equation, efforts are required to improve food accessibility both in terms of quality and quantity for all the people.

## REFERENCES

Amani, H.K.R., S.M. Kapunda, N.H.I. Lipumba, and B.J. Ndulu.  1988.  Effects of Market Liberalisation on Food Security in Tanzania.  In:  M. Rukuni and R.H. Bernsten (eds) *Southern Africa: Food Security Policy Options.*  UZ/MSU Food Security Project. Department of Agricultural Economics and Extension. University of Zimbabwe. Harare.

Amani, H.K.R., S.M. Kapunda, N.H.I. Lipumba, and B.J. Ndulu. 1988. Impact of market liberalisation on household food security in Tanzania 1989. In: G.D. Mudimu and R.H. Bernsten (eds) *Household and National Food Security in Southern Africa.* UZ/MSU Food Security Research Project. Department of Agricultural Economics and Extension. University of Zimbabwe. Harare.

Ndulu, G. 1987. *Stabilisation and Adjustment Policies and Programmes Country Study:* Tanzania WIDER.

United Republic of Tanzania. 1983. *Agriculture Policy.* Government Printer. Dar-es-Salaam.

United Republic of Tanzania. 1984. *Tanzania: National Food Strategy.* FAO.

United Republic of Tanzania. 1988. *1989-90 Budget Speech.* Ministry of Agriculture and Livestock Development. Government Printer Dar-Es-Salaam.

United Republic of Tanzania. 1988. *Second Union Five Year Development Plan, 1988-89 to 1992-93, Vol.II.* Government Printer. Dar-es-Salaam.

United Republic of Tanzania. June 1989. *Food Security Bulletin*: June, Food Security Unit.

United Republic of Tanzania, WHO and UNICEF. 1983. *Joint Nutrition Support Programme. Plan of operations and plan of actions 1982-1987.* UNICEF.

United Republic of Tanzania, WHO and UNICEF. 1988. *Joint Nutrition Support Programme 1983-1988 Evaluation Report.*

United Republic of Tanzania and UNICEF (undated) *Household Food Security Nutrition and Child Survival Programme.*

# 7

# Zambia : Food Security Issues
# And Challenges For The 1990s

*A.K. Banda*[1]

## INTRODUCTION

Zambia launched the Fourth National Development Plan in January 1989. The plan is of five years' duration and will extend to 1993. The theme for the plan is "growth from own resources" meaning that the country will as much as possible use local resources in its development endeavours.

The agricultural sector will continue to be given prominence under the five year plan. In fact, agriculture has been identified as the 'target sector' to replace mining in the promotion of growth.

To emphasise the role of the agricultural sector during the plan period, the Fourth National Development Plan (FNDP) outlines the overall objectives of the sector as being to increase production and productivity, to streamline the marketing of both products and inputs and to contribute to improved living conditions of the population. The plan further outlines the specific objectives of the sector as follows:

o   increase the capacity utilisation of all private and  public sector capital investment in agro-industries;

o   achieve a satisfactory level of self-sufficiency at the household, community and national levels in the production of staple foods;

o   expand the production of agricultural exports;

o   increase the import substitution and replacement of agricultural products and inputs;

o   promote the use of animal draught power with emphasis on oxen;

o   improve rural employment and incomes;

o   balance agricultural production with environmental concerns by minimising the effects of natural catastrophes in agriculture (such as drought, floods) while simultaneously curtailing erosion and other environmental damages;

---

[1]Principal Economist, Planning Division, Ministry of Agriculture and Cooperatives, Zambia.

o    develop and promote a national irrigation programme aimed at both small-scale and large-scale producers;

o    promote the efficient and orderly exploitation of Zambia's natural resources, with particular emphasis on forestry;

o    support training and extension activities for farmers and other rural dwellers, particularly those designed to improve their productivity and their nutritional and health standards;

o    ensure that rural women are active participants in and beneficiaries of agricultural and rural development activities;

o    integrate nutritional concerns into agricultural planning and projects;

o    integrate population education into agricultural extension services; and

o    balance agricultural production targets with changes in the size and growth rate of the nation's population so as to achieve the desired self-sufficiency in food production.

To achieve the above objectives, the agricultural sector will continue to combine price and non-price incentives as well as to consolidate the necessary support services. Price incentives, foreign exchange retention schemes and tax incentives are expected to encourage increased production. The strategies for the sector during the plan period are to include a concerted effort in improving the living standards of the rural population by increasing food availability and employment opportunities and incomes.

The Zambian government has therefore put emphasis on not only increasing national food self-sufficiency *per se* but also on ensuring food security at national, community and household levels. These are noble goals and the stage has been set for agriculture to occupy that important spot in Zambia in the 1990s. The FNDP will play a very important role towards the improvement of food security.

The Zambian definition of food security conforms to the generally accepted international definition which is "access by all people at all times to enough food for an active and health life" (World Bank, 1986 : 1; Rukuni and Eicher 1987 :8).

## CURRENT STATUS OF FOOD INSECURITY IN THE COUNTRY

Zambia enjoyed a food surplus in the 1988-89 marketing season especially in maize, meaning that the effective demand for maize fell short of production[2]. Indications also show that there is another surplus expected in the 1989-90 marketing season. Table 1 presents the import position of major cereals for the past five years.

---

[2]Maize is the staple food in Zambia. Over 60 percent of food consumed in the country is maize. It is safe to say that in Zambia, food means maize.

The table reveals a declining trend of maize imports in the last two years indicating that the country has been meeting an increasing share of national food demand.

Central, Eastern and Southern Provinces accounted for the surplus enjoyed in the 1988-89 marketing season (Table 2). Expected production and consumption in the 1989-90 season will also result in a surplus for the season. Some deficit provinces such as North Western, Luapula and Western consumed cassava, millet and sorghum. This reduced the pressure on the demand for maize.

## Table 1
### Cereal imports
### ('000 tonnes)

| Consumption Year | 1985-86 | 1986-87 | 1987-88 | 1988-89 | 1989-90 |
| Production Year | 1984-85 | 1985-86 | 1986-87 | 1987-88 | 1988-89 |
| --- | --- | --- | --- | --- | --- |
| Maize[a] | 115,7 | 14,4 | 20,7 | 125,2 | 0 |
| Wheat | 77,6 | 57,4 | 73,5 | 47,8 | 34,5 |
| Rice[b] | na. | 5,55 | 2,0 | 0 | 0 |
| Total | 193,3 | 77,35 | 96,2 | 173,0 | 34,5 |

na. means not available
[a]  The figure shown in 1988-89 consumption year is for stocks which were supposed to have arrived in 1987-88 consumption year. The stocks came in late. Otherwise Zambia had a surplus in the 1987-88 production year.
[b]  Official rice imports were banned in 1987.

## Table 2
### Maize production and consumption 1988 and 1989

| Consumption Year | | 1988-89 ('000 tonnes) | | | 1989-90 ('000 tonnes) | | |
| Province | Population ('000) | Produc-tion | Consum-ption | Surplus/ Deficit | Produc-tion | Consum-ption | Surplus/ Deficit |
| --- | --- | --- | --- | --- | --- | --- | --- |
| Central | 696 | 310,0 | 131,9 | +179,1 | 406,1 | 152,6 | +253,5 |
| Copperbelt | 1 787 | 75,8 | 338,8 | -263,0 | 61,5 | 396,7 | -335,2 |
| Eastern | 805 | 299,6 | 152,5 | +147,1 | 569,0 | 256,3 | +312,7 |
| Luapula | 511 | 28,6 | 96,8 | -68,2 | 44,2 | 36,6 | +7,6 |
| Lusaka | 1 091 | 94,7 | 206,8 | -112,1 | 72,3 | 354,6 | -282,3 |
| Northern | 814 | 113,7 | 154,3 | -40,6 | 204,7 | 109,7 | +95,0 |
| N/Western | 385 | 25,4 | 72,9 | -47,5 | 35,7 | 37,4 | -1,7 |
| Southern | 878 | 477,0 | 166,5 | +310,5 | 413,8 | 165,1 | +248,7 |
| Western | 565 | 27,9 | 107,2 | -79,3 | 53,5 | 40,9 | +12,6 |
| Total | 7 532 | 2 452,7 | 1 427,7 | +25,0 | 1 860,0 | 1 549,9 | 310,9 |

The free movement of maize and drought resistant crops like sorghum and millet does not imply that there are no food shortages in the country. Not all areas for example receive their share of maize in time because of the bad conditions of the roads in some parts of the country. There are also some areas which are regularly affected by floods such as Mpika district (Northern Province), Lundazi and Chama districts (Eastern Province). When such areas experience floods it is virtually impossible to supply food except by helicopter. This is usually at a very high cost. Food shortages in the country are also caused by pest infestations like the cassava mealy-bug which affected some parts of the northern high rainfall areas in the 1986-87 season.

In general, food shortages do not affect a large population nor extensive areas. The effects of drought and floods are generally limited to relatively isolated pockets of the country and vary considerably at provincial as well as district and ward levels.

When there are natural calamities, the government usually distributes food to the affected families through the famine relief programme coordinated by the Ministry of Agriculture and Cooperatives and the Contingency Planning Unit in the Cabinet Office. Some famine relief food has been distributed free of charge at times while some has been given to relief victims at subsidised prices.

It is very difficult to pinpoint the reasons for some types of food shortages. One argument that has been advanced is the over emphasis on maize production in some areas where the crop cannot grow easily. The bias towards maize production has been experienced because of the marketing arrangements which favour the transportation of maize, and the lack of price support and marketing infrastructure. The poor performance and frequent failure of the maize crop in drought prone areas has exacerbated the shortages in these areas.

In addition to major food shortages in specific areas, there are also seasonal shortfalls of some staple and relish foods. These shortfalls result from changes in production patterns, intercropping of traditional staples with relish crops and monocropping of cash crops, notably hybrid maize. Households in early stages of commercialised production are especially vulnerable.

## CURRENT STATUS OF FOOD SECURITY POLICIES, PROGRAMMES AND PROJECTS

Zambia will continue to encourage people to produce maize through the provision of incentives while the country is looking at ways of promoting the marketing of such crops as sorghum, millet and cassava.

The marketing system was recently reviewed and changed. Provincial Cooperative Unions (PCUs) are responsible for the buying of all maize in their respective provinces. The Zambia Cooperative Federation (ZCF) is responsible for the inter-provincial marketing of maize[3]. ZFC, the apex body of the cooperative movement, has recently taken over the functions of the National Agricultural Marketing Board (NAMBOARD) which was responsible for the importation of grains, whenever a deficit occurred. NAMBOARD was also responsible for the importation of grain bags and fertilizers. The function of importing fertilizer has now been transferred to the Nitrogen Chemicals of Zambia (NCZ).

---

[3]Provincial Cooperative Unions were given more power to market grains in their Provinces in 1985. The dissolution of NAMBOARD and the transference of NAMBOARD functions to ZCF was done in 1989.

Under the present marketing system, where PCUs play a leading role, it is hoped that distribution of food will improve and that PCUs will purchase grains from the remotest areas and also distribute to the same in times of need.

It is however still too early to assess how effective the present marketing system has been in reaching remote areas. Marketing of grain has improved but we still have to wait and see before attributing these successes to Provincial Cooperative Unions.

In an effort to improve food availability and food security at national, community and household levels, discussions are underway on a National Food Security Reserve. The purpose of the reserve is to have easy access to readily available maize to draw from whenever there is localised famine in some areas. NAMBOARD had been keeping 250 000 tonnes of reserve maize before the start of any marketing season.

The Zambian government has also embarked on the coupon system to reduce subsidies on mealie meal. The coupon system was introduced so that subsidies could be targeted to people in urban and peri-urban areas. The coupon system is limited to people who have an income of less than 20 500 Kwacha per year either in formal or informal employment. Rural areas, including farm labourers, do not benefit from the coupon system.

The coupon system is less than a year old and it is encountering problems of fraud and cheating. The Government is working on measures to seal the loopholes. The aim of the coupon system is to reduce maize subsidies to producers and millers.

Other government programmes for combating drought and floods are being implemented through the Ministry of Agriculture and Cooperatives. The Government has mandated the Ministry of Agriculture and Cooperatives through the Land Husbandry and Irrigation branch to formulate programmes and projects which will aim at combating drought and flooding. The objectives of the Land Husbandry and Irrigation Sector of the FNDP will be to:

o    develop a strong institutional framework that will spearhead the development of irrigation; and

o    promote the diversification of cropping patterns with a view to increasing food and agricultural production.

The irrigation sector aims to increase the area under irrigation by 6 000 hectares per year during the FNDP period. The Land Husbandry and Irrigation branch of the Ministry is also operating an irrigation fund for the benefit of small-scale and commercial farmers. All these efforts are aimed at improving food production and increasing food security.

The Government with assistance from the international donor community has also put in place a National Preparedness Plan to cope with food disasters, including a programme of rehabilitation and construction of boreholes, wells and dams in drought-prone provinces.

## ORGANISATIONAL STRUCTURE FOR MANAGING FOOD SECURITY

The government has established institutions to cope with food shortages. The crop forecasting and Early Warning System is responsible for estimating crop production, marketed surplus for maize and import needs. Based on meteorological and statistical information collected by various participating government institutions and departments. The Early Warning Unit, attached to the Planning Division of the Ministry of Agriculture and Cooperatives, in conjunction with the Early Warning Coordinating Committee, estimates crop production and marketed quantities of maize in February and April each year. These estimates are given to the National Committee on Early Warning (NCEW) which is composed of directors of the departments and institutions supplying information to the Early Warning Unit, the Food and Nutrition Commission, the National Contingency Planning Committee, Zambia Cooperative Federation and the National Commission for Development Planning. The NCEW meets twice a year to discuss the reports on preliminary and final crop forecasts and resulting supply situation at the national level.

It is important to mention that the crop forecasting and Early Warning System is able to come up with estimates of production and import requirements but is not sufficiently developed at present to identify specific areas in possible risk of hunger.

Funding for the purchase of relief food is provided by Government and donor organisations through the Contingency Planning Unit and the Relief Coordinating Unit at the Ministry of Agriculture and Cooperatives which purchase food from cooperative unions, which is later sold to famine Relief victims at a charge (sometimes subsidised).

The Government recently started selling relief food to famine victims to avoid making the famine victims dependent on free food from Government. In exceptional cases, food is given free of charge and this is only after a thorough analysis is done on the conditions of the famine victims.

## ANTICIPATED PROBLEMS

### Roads and Transport Systems

The Zambian government experienced a surplus in maize availability in the 1988-89 marketing season and another surplus is expected in the current (1989-90) marketing season but these surpluses will not mean much if the maize does not reach the intended market. The transport distribution network in the country is still not sufficiently developed. Maintenance of roads during and after the rains is a particular problem.

### Storage

Zambia has plans to build strategic reserves especially of maize in provincial centres so that a province can have easy access to such resources in times of need. Storage facilities have to be developed and these require enormous financial resources. People also have to be trained in the management of storage facilities. All these are problems which need to be looked into.

## Timely Provision of Inputs

Late provision of fertilizer, bags and credit can also reduce production and hence bring shortages in a country. So unless all the above things are looked at seriously by any government, a country's food security position could be at stake.

## SADCC INITIATIVES

The Southern African Development Coordination Conference (SADCC) should cushion the effects of drought and such natural calamities. SADCC countries should expand food trade. Transportation costs can be reduced if trade is encouraged among the countries.

A serious problem which has discouraged trade in the region is the lack of foreign exchange. SADCC should look at ways of promoting trade in the region without this strain on foreign exchange.

Trade in the region has also been minimal because of quality problems and late delivery. There is need for collective initiatives by SADCC to improve the quality of tradeable products. SADCC, possibly through the Southern African Centre for Cooperation in Agricultural Research (SACCAR), should examine ways of improving quality and packaging of food products.

## RESEARCH REQUIRED

Famine caused by drought, flooding and pest infestation still remains a serious problem in SADCC. Priority should therefore be given to research in these areas. Researchers should also find ways of reducing the effects of seasonal food shortages. This is a serious problem which requires concerted efforts by all researchers in the SADCC region.

## REFERENCES

Bolt Richard et al. 1988. *Food availability and Consumption Patterns in Northern Province ARPT Trial Areas: Implications for Research, Extension and Policy.* Kasama. Adaptive Research Planning Team. Economic Studies No.3.

FAO. 1986. *National Preparedness Plan for coping with Food Emergencies.* Rome.

National Commission for Development Planning. 1989. *Zambia New Economic Recovery Programme.* The Fourth National Development Plan. Lusaka.

Rukuni, M. and Carl K Eicher (eds). 1987. *Food Security for Southern Africa.* UZ/MSU Food Security Project. Department of Agricultural Economics and Extension. University of Zimbabwe. Harare.

# 8

# Zimbabwe : Perspectives On Food Policy Options

*T. Takavarasha and A. Rukovo*[1]

## INTRODUCTION

With the attainment of independence in 1980, the Government of Zimbabwe adopted a path of socialism. The major objective of the nation was growth with equity and transformation to a socialist society. The immediate aim was to improve the economic and social welfare of the majority of the people who had been neglected. Under this noble objective, rehabilitation of the damaged economy, resettlement, reconciliation and minimum wage legislation were priority areas for the Government. The successful attainment of this objective needed proper planning. The Transitional National Development Plan 1982-83 to 1984-85 and subsequently the first Five Year National Development Plan 1986-1990 were formulated. These plans set out the objectives and strategies of the Government.

In the sphere of food and agriculture, the Government aims to achieve food self-sufficiency for staple foods and food security at national and household levels. Food security is achieved when a country can assure all its citizens of both physical and economic access to food of an appropriate nutritional quality (SADCC, 1986). The contribution of Zimbabwe to regional food self-sufficiency is also important since the country plays a leading role in the SADCC food security situation. Clearly, the definition of food security involves both the supply and effective demand side.

Zimbabwe has produced most of its staple food (maize) and has also managed to export substantial quantities over the past three years. Even though the achievement of food security is threatened by various calamities, *e.g.*, drought, that are beyond Government's control, there are strategies which the Government can adopt in an effort to avoid food insecurity among the rapidly increasing population. When food insecurity takes place due to drought, various actions are implemented. These include food-for-work and supplementary feeding for the less privileged, mainly children, women, the aged and the disabled.

In the fight to combat food insecurity, Government has developed positive measures, giving first priority to the development of the agricultural sector because of the dynamic role which it plays in the economy of the country. Over 70 percent of the population live in the rural areas and their primary source of livelihood is farming. The growth of the economy is largely conditioned by the performance of the

[1]Economics and Markets Branch, Ministry of Lands, Agricultural and Rural Resettlement, Harare, Zimbabwe

agricultural sector. It provides over 90 percent of domestic food requirements and accounts for 41 percent of total merchandise exports.

## CURRENT STATUS OF FOOD INSECURITY

Food insecurity is present at both micro and macro levels of the economy. In Zimbabwe, the major area of concern is the availability of food at the household level. The country is able to produce most of its cereal requirements and in normal years manages to export to surrounding countries. However, there is a need to address the issue of distribution and effective demand. Household food insecurity is seasonal due to poverty and the lack of effective distribution machinery. At the national level, food insecurity is caused by: droughts, the limited funds available for the development of the agricultural sector, poor road infrastructure and the lack of skilled manpower to implement government policies. Currently, the production of wheat and rice is significantly below the market demand at current prices. The Government has adopted a policy of triangular transaction, involving the importation of both wheat and rice for the export of maize. The high urbanisation rate, increases in minimum wages, changes in consumer tastes and the decline in consumer price of wheat relative to substitutes has led to significant increases in the demand for wheat products, mainly bread.

Erratic droughts have been a common feature in the 1980s with four drought years (1982-83; 1983-84; 1984-85 and 1986-87). The country's weather pattern is also erratic. Not only is rainfall unreliable, but it is poorly distributed geographically and there is a high frequency of mid-season droughts. This erratic rainfall pattern affects the rural poor particularly. The rural poor are mainly those that do not have any member of their household formally employed in the urban area.

## Table 1
### Distribution of land by natural region and by sector

| Region | Hectares ('000) | Large Scale Commercial (%) | Small Scale Commercial (%) | Communal (%) | Average Annual Rainfall (mm) |
|--------|-----------------|----------------------------|----------------------------|--------------|------------------------------|
| I      | 700             | 74                         | 2                          | 24           | 1 050                        |
| II     | 5 860           | 74                         | 4                          | 22           | 700 - 1 050                  |
| III    | 7 290           | 49                         | 8                          | 43           | 500 -   700                  |
| IV     | 14 880          | 34                         | 4                          | 62           | 450 -   600                  |
| VI     | 10 440          | 35                         | -                          | 65           | <   500                      |
| Total  | 39 170          |                            |                            |              |                              |

Source: Ministry of Lands, Agriculture and Rural Resettlement.

The country is subdivided into five natural regions according to the total annual rainfall. Table 1 shows the percentage distribution of the natural regions into farming areas.

The rural poor residing in Natural Regions III, IV and V are most affected by drought. In these areas, rainfall is below 700mm *per annum* and is very erratic. Even when Natural Regions I and II receive adequate rainfall, Regions III, IV and V may fail to meet the crop water requirements and people in these areas may find themselves requiring food from other regions. This has been the case in 1989 when the people in the southern part of the country had to rely on food from other regions.

The other groups that are affected by food insecurity include the urban poor earning below the poverty line, some commercial farm labourers and the unemployed. These groups have insufficient food to meet their nutritional requirements and malnutrition is a potential problem among these groups. The problem is currently not very serious but if the present trend of population growth and unemployment is maintained, a crisis could become evident in the 1990s.

## CAUSES OF FOOD INSECURITY

The definition of food security embodies supply and effective demand. The supply of food is determined by production, importation and strategic stocks. In a landlocked country such as Zimbabwe, which has high transport costs and shortages of foreign currency, the major issues on the supply side is production. The country cannot afford to import substantial quantities of food on a commercial basis, given the shortage of foreign currency. A close proxy of production fluctuations in the 1980s is the erratic deliveries of grain to the Grain Marketing Board. The unreliable rainfall and four drought years have been the major cause of production fluctuation. The intensity of drought increases from Natural Region I to V; thus farmers situated in the low rainfall areas (III, IV and V) are more vulnerable to food insecurity. The communal farming population forms the greater part of the total population in the country residing in these low rainfall areas. When high production levels have been achieved, appropriate stock levels need to be maintained in order to bridge the gap between seasonal production and year-round consumption.

On the effective demand side, various problems have emerged. The majority of people that do not own the means of production, *i.e.* land and capital, lack effective demand for food. The unemployed are not able to purchase their food requirements with certainty, thus putting their families at risk. The country now has a large proportion of children under the age of fifteen, which results in a high burden on the employed people. The long term effect of such a situation is malnutrition for those members of society who fail to compete successfully in the market to acquire food. Thus a summary of people that are affected by food insecurity included the following:

o   poor farmers in low rainfall areas;

o   some farm labourers and their households who have limited disposable incomes;

o   unemployed urban and landless rural;

o   people earning below the poverty datum line.

All the people listed above lack effective demand. The number of unemployed and underemployed has grown in the urban areas because of the rural-urban migration which has been increasing in the 1980s. The persistent droughts plus low productivity of the communal areas has made rural life unattractive and insecure; thus people find themselves moving into towns in anticipation of being employed sometime. There is also the belief that students that complete their "O" levels (four years of secondary school education) are not prepared to work on the land. This may well be true because rural life is unattractive since the terms of trade in the economy are generally in favour of urban areas and against the rural sector.

## CURRENT STATUS OF FOOD SECURITY POLICIES, PROGRAMMES AND PROJECTS

When people talk of food security, they usually focus on the agricultural sector. But this is a narrow approach because food security is multi-dimensional. Food is a basic need of human life. Thus every individual works for his food first, then for shelter, clothing and other needs. Focusing on the agricultural sector alone often leads to an over emphasis on food self-sufficiency. All the people should have adequate food at all times to lead a healthy and active life. Thus all programmes that encourage earning of a living and generating economic activity, contribute to the food security objective through the multiplier effect. Thus with the above in mind, one can look at the food security equation and assess how Government can increase both food availability and access to food.

### Programmes to Increase Food Availability

Soon after independence, the Government adopted a policy of growth with equity and transformation.

> *The welfare of the people of Zimbabwe depends largely on the attainment of sustained rapid economic growth and development and an equitable distribution of income and wealth. Given a rapidly growing population, distribution without economic growth and development leads to a decline and deterioration in living standards and hence to a decline in the welfare of the people. Conversely, growth with unequitable distribution of income and wealth, while benefiting a few, diminishes the welfare of society as a whole and invariably leads to socio-political instability. For these and other reasons, Government has adopted growth with equity and transformation as its development strategy.* (Republic of Zimbabwe, 1982).

This clearly shows the problem which the Government was facing: political stability was the major concern after independence, since in the absence of political stability the development of the country is at risk.

In a bid to promote production, the Government has adopted various policy incentives. These include guaranteed producer prices, resettlement, reconciliation, increased credit facilities and extension services, improvement in the marketing infrastructure in the previously neglected communal areas and encouraging irrigation development to make maximum use of water. Favourable producer prices help to maintain farmer confidence in farming, thus encouraging production. The resettlement policy is aimed at providing the landless with land so that they could directly participate in agricultural production.

The agricultural parastatals have played a crucial role in the agricultural transformation process in Zimbabwe. The Agricultural and Rural Development Authority (ARDA), a parastatal, has been given the responsibility for state-controlled agricultural development. The Agricultural Finance Corporation (AFC) is responsible for providing low interest credit to farmers. The Grain Marketing Board (GMB) is responsible for all marketing activities for grain cereals between producers and wholesalers. All these efforts have resulted in the country being able to produce enough staple grain (maize) to meet its requirements and for export. When considering production, one should not only focus on food crops but also the meat industry, which plays an important part in promoting a balanced diet. The Cold Storage Commission (CSC) is a parastatal responsible for promoting the development of the beef industry. There is also the Dairy Marketing Board (DMB) which is responsible for marketing of milk and milk products.

The Department of Research and Specialist Services is responsible for the development of suitable crop varieties. These varieties have to be complemented by appropriate technology. Thus AGRITEX is responsible for providing technical extension services to the farmers. Substantial increases in irrigation development have been realised due to technical assistance from AGRITEX. The Government has also approved the formalisation of a Secretariat to handle irrigation development projects.

All these government efforts have resulted in increased crop production. The challenge that now faces the country is how to maintain production in line with increases in demand. Given a situation where production increases in arithmetic progression and population increases in geometric progression, the country could find itself faced with a difficult food security problem. The United Nation's Economic Commission on Africa (ECA) reported that Zimbabwe's Gross Domestic Product is keeping pace with the population growth rate. *Zimbabwe economy grew by about six percent in 1988 ... it would be difficult for Zimbabwe to repeat such an achievement in 1989.* (*Chronicle,* 18 May, 1989).

## Post Harvest Losses and Grain Storage

There is a need to reduce post-harvest losses. This will help to increase available food. However, farmers are prepared to invest only if the benefits exceed the costs of reducing post-harvest losses. The storage of grain is a very important factor in the marketing of grain. Storage helps to link seasonal production and the daily demand. The Grain Marketing Board (GMB) is the statutory board that is responsible for storing all the grains in Zimbabwe at the national level. A pilot project to develop bunker storage for maize is also being developed in conjunction with the GMB in Zimbabwe. The aim of the current Government's pan-seasonal pricing policy is to encourage delivery to the Board where economies of scale can be attained with bulk storage. At the farm level, farmers tend to store most of their home consumption requirements. What is stored by the board is mainly sold to milling companies, which in turn market to the urban consumers. The development of storage facilities will help to reduce food insecurity, provided the costs of storage are less than the benefits achieved.

## Other Initiatives to Increase Food Production

When there is a drought, in the following year the Government encourages production by providing farmers in the affected areas with some crop packs. These crop packs contain hybrid seeds, fertilizers and other inputs that may be required to assist farmers to recover from the effects of drought. Most of the small scale farmers rely on ox-drawn power to plough their fields. Tractor hire schemes are also used in other districts where the farmers are able to pay for the costs involved.

## Use of World Market to Meet Domestic Food Shortage

Based on Zimbabwe's recent record of exports of maize, the World Bank and SADCC forecasts anticipate exports of 400 000 tonnes *per annum* from Zimbabwe in the coming year, and imports of about 120 000 tonnes of rice and wheat. In addition, it would appear that there is potential for significantly increasing the volume of maize exported through Beira. Between 1985-86 and 1987-88 exports fluctuated between 285 000 and 495 000 tonnes, as shown in Table 2.

### Table 2
### Zimbabwe: maize exports by destination
### (tonnes).

| Destination | 1985-86 | 1986-87 | 1987-88 | 1988-89 [Committed] |
|---|---|---|---|---|
| Angola | 0 | 1 309 | 3 196 | 0 |
| Botswana | 3 030 | 25 847 | 52 354 | 12 836 |
| Cape Verde | 0 | 11 231 | 0 | 0 |
| Europe | 36 | 159 | 0 | 0 |
| Ethiopia | 12 384 | 15 815 | 500 | 0 |
| Far East | 0 | 32 179 | 0 | 0 |
| Kenya | 1 150 | 0 | 0 | 0 |
| Lesotho | 688 | 2 537 | 16 098 | 3 721 |
| Malawi | 0 | 0 | 67 506 | 153 963 |
| Mauritius | 4 104 | 0 | 0 | 0 |
| Mozambique | 45 383 | 177 361 | 111 503 | 105 309 |
| Namibia | 0 | 2 150 | 1 693 | 0 |
| Reunion | 28 255 | 17 237 | 6 778 | 10 107 |
| Somalia | 0 | 6 844 | 0 | 0 |
| RSA | 91 345 | 115 709 | 9 917 | 0 |
| Swaziland | 0 | 7 617 | 0 | 5 180 |
| Tanzania | 750 | 3 000 | 0 | 0 |
| Venezuela | 18 696 | 0 | 0 | 0 |
| Zaire | 4 616 | 2 455 | 11 418 | 4 450 |
| Zambia | 68 210 | 13 244 | 6 292 | 78 780 |
| Overseas | 0 | 28 461 | 66 223 | 0 |
| Processed products | 5 859 | 21 370 | 32 910 | 0 |
| Total | 284 817 | 494 525 | 386 388 | 374 076 |

Source: Grain Marketing Board

It can be seen that 50 percent or more of Zimbabwe's exports were to SADCC and other Southern Africa countries. Moreover, significant quantities of exports have been shipped to Reunion, Venezuela and, as food aid, to Ethiopia.

The Government's declared policy is to aim for domestic self-sufficiency in white maize production, maintain strategic stocks and report any surpluses. Due to the nature of the uncertainty of the rainfall pattern, and the consequent variations in maize production in Zimbabwe from year to year, the policy of self-sufficiency unavoidably results in substantial surpluses in most years, which are either exported or stored as reserves.

Zimbabwe is expected to continue to be a significant importer of wheat, given the increasing demand for bread and other wheat flour products in both urban and rural areas. Import restrictions on wheat due to foreign exchange constraints result in suppressed demand and *de facto* rationing. Current domestic production is about 260 000 tonnes with imports averaging between 80 000 and 90 000 tonnes *per annum*. Domestic production is expected to increase, but wheat as a winter crop production is constrained by the availability of irrigation facilities. Table 3 shows Zimbabwe's supply and disposal.

Table 3
Zimbabwe wheat supply and disposal
('000 tonnes)

| Year | 1984 | 1985 | 1986 | 1987 | 1988 |
|---|---|---|---|---|---|
| GMB Intake | 124 | 98 | 206 | 248 | 215 |
| Imports | 55 | 104 | 86 | 56 | 91 |
| Local Sales | 227 | 220 | 248 | 258 | 271 |
| Exports | - | - | - | - | - |
| Closing Stocks | 80 | 60 | 106 | 152 | 187 |

Source: Grain Marketing Board

Rice import requirements are estimated to be 15 000 tonnes *per annum*, coming mainly from the Far East and Malawi. The bulk of wheat imports have involved swap arrangements with maize purchased by donors. Rice imports have varied between commercial and barter sources.

### Increasing Access to Food

Increasing access to food is another important component of the food security equation. Food entitlement is an important aspect of the various ways of increasing food accessibility. These include increasing rural income and employment, nutrition programmes, school feeding, food-for-work, food transfer programmes and others. In Zimbabwe, increasing the welfare of other rural sectors has been the major objective of policy since independence. Decentralisation has been emphasised as a means of increasing rural welfare. Cooperative development has also been encouraged in order to improve the income levels of the rural people. The Government also adopted a policy of minimum wage legislation as a means of raising the income of the peasant and farm labourers. The subsidisation of basic food such as mealie-meal has also been used in order to increase the effective demand for these commodities. There are, however, arguments that blanket subsidisation may not achieve the intended objective of closing the gap between the poor and the rich. Moreover, administering subsidies may add to the financial burden of the Government.

In a situation where there is malnutrition because of poverty, especially among children, the Government has adopted supplementary feeding and school feeding programmes. Properly planned school feeding programmes can be used as a means to encourage grain consumption in surplus commodities, such as small grains. During drought years, able-bodied people are encouraged to work for food. Programmes implemented include building of dams, construction of irrigation schemes, road maintenance, gully reclamation, school building, *etc*. Botswana's food-for-work programme has been successfully adopted in Zimbabwe. This strategy seems to have gained momentum in 1989 when the southern part of the country was hit by drought. The advantage of food-for-work programmes is that it removes the food dependence syndrome and helps to increase people's self-esteem. Food-for-work programmes help to develop the areas where the people reside, by improving their roads, construction of dams and irrigation schemes, building of schools, reclamation of gullies, and so on.

In households where there are no individuals that can work because they are old or disabled, food transfer programmes are used. This clearly shows that proper administration of both finance and food is necessary at the district level. Problems envisaged are mainly the shortage of skilled manpower and transport.

In a severe drought year, a drought tax may be imposed to purchase food for the drought victims. Government encourages the maintenance of family linkages. Under such linkages, members of families with formally-employed family members are not given food, since it is assumed that their urban relatives will remit food/cash to them. This has been successful in some parts of the country.

In the 1980s the country was hit by four droughts. Various ministries were coordinated to form a Drought Relief Committee, including the Ministry of Lands, Agriculture and Rural Resettlement, Ministry of Health, Ministry of Labour, Manpower Planning and Social Welfare, Ministry of Local Government and Rural Urban Development, Ministry of Energy and Water Development, Ministry of Finance, Economic Planning and Development, Ministry of Transport, Ministry of National Supplies, and Ministry of Cooperative Development and Women's Affairs. The ministries were responsible for coordinating the supply and distribution of food to the affected people. In implementing the above drought relief programmes, various problems were encountered:

o    lack of transport and inadequate subsistence and travel allocations;

o    lack of financial management at the district level;

o    non-availability of materials and tools, especially cement and piping, which has delayed the implementation of some projects;

o    inadequate supervision of projects and control of assets.

The above ministries help in the implementation and coordination of various programmes such as construction of bridges, weirs, dams, dip tanks, grazing schemes, piped water schemes, gully reclamation, and brick moulding, *etc*. The Ministry of Health is also responsible for coordinating supplementary feeding programmes, while the Ministry of Labour, Manpower Planning and Social Welfare is responsible for food transfers.

Currently, the Crop Forecasting Committee can be used as a means of detecting the likely food situation. In the future, the Early Warning Unit of the country can play a leading role in the crop forecasting committee.

## ANTICIPATED PROBLEMS

The major problems that are likely to cause food insecurity in the 1990s are unemployment, drought, population growth, lack of foreign currency, lack of adaptable technology and land tenure.

The increase in unemployment caused by the fast growing population is going to be the major problem of the 1990s. In the bid to combat the problem, the President, His Excellency Cde R.G. Mugabe has approved a Secretariat for Population Policy and Development in Zimbabwe (Herald, 1989). The primary task of the Secretariat will be assisting the drafting of a government population policy. The population policy will be a set of national priorities in terms of size and growth of the population in line with sustainable social and economic growth and development. There are various alternatives that can be applied to counter the unemployment problem. The provision of the means of production (land and capital) will help to reduce the unemployment problem.

If the drought pattern follows the pattern of the 1980s, then its effect will be very severe, given the current population growth rate, which is almost 3 percent *per annum*. The challenge is to increase the gross agricultural output at least as fast as the population growth rate. The increase in agricultural output in the 1980s has been due mainly to an increase in the area under cultivation, use of hybrid varieties and increased use of other inputs. The possible areas of increasing production in the future would be through improved husbandry, use of appropriate technology and use of hybrid varieties, since the land resource is finite. Intensive agriculture in the form of irrigation development will help to increase production and employment.

Policymakers are concerned with devising ways of encouraging fixed investment in various sectors of the economy. Given a situation where the capital development of the economy is seriously affected by the shortage of foreign currency, it is necessary to determine how to acquire additional foreign currency.

Thus the problems of the 1990s can be ranked as:

o   unemployment;

o   drought;

o   rapid population growth;

o   lack of appropriate technology;

o    foreign currency constraints;

o    sustainable economic development.

## RESEARCH AREAS

Research should focus on how the problems of drought, unemployment, rapid population growth and shortage of foreign currency can be solved. Research should be carried out to determine the impact of changes in micro- and macro-economic policies on household food security. Policymakers are willing to accept theory that can be put into practical use. This will contribute very much to the development of the country. There is a great need to synchronise population growth, employment growth and food production in order to maintain the food security status of the country.

## CONCLUSION

The analysis in this paper focused on the people that are affected by hunger and malnutrition. Zimbabwe's future food security will depend on population growth, development of appropriate technology, employment creation, efficient growth and the distribution of resources. A country can produce all its nutritional requirements but, without proper education about a balanced diet, this production effort will be nullified, thus resulting in a situation of hunger and malnutrition amidst plenty. More information needs to be collected in order to determine the current status of food insecurity in Zimbabwe. This information can be used to identify the "silent" hunger and malnutrition problem which is currently not receiving sufficient public attention.

## REFERENCES

Gentleman, T. Deputy Secretary, Economics and Markets. and E.A. Attwood. Technical Advisor, Ministry of Lands, Agriculture and Rural Resettlement. (1989). Personal contact.

The Herald. Harare. May 16 1989.[Incomplete]

Republic of Zimbabwe. 1982. *Transitional National Development Plan   1982/83-1984/85 Vol. 1.* Government Printers. Harare.

Republic of Zimbabwe. 1983. *Transitional National Development Plan   1982/83-1984/85 Vol.2.* Government Printers. Harare.

Republic of Zimbabwe. 1986. *First Five Year National Development Plan 1986-1990 Vols. 1 and 2.* Government Printers. Harare.

Rukuni, M. and R.H. Bernsten (eds). 1988. *Southern Africa: Food Security Options.* University of Zimbabwe/Michigan State University Food Security Research Project. Department of Agricultural Economics and Extension. University of Zimbabwe. Harare.

Rukuni, M. and C.K. Eicher (eds). 1987. *Food Security for Southern   Africa.* University of Zimbabwe/Michigan State University Food Security Project. Department of Agricultural Economics and Extension. University of Zimbabwe. Harare.

SADCC. 1986. *Food and Agriculture.* Southern Africa Development Coordination Conference. Harare 30-31 January 1986. Printing and Publishing Company. Botswana (Pvt) Ltd.

# III

# The Market Reform Process: Emerging Results And Policy Implications

# 9

# Agricultural Market Reform In Tanzania : The Restriction Of Private Traders And Its Impact On Food Security

*H.K.R. Amani and S.M. Kapunda*[1]

## INTRODUCTION

The main broad objective of any government with respect to food security is to assure at all times access to food for all members of the population of the country. To achieve this objective a range of policies are required, including production (availability), marketing, processing, as well as nutrition education programmes.

The role of food marketing policy is to:

a)    Ensure that basic food stuffs are available at all times at affordable prices to consumers; and

b)    Ensure that a market is available for domestic food producers and prices received by producers are reasonable enough to make them continue production.

How should marketing policy be formulated so that it contributes positively to the achievement of food security objectives?

The role of Government in food markets is sometimes questioned unjustifiably. The argument against government intervention often centres on it being costly and ineffective. To improve food marketing it is often recommended to leave it wholly to the private sector. The shortcomings of such a recommendation have been shown elsewhere (Amani *et al.*, 1987).

Since 1984 Tanzania has been going through a process of macro-economic crisis brought about by internal and external causes. In food marketing the crisis was particularly manifested in food shortages (Amani *et al.* 1987). Consequently administrative enforcement of official subsidised prices was almost completely eroded. The majority of consumers bought most of their food requirements from parallel (unofficial) markets. Furthermore, as expenditures on subsidised staple

---

[1]Department of Economics, University of Dar es Salaam, Tanzania.

foods escalated, budgetary pressures built up, forcing the government to reconside its policy.

Starting July 1984 the Government has undertaken several measures to deregulate markets. The main food marketing policy changes were:

   o    allowing individuals to buy and transport up to 500 kilograms of foo grains;

   o    the introduction of Cooperative Unions to replace Crop Authorities;

   o    allowing individuals with foreign exchange to import "incentive" good and sell them at market clearing prices;

   o    the withdrawal of subsidies on consumer goods and agricultural inputs

   o    substantial increases in real official producer prices for major agricultura crops - 31 percent in the case of maize, 7,8 percent for rice, and 1,2 percent for export crops;

   o    devaluation of the Tanzanian Shilling (Tshs) by about 31 percent with inflation running at 30 percent.

With the introduction of the Economic Recovery Programme in 1986 further changes were introduced:

   o    a major devaluation was undertaken; from Tshs17 to the US dollar to about Tshs52 to the US dollar between March and June of 1986. Thereafter, a crawling peg mechanism was instituted to adjust for inflation;

   o    all consumer commodities were decontrolled except for a maximum of 12 categories which were considered to be essential items;

   o    official producer prices were increased by five percent in real terms annually.

The following year (1987) additional measures were taken by the government:

   o    the restriction on the movement of food grains was removed by eliminating the requirement to obtain permits from the National Milling Corporation (NMC);

   o    the role of NMC was formally limited to operating the strategic grain reserve, undertaking imports of food, and managing food aid and grain milling;

   o    official producer prices were further increased by 30 percent to 80 percent depending on the crop;

o    controls were removed on the importation and distribution of all agricultural inputs except fertilizer and seed;

o    transport infrastructure was made a priority policy.

The impacts of these measures on food availability and accessibility at the macro and household level have been already been discussed (see Amani *et al.*, 1987 and 1988). Inspite of the studies already done, many issues require further research such as the role of the private traders.

### SETBACK?

During the 1989-90 budget session the Government announced some changes in food grain marketing. Private traders are no longer "allowed" to buy directly from farmers; they can only buy from the Cooperative Union and the NMC.

Why was such a change introduced? The most common explanation centres on the modality of operation and the resulting profitability. Private traders have a choice to buy from anywhere, including accessible producing and deficit areas. Traders are thus able to make good profits, especially because of their relatively low cost of transport and zero storage costs. The Cooperative Unions and the NMC have not been able to compete with them and thus remain confined to the more inaccessible areas where operational and overhead costs are higher. Private traders have also been blamed for high food prices even though inflation has remained at about 29 percent. In addition, since 1967, the role of private traders in the food marketing system has never been politically and legally accepted. The main food staples such as maize, rice, cassava, beans, sorghum, millet and wheat have traditionally been regarded as vital to the nation's welfare. Hence food shortages and high consumer prices, particularly in urban areas, are considered to be politically dangerous.

This paper deals with policy issues emanating from the reforms. In particular the paper focuses on the roles of private traders, Cooperative Unions and the National Milling Corporation (NMC) under the evolving marketing arrangement. Implications of the market reforms on farmers, consumers and marketing agencies are discussed.

### PRIVATE TRADERS AND OPEN MARKET PRICES

Since 1984 many private traders have been encouraged to proceed with internal trade largely because some trade obstacles have been removed and in 1987 all restrictions on food (grain) transport, movement and permits were abolished and inter-regional trucking rates were allowed to be determined by market forces.

According to 105 private traders interviewed[2] in Mwanza, Moshi and Arusha, the removal of trade restrictions was practical. About 74 percent of those interviewed started trading in food grains after 1984. This implies that domestic trade liberalisation has attracted more private traders into food trading.

---

[2]The interviews were carried out between October 8, 1988 and January 7, 1989. For details see Scarborough (1989)

The high entry rate of traders has some implications for competition. New traders felt that an increase in the number of traders made business more difficult and that this was exacerbated by declining open market consumer prices which led to a decline in profits. Nevertheless, established traders claimed they were unaffected by entry of new traders in the market.

Food trade was regarded by farmers as the easiest business to start; they might start the trade by selling their own crops. Additionally such trade could be combined easily with farming in terms of labour allocation. Almost 73 percent of traders interviewed in the three towns obtained at least part of their initial start-up capital from agriculture. Other credit sources identified included mutual lending, credit in kind, and to a lesser extent, informal credit markets. Mutual lending included lending among traders, relatives and friends and was interest-free. Credit in kind was more often given by farmers to traders, *i.e.*, farmers handed over their produce to traders who returned later to pay the farmers. Informal credit markets were not well established in the three towns; 86,8 percent of all traders said they had no access to credit at all. The credit situation was similar in Morogoro, Iringa and Dodoma. In Dar es Salaam, however, traders had access to informal credit markets and the interest rate was about 100 percent over six months and 5.8 percent over two weeks.[3]

## Marketing Chains and Marketing Functions

Marketing chains are similar in all towns. They tend to indicate where and between whom exchange occurs, marketing functions and the actors involved. An illustration from Dar es Salaam for maize will suffice.

|  | S,L,T |  | U |  | P,T |  |
|---|---|---|---|---|---|---|
| FARMER | ------> | WHOLESALER | ------> | RETAILER | ------> | CONSUMER |
| (V) | | (DSM) | | (DSM) | | |

| Where | ---> | Represent action and direction of exchange of goods - for cash or credit. |
|---|---|---|
| V | = | Villages in Ruvuma, Mbeya, Iringa, Morogoro, regions. |
| DSM | = | Dar es Salaam. |
| S,L,U,P | = | Marketing functions |
| S | = | Storage for more than a brief period |
| L | = | Loading maize bags into lorries/trucks using hired labour. |
| T | = | Transport |
| U | = | Unloading in Dar es Salaam especially at Tandale/Manzese using hire labour. |
| P | = | Processing |

The wholesalers, retailers and consumers are essentially Dar es Salaam residents (Gordon, 1988 :181). It follows from the illustration that the functions of private traders include buying and selling, storing, transporting and processing commodities. Other functions which are not directly deducible from the illustration include gathering information and seeking credit. The details of these functions is in order.

---

[3]Gordon (1988). The interviews covered 75 traders between June and August, 1988.

## Buying and Selling

This is a key function of the private traders. This process is, however, affected by seasonality. In Mwanza, Moshi and Arusha, for instance, it has been found that trade business is slow during harvest season since there are few buyers and, due to lack of storage facilities, there is little buying on the part of traders (Scarborough, 1989). However, before and after harvest, business is very active because traders, consumers and institutions are all in the market for food.

During the research period, wholesalers bought directly from farmers in most cases, but the buying centres varied according to season. Immediately after harvest,[4] farmers delivered their produce to market places usually using hand-drawn carts, ox-carts, tractors, lorries, trucks, buses and rented vehicles.

Buying directly from farmers, however, was an illegal activity although at the time of the fieldwork a shift in the Government's attitude towards this was being expressed through radio broadcasts.

## Storage

In general traders have no permanent storage facilities partially because the construction of such facilities is very expensive.[5] Furthermore, many traders regard storage as a risky project due to crop deterioration, governmental policy changes and the usual problems of predicting supply and demand fluctuations.

In Mwanza, Moshi and Arusha, traders stored not more than 100 bags of grain in the market places. In the case of wholesalers and many retailers the bags were merely kept under tarpaulins or polythene sheeting. Thus crop damage was not uncommon (Scarborough, 1989).

In Manzese/Dar es Salaam traders had no permanent storage, only an open plot at the market which was watched at night by hired guards. The plot had a capacity of 15 tonnes of stacked bags. The situation was similar for Morogoro, Iringa and Dodoma. However, turnover of goods was extremely fast since traders did not want their grain to spoil and be in the open (Gordon, 1988).

Storage capacity is currently available at the household (farm) level and in official institutions such as the NMC, primary societies and Cooperative Unions.

Household storage in rural areas is the backbone of food security in Tanzania. The 1987 FAO report estimated that between 70 to 80 percent of total grain production was kept at the household level in traditional storage structures either for consumption or for sale. However, there was little storage from one year to the next.

---

[4]June/July in Mwanza and Moshi and also January in Arusha.

[5]Out of 105 traders interviewed in Mwanza, Moshi and Arusha, for instance, only one had managed to build a permanent store with a capacity of 500 bags of grain.

The traditional storage methods and structures differ widely -- from trees and open platforms to well constructed bins or granaries. In many areas these storage structures are known as *Kihenge* while in southern part of Lake Victoria, Mwanza in particular, they are called *Maluli/Mafuma/Makologoto* (Mpuya, 1989). However, much remains to be done to improve household storage facilities in order to minimise food losses.

## Transport

Generally speaking private grain traders have no transport facilities, essentially because they are expensive to buy, maintain and manage. In Mwanza, Moshi and Arusha, for instance, wholesalers travel to villages during the post-harvest period to buy food crops usually using 1-20 tonne vehicles hired in towns. They usually take them empty to villages and the potential savings involved in trying to operate two way trade are ignored. Transport services are readily available in towns. Prices are negotiated between traders and transporters and they are relatively uniform. In some cases private traders travel to rural areas by buses and hire trucks there for the return journey.

In Dar es Salaam it was found that much grain comes to the city in backloads on large trucks including those returning from Zambia, Malawi, Burundi or other locations linked to the Tanzania or Dar-Burundi roads (Gordon, 1988 :19).

## Processing

Food processing or milling is done by either official institutions such as the NMC or private mill owners. Traders prefer to sell maize rather than maize flour, but they prefer to sell rice rather than paddy.

## Gathering information

Collecting information about prices, supply and demand fluctuations, availability of advice and cash assistance is usually done mutually among traders themselves despite the existence of competition. The information is usually gathered by word of mouth among traders and farmers.

Currently there is an increasing number of newspapers that carry some information about prices of grain and other food crops. However, this is more effective in the city of Dar es Salaam where most of the newspapers are printed, than in regional towns and villages. In rural villages, there is a time lag due to long distances and transport problems and newspaper information is usually outdated.

## Seeking Credit

Credit is usually obtained through mutual lending as explained earlier. In Dar es Salaam, resident traders help link sellers from rural areas with urban buyers, and they provide credit and/or cash advances to farmers and incoming non-resident traders to pay for transport, lodging and other expenses (Gordon, 1988 :6).

## OPEN MARKET PRICES AND MARKET MARGINS

### Open Market Prices of Food Commodities

One of the most persistent prejudices about open food markets is that consumer prices are always far above official prices while producer prices are always lower than official producer prices.

An open market may exist because:

a)　Expected informal price margins are high enough to attract private traders to enter the market. Sometimes it is possible for a private trader to buy from farmers at a price equal to or above the official producer price and resell to consumers at a price equal to or less than the official consumer price. Since the official price margin is relatively high due to the fact that official agencies have to include the cost of the expensive long-haul transport into their margin, a private trader who confines himself to short distance transport from farmer to consumer can operate profitably within the official price margin. This type of open market probably explains the low price levels in many markets in October 1985 (MDB, 1986). This is a rare phenomenon in Tanzania.

b)　Food shortages are characterised by prices above the official levels. Shortages may arise because of crop failure and/or failure on the part of the official marketing agencies to bring the food to where it is demanded. The main problem with this type of open market is that consumer prices are not below official prices. Both the producer and the consumer prices will be determined by the forces of supply and demand. Producers in the more inaccessible areas will get a price below the official price. On the other hand, consumers in areas with acute shortages and/or where the cost of bringing food is high will pay prices above official prices. This type of open market is more common in Tanzania.

Open markets for food commodities in Tanzania seem to have established themselves as a permanent feature of the agricultural sector whereas for many commodities, particularly perishables such as vegetables, fruits and fish, the open market is the only marketing channel in operation. Other commodities, notably the main staples such as maize, rice, cassava, beans and sorghum, are partly marketed through official marketing agencies. Sometimes the government attempts to control directly consumer prices of rice and maize.

### The Need to Study Market Margins

It is sometimes argued that private traders have the ability to collude against producers and consumers in order to ensure large profits.

The Mwanza-Moshi-Arusha study, however, has revealed that wholesalers and retailers did not make unreasonable profits as shown in Table 1. However, these are rough estimates since real profit rates, the opportunity cost of capital, real cost of transport, storage costs and fluctuations of profit rates throughout the year were rough calculations.

Although Dar es Salaam gross profits were found to be rather high these findings are preliminary. There is therefore a need to undertake further research on market margins.

### Table 1
### Gross profit made by traders in Mwanza, Moshi and Arusha
(%)

|  | Mwanza | Moshi | Arusha |
|---|---|---|---|
| Wholesalers gross 'profit'[a] (% of wholesale price) | 6,0 | 7,9 | 5,1 |
| Retailers gross 'profit'[b] (% of Retail price) | 2,6 | 2,7 | 2,0 |

[a] Wholesale price *less* (buying price + transport costs + other costs *i.e.* hired labour, price of sacks and market taxes).
[b] Retail price *less* (wholesale price + transport costs + other costs, *e.g.* stall rental fees).
Source: V. Scarborough (1989 :37)

### The Need to Study Parallel Markets for Food

It is estimated that 65 percent of marketed surplus is handled by the private sector (MDB 1988). However, so far very little is known about its structure, function, performance potentials and constraints. Traders operating in the parallel market have no legal status in Tanzania. Nevertheless, since 1984 they have been encouraged to undertake marketing functions by the Government and by Presidential directives. Operators in official markets, namely NMC and cooperative unions, view their activities as illegal but to be tolerated. Because they have no legal status, there is very little investment by private traders in the marketing field.

There is, therefore, a great need for data collection and analysis of the role of private traders. This type of information will be crucial in terms of the political sustainability of market liberalisation, and will help to inform future policy changes in food marketing.

### THE ROLE OF THE NMC

The re-establishment of cooperatives in 1984 as the major official channel for purchasing crops from farmers and the decontrol of private traders in grain trading have changed the role of the NMC from a virtual monopoly in grain trading to a restricted role of maintaining a strategic grain reserve, handling food imports and exports, grain milling as well as selling food grains and flour to deficit regions at a defined selling price. These market reforms are causing new problems for NMC. The main problems are outlined below.

### The Impact of Increased Participation by Private Traders

The progressive removal of restrictions on the marketing of grains by private traders since 1983 has partly affected the performance of the NMC. Apparently NMC purchases of preferred staples have not been adversely affected, with the exception of intra-regional distribution of surpluses. All cooperative unions sell surplus food to the NMC. NMC purchases of preferred staples have generally increased during the last five years (Table 2).

### Table 2
### NMC purchases of preferred staples 1983-84 to 1987-88
### ('000 tonnes)

| Year | Maize | Rice[a] | Wheat | Total |
|------|-------|---------|-------|-------|
| 1983-84 | 71 | 22 | 28 | 121 |
| 1984-85 | 85 | 12 | 33 | 130 |
| 1985-86 | 178 | 16 | 50 | 244 |
| 1986-87 | 173 | 11 | 34 | 218 |
| 1987-88 | 229 | 43 | 43 | 315 |

[a]Paddy converted to rice equivalent.
Source: MDB (1988).

However, a slightly different picture emerges if we look at Regional NMC purchases of these staples (Appendices 1 - 3). In the case of two of the most productive but less accessible regions, Rukwa and Ruvuma, maize purchases have generally declined between 1984-85 and 1987-88. This decline is not a result of a fall in output. In the case of Ruvuma for example, maize production during 1986-87 and 1987-88 far exceeded production in any of the previous three seasons and yet purchases by NMC (and also by cooperative unions) have been declining. This is partly explained by the increased role of private traders in intra-regional trade and partly by financial problems faced by NMC. In the other most productive and accessible regions like Arusha, Iringa and Mbeya, NMC purchases have been increasing irrespective of strong competition from private traders. Such increases in purchases are mainly explained by increased production during 1984-85 to 1987-88.

While aggregate purchases have increased (Table 3), NMC stocks are moving slowly as a result either of generally low open market consumer prices, consumers' perceptions of NMC grains (mainly maize) as being below quality and/or due to less time spent in buying from the open market. This is particularly true when open market prices are slightly higher than official prices.

### Table 3
### Available supply of maize grain at NMC
### ('000 tonnes)

|                    | 1984-85 | 1985-86 | 1986-87 | 1987-88 |
|--------------------|---------|---------|---------|---------|
| Domestic Purchases | 90      | 178     | 128     | 229     |
| Imports            | 128     | 6       | 94      | -       |
| Opening Stock      | 18      | 19      | 43      | 183     |
| Total Supply       | 236     | 203     | 265     | 412     |

Source: MDB (1988).

Lack of aggressiveness and imagination by the NMC in promoting sales has also been mentioned as a factor contributing to low sales. For example, part of the reason for the build-up of maize stocks in 1986-87 was NMC's insistence on selling first yellow maize which it had in stock. Since yellow maize is less preferred to white maize, consumers bought their requirements from the open market. The NMC decision to sell yellow maize first was definitely unwise in the face of abundant supplies of white maize on the open market and the resulting low prices. Low sales have been registered during the last three marketing seasons (Table 4).

### Table 4
### NMC sales of maize, rice and wheat
### ('000 tonnes)

| Year    | Maize[a] | Rice | Wheat[b] | Total |
|---------|----------|------|----------|-------|
| 1974/74 | 210      | 38   | 60       | 308   |
| 1975/76 | 137      | 38   | 59       | 234   |
| 1976/77 | 134      | 56   | 74       | 264   |
| 1977/78 | 109      | 77   | 86       | 272   |
| 1978/79 | 156      | 70   | 93       | 319   |
| 1979/80 | 223      | 61   | 55       | 339   |
| 1980/81 | 293      | 77   | 42       | 412   |
| 1981/82 | 286      | 78   | 58       | 422   |
| 1982/83 | 209      | 72   | 57       | 338   |
| 1983/84 | 254      | 79   | 34       | 367   |
| 1984/85 | 220      | 58   | 67       | 345   |
| 1985/86 | 157      | 28   | 51       | 236   |
| 1986/87 | 76       | 63   | 33       | 172   |
| 1987/88 | 120      | 62   | 76       | 258   |

[a] Includes sales of sembe - expressed as maize equivalent.
[b] Includes wheat flour - expressed as wheat equivalent
Source: MDB (1988)

The substantial increase in maize sales in 1987-88 is mainly explained by relatively high open market consumer prices (Table 5) caused by tight supply conditions in the open market.

### Table 5
### Official and open market consumer prices of food
### staples in urban areas

| Staple Food | 1984-85 | | 1985-86 | | 1986-87 | | 1987-88 | | 1988-89 | |
|---|---|---|---|---|---|---|---|---|---|---|
| | Open | Official | Open | Official | Open | Official | Open | Official | Open | Official |
| Maize grain | 10,78 | 5,40 | 9,65 | 7,60 | 10,17 | 12,20 | 13,76 | 12,20 | n,a | 17,00 |
| Rice | 36,07 | 13,40 | 37,57 | 14,50 | 35,72 | 19,00 | 44,33 | 32,00 | n,a | 59,70 |
| Wheat flour | 41,31 | 14,50 | 35,53 | 17,20 | 49,59 | 25,15 | 55,99 | 35,00 | n,a | 55,85 |
| Maize flour | 13,29 | 8,0 | 17,14 | 13,75 | 19,57 | 13,75 | 25,37 | 13,75 | n,a | 13,75 |

Source : MDB various reports

### Financial Losses

First it is important to mention that in the period up to 1984-85 the NMC had incurred significant financial losses. As a result the government periodically wrote off losses in the form of accumulated debt to the banking system. Since the re-establishment of cooperatives and the decontrol of private sector grain trading, NMC has been incurring losses by accumulating bank overdrafts. The magnitude of such debt to the National Bank of Commerce is shown in Table 6.

### Table 6
### Bank lending to NMC
### (Shs. million)

| | 1985-86 | 1986-87 | 1987-88 |
|---|---|---|---|
| Cumulative overdraft | 1 071 | 3 742 | 10 738 |

According to NMC accounts, net losses (after overheads, financial charges and depreciation) for 1985-86 and 1986-87 were Tshs709,2 million and Tshs1 842,7 million respectively. Estimates of losses for 1987-88 have been put at Tshs4 billion. Thus the cumulative losses over the 1985-86 to 1987-88 period was about Tshs6,5 billion.

There are three sources of these financial losses, namely: (a) losses on commodity exports; (b) financial losses arising from interest charges on previous years losses; and (c) losses caused by internal inefficiencies and operational constraints imposed by the government. Each of these sources of financial losses is briefly summarised below.

### *Losses on Commodity Exports*

In year of surplus food staples NMC is forced, by inadequate storage capacity, to export some of that food surplus. Commodity exports for 1987-88 are shown in the table below as an illustration.

## Table 7
### Estimate of losses on commodity exports : 1987-88

|  | Maize | Beans | Cassava Roots | Sorghum | Total |
|---|---|---|---|---|---|
| Export price (US$) | 76 | 95 | 65 | 49 | |
| Volume (MT) | 100 000 | 30 000 | 10,000 | 20 000 | 160 000 |
| NMC selling price(Tshs) | 10 900 | 40 229 | 13,646 | 18 125 | |
| Loss (Million Tshs) | 1 083 | 1 162 | 143 | 402 | 2 790 |

Source: NMC

### Losses Arising from Interest Charges

As the role of the private sector in domestic grain marketing increases, the cost structure of NMC will continue to be adversely affected by increasing grain stocks. In particular the cost structure will be affected by costs emanating from the loss of value of grain held in storage for prolonged periods, increased depreciation charges on the large physical capacity, and more importantly, from interest cost of capital tied up in grain stocks.

### Losses Emanating from Internal Inefficiencies and Operational Constraints

It is important to make a distinction between losses emanating from NMC's internal inefficiencies and those caused by operational constraints imposed by the Government.   One indication of internal inefficiencies is a substantial increase in total overhead costs in general and in administrative costs in particular.   For example, administrative costs of sales and marketing increased by about 47,5 percent between July 1984 and July 1985.   Whereas administrative costs as a proportion of total overhead was 34,8 percent as of 31 July 1984, this proportion increased to 51 percent by 31 July 1985.   Of course, part of the increased administrative cost is due to the enlarged network of depots and stores requiring increased personnel. However, improvement in management and to some extent restructuring of NMC's operations should help reduce such costs.

Losses emanating from operational constraints are beyond the control of the NMC. Such losses are caused by the marginalisation of the NMC in terms of being left with the non-profitable high-cost elements of grain marketing; high-cost elements include servicing uneconomic supply routes, holding stocks for longer inter-annual periods, and purchasing and handling low quality grains.   The Government is aware of such problems and the restriction of private traders from buying directly from farmers (as announced in July 1989) is partly a response to those operational constraints.

### COOPERATIVE UNIONS

In 1984 cooperatives were reintroduced and crop authorities were abolished.   This move may be viewed as a compromise between privatisation and parastatal monopolies.

At present there are 8 147 primary societies and 24 main regional cooperative unions in Mainland Tanzania. Zanzibar has 1 281 primary societies and five unions. These societies and unions are supposed serve the economic interests of peasants. However, experience has shown that the peasants' efforts have not been rewarded enough; as a result some of them have abandoned producing traditional export crops (coffee, cotton, tea, *etc.*) and have concentrated on the production of food and 'new cash crops' like tomatoes and onions which give them quick and reliable returns generally not shared with the unions. Worse still the unions' problems seem to be increasing over time. An examination of the major problems facing the unions are in order:

o Liquidity problems and delay in paying bank loans lead to delay in paying the peasants after they have sold their crops. The Cooperative and Rural Development Bank (CRDB) and National Bank of Commerce (NBC) have been giving loans to the unions but the loans have never been repaid or have been paid very late. By the end of June 1989, money tied up with creditors had reached 5,5 billion shillings and NBC loans between 1985-86 to March this year reached 16,3 billion shillings. As a result, the CRDB and NBC are becoming reluctant to extend loans.

o Another problem is related to diversion of funds, embezzlement/theft and buying fictitious crops. These activities make the peasants and their sympathisers lose confidence in the top personnel especially when the peasants are paid unfairly and late.

o Lack of proper accounting, lack of an adequate accounting information system to assist the management of the unions and societies, and failure by cooperatives to make use of accounting information in the measurement and evaluation of all business activities, are a constraint on the progress of cooperatives.

o Lack of competent and qualified top personnel in some unions, *i.e.*, the general manager, chief accountant and internal auditor and other key officers lead to managerial problems and inefficiency.

o Bad roads and low capacity to transport commodities from rural areas despite the arrangements of unions to hire both public and private vehicles, is another thorny problem facing the unions. The problem is heightened by the existence of bad roads and bridges. As a result, crops remain stranded in villages and some crops eventually spoil. By mid-August 1988, over 270 000 tonnes (about 36 percent total purchases) were stranded in villages.

o Cost escalation in the Cooperative Union. The main sources of these high costs include a sharp rise in the interest rates (*e.g.*, from about 1 percent of the producer price in 1985-86 to 18 percent in 1987-88) reflecting government policy towards interest rates; large non-marketing costs in which societies, unions and local authorities levy; and increases in the cost of bags and twine from 7 percent in 1986-87 to 13 percent in 1987-88

(Table 8).  As a result the margin of societies and cooperatives has risen from 53 percent in 1985-86 to 77 percent in 1987-88.

o  Competition for market share of staple food grains, particularly maize and rice from private traders, is another problem facing the cooperative unions. The competition is more acute in accessible areas/regions such as Mbeya and Iringa.  Normally private traders confine themselves to short-distance transport from farmer to consumer.  In cases where long distances are involved, the roads must be good.  Financial and management problems have often left cooperative unions in a weak position relative to private traders in the accessible food surplus regions.  Hence the unions have to buy from distant and partially accessible areas.  Sometimes a bigger part of what is purchased gets stranded in villages and primary societies due to the reasons explained earlier.  In more remote areas, farmers fail to sell their surplus produce because the unions cannot reach them or lack the funds to do so.

### Table 8
### Cooperative maize marketing cost structure

|  | 1985-86 | 1986-87 | 1987-88 |
|---|---|---|---|
| Producer price | 5 226 | 6 223 | 8 077 |
| Society Levy | 261 (5) | 290 (5) | 380 (5) |
| Union Levy | 523(10) | 500 (6) | 650 (8) |
| Transport | 1 200(23) | 1 600(26) | 2 079(26) |
| Bags and Twine | 330 (7) | 444 (7) | 1 020(13) |
| Cash Insurance | 60 (1) | 71 (1) | 24 (-) |
| Handling | - (-) | 100 (2) | 50 (1) |
| Fumigation | - (-) | 44 (1) | 30 (-) |
| Crop Insurance | 40 (1) | 48 (1) | 46 (1) |
| Shrinkage | 105 (2) | 62 (1) | 247 (3) |
| Interest | 64 (1) | 460 (7) | 1 449(18) |
| Local Authority | - (-) | - (-) | 200 (3) |
| Stamp Duty | - (-) | 25 (-) | 30 (-) |
| Overall margin | 2 583(53) | 3 619(59) | 6 205(77) |
| Into-Store Price | 8 000 | 9 888 | 14 213 |
| Cost Reduction Required | - | - | - |
| Selling Price to NMC | 8 008 | 8 008 | 12 313 |

*Parenthesis contain percent of production price
Source:  Marketing Development Bureau, (1987).

Because of increased competition, the purchases by unions have been falling except for special cases such as during bumper harvests (Tables 9-11).  Purchases of maize in Iringa and Mbeya for instance increased essentially because of bumper harvests and because the regions are very accessible.  But in the case of Rukwa maize purchases declined even when production had increased substantially.  Apparently the region is quite inaccessible.  Since private traders shy away from such remote areas and the Cooperative Union is financially constrained to buy from all over the region, purchases have declined.

## Table 9
### Cooperative Union purchases of preferred staples
### marketing year 1986-87 to 1987-88
### (tonnes)

| Region | Maize | | Paddy | | Wheat | |
|---|---|---|---|---|---|---|
| | 1986-87 | 1987-88 | 1986-87 | 1987-88 | 1986-87 | 1987-88 |
| Iringa | 43 868 | 77 393 | 34 | 1 227 | 102 | 200 |
| Mbeya | 7 996 | 15 737 | 1 795 | 12 145 | 2 | 1 |
| Rukwa | 30 079 | 22 195 | 229 | 2 250 | na | 11 |
| Ruvuma | 35 211 | 28 566 | 231 | 1 902 | 0 | 0 |
| Coast | na. | 41 | na | 10 | 0 | 0 |
| Dar es Salaam | 0 | 0 | 0 | 0 | 0 | 0 |
| Kagera | 1 522 | 539 | 21 | na | 0 | 0 |
| Kigoma | 1 233 | 572 | na | 0 | 0 | |
| Lindi | 555 | 242 | na | 741 | 0 | 0 |
| Mara | 488 | 2 888 | 347 | 364 | na | 50 |
| Morogoro | 921 | 2 346 | 665 | 1 581 | 0 | 0 |
| Mtwara | 310 | 45 | 541 | 629 | 0 | 0 |
| Mwanza | 581 | na | na | 14 124 | 0 | 0 |
| Shinyanga | 5 228 | 504 | 4 629 | 25 167 | 0 | 0 |
| Singida | 3 300 | 9 610 | na | 413 | 69 | 8 |
| Tabora | 3 406 | 583 | 757 | 7 628 | 0 | 0 |

Source: MDB, (1987 and 1988).

## Table 10
### Maize production
### ('000 tonnes)

| Region | 1986-87 | 1987-88 |
|---|---|---|
| Iringa | 388 | 436 |
| Mbeya | 262 | 336 |
| Rukwa | 143 | 187 |
| Ruvuma | 310 | 179 |
| Coast | 3 | 12 |
| Dar es Salaam | - | - |
| Kagera | 62 | 51 |
| Kigoma | 51 | 47 |
| Lindi | 12 | 5 |
| Mara | 30 | 28 |
| Morogoro | 97 | 97 |
| Mtwara | 44 | 25 |
| Mwanza | 118 | 106 |
| Shinyanga | 103 | 226 |
| Singida | 41 | 64 |
| Tabora | 232 | 155 |
| Arusha | 265 | 242 |
| Dodoma | 56 | 45 |
| Kilimanjaro | 41 | 61 |
| Tanga | 60 | 34 |

Source: MDB (1988)

## Table 11
### Production levels for paddy 1986-87 to 1987-88
### ('000 MT tonnes)

| Region | 1986-87 | 1987-88 |
|---|---|---|
| Iringa | 4 | 1 |
| Mbeya | 59 | 45 |
| Rukwa | 9 | 13 |
| Ruvuma | 42 | 36 |
| Coast | 39 | 33 |
| Dar es Salaam | - | |
| Kagera | 6 | 5 |
| Kigoma | 1 | 1 |
| Lindi | 24 | 3 |
| Mara | 1 | 2 |
| Morogoro | 122 | 80 |
| Mtwara | 21 | 29 |
| Mwanza | 107 | 181 |
| Shinyanga | 131 | 103 |
| Singida | 2 | 1 |
| Tabora | 40 | 56 |
| Arusha | 5 | 9 |
| Dodoma | 2 | 0 |
| Kilimanjaro | 16 | 12 |
| Tanga | 14 | 5 |

Source:  MDB (1988).

To conclude this section a note on the structure of the unions is also in order.  It seems that the structure of the unions is not conducive enough to improve the welfare of the peasants/farmers since the top personnel are not answerable to the farmers themselves.   However, because of the various views from politicians, economists and others, there is a need for more detailed research on the issue.

## UNSOLVED ISSUES

By requiring private traders to buy from the NMC and cooperatives, the Government expects to reduce the degree of competition in primary marketing and thus enable official agencies to:

o  buy not only from remote and high cost areas but also from accessible areas in which the private sector had an upper hand;

o  buy high quality grains which could be stored for longer periods without extensive deterioration in quality;

o  increase the turnover of stocks (this is particularly relevant to the NMC which has accumulated large stocks of maize).

However, the Government's action to restrict the marketing activities of private traders is most likely to adversely affect consumers (particularly in major urban centres like Dar es Salaam) and producers, particularly in remote areas.

Consumers are likely to pay higher prices either because private traders will be paying high into-store prices and/or because they will resort to "illegal" purchases. Private traders may be forced to pay their way by bribing road block officials. This additional cost may force some, and probably many, of the private traders out of business. This will have a negative impact on food availability in urban and food deficit rural areas as food prices may increase faster than consumers' incomes and their purchasing power will decline unless the NMC is capable of influencing food availability and prices on open markets through guaranteeing its ability to buy and sell at announced prices.

Producers of food grains are likely to experience more or less the same problems that they experienced prior to the 1984 and 1987 market reforms. The absence of competition in the accessible food surplus areas would enable cooperatives and NMC to concentrate their purchases in such areas and thus penalise the more remote producers. In areas where farmers earn income mainly from the production of staple grains (*e.g.*, Rukwa, parts of Ruvuma, Iringa and Mbeya) and where a shift to export crops is currently impossible (due to unfavorable agronomic conditions) the standard of living of the farmers is most likely to decline.

In addition, the restriction imposed on private traders is likely to increase the requirement for public sector credit for crop procurement from the levels which would otherwise have been required. Given the current debt problems as faced by NMC and cooperatives, financial institutions will be even more reluctant to give additional loans. The consequence of this will be to aggravate the existing problems of crop procurement at the primary level.

## OTHER POLICY MEASURES

From the above discussion it seems that the restriction of private traders from engaging in primary level marketing is unlikely to solve the financial problems of NMC and cooperatives or the problems of farmers in remote areas. If anything the problems are likely to get worse and consumers may be worse off. Are there alternative and more effective policy options?

One possible policy measure is to reform pricing policy so that it is consistent with the role of the NMC which is supplying distant but major deficit regions like Dar es Salaam. The pricing reform often considered is the introduction of a producer price structure based on economic suitability of different locations. This implies that higher prices should be paid to producers located near food deficit areas and discount prices paid to remote areas. This measure may benefit NMC but it may discourage production in remote areas; the implications of this on producers in remote areas may have to be clearly understood.

This policy measure appears not to provide solutions to problems faced by the NMC and the cooperatives and may even lead to a setback in the welfare of consumers and producers. There is likely to be no one policy measure that can effectively deal with the problems discussed in the paper.

It is our view that a combination of the following measures may be necessary:

o The government should legalise and regulate the role of the private traders in primary marketing. This is likely to benefit consumers and producers as well as reduce the financial burden of the public sector in purchase.

o The NMC should primarily deal with the food security role of assuring the availability of basic food grains in the country. On the other hand the main role of cooperatives should be to provide a mechanism for producers to benefit from the income and value-added arising from their performance. This may require them to compete with private traders.

More research needs to be done on the role played by the private sector in food marketing in Tanzania.

## REFERENCES

Amani, H.K.R. *et al.* 1987. Effects of Market Liberalisation on Food Security in Tanzania. In: M. Rukuni and R.H. Bernsten (eds) *Southern Africa : Food Security Policy Options.* University of Zimbabwe/Michigan State University Food Security Research Project. Department of Agricultural Economics. Harare.

Amani, H.K.R. *et al.* 1988. Impact of Market Liberalisation on Household Food Security in Tanzania In: G.D. Mudimu and R.H. Bernsten (eds) *Household and National Food Security in Southern Africa.* University of Zimbabwe/Michigan State University Food Security Research Project. Department of Agricultural Economics. Harare.

Gordon, H. 1988. *Open Markets for Maize and Rice in Urban Tanzania. Current Issues and Evidence.* Paper presented at the Economic Research Bureau. Dar es Salaam. November.

Gray, John G. *et al.* 1986. *The Pricing and Distribution of Basic Food Commodities in Tanzania.* Government of Tanzania. April.

Market Development Bureau (MDB). *Annual Review of Maize Rice and Wheat, 1984-1988.*

Market Development Bureau (MDB). 1986. *Aspects of the Open Market for Food Commodities in Mainland Tanzania.*

Mpuya, M. 1989. Peasants Need Better Storage Facilities. *Business Times.* 29/9/1989.

Scarborough, V. 1989. *The Current Status of Food Marketing in Tanzania.* Research paper. Wye College. Ashford. UK.

# APPENDICES

## Appendix 1
### Regional NMC purchases of maize grains
### (tonnes)

| Region | 1984-85 | 1985-86 | 1986-87 | 1987-88 |
|---|---|---|---|---|
| Coast/DSM | 25 | 0 | 0 | 0 |
| Morogoro | 584 | 776 | 640 | 1 683 |
| Tanga | 3 046 | 623 | 3 591 | 1 104 |
| Mtwara | 36 | 588 | 214 | 9 |
| Lindi | 89 | 627 | 774 | 46 |
| Arusha | 2 969 | 36 060 | 46 398 | 70 491 |
| Kilimanjaro | 50 | 769 | 23 | 2 228 |
| Dodoma | 1 143 | 12 020 | 7 057 | 25 694 |
| Singida | 67 | 5 084 | 4 750 | 9 806 |
| Tabora | 376 | 1 428 | 2 189 | 452 |
| Kigoma | 198 | 90 | 881 | 260 |
| Rukwa | 16 563 | 29 338 | 28 196 | 18 400 |
| Mwanza | 10 | 5 016 | 2 009 | 2 386 |
| Mara | 149 | 0 | 377 | 1 868 |
| Shinyanga | 187 | 2 745 | 4 140 | 404 |
| Kagera | 21 | 221 | 1 000 | 312 |
| Iringa | 22 982 | 38 006 | 36 428 | 63 575 |
| Mbeya | 7 341 | 15 987 | 11 804 | 14 236 |
| Ruvuma | 33 641 | 29 116 | 22 305 | 16 446 |
| Total | 89 477 | 178 494 | 172 776 | 229 400 |

Source: MDB (1988).

## Appendix 2
### Regional NMC purchases of rice
### (tonnes)

| Region | 1984-85 | 1985-86 | 1986-87 | 1987-88[a] |
|---|---|---|---|---|
| Coast/DSM | 18 | 65 | 0 | 0 |
| Morogoro | 834 | 258 | 1 477 | 1 442 |
| Tanga | 65 | 40 | 26 | 259 |
| Mtwara | 1 | 5 | 536 | 280 |
| Lindi | 1 | 0 | 423 | 342 |
| Arusha | 1 | 25 | 0 | 0 |
| Kilimanjaro | 0 | 33 | 65 | 1 568 |
| Dodoma | 0 | 0 | 0 | 251 |
| Singida | 0 | 0 | 0 | 36 |
| Tabora | 80 | 326 | 367 | 3 805 |
| Kigoma | 142 | 39 | 187 | 295 |
| Rukwa | 193 | 194 | 391 | 1 103 |
| Mwanza | 70 | 736 | 776 | 6 081 |
| Mara | 1 | 0 | 5 | 62 |
| Shinyanga | 55 | 2 601 | 2 092 | 15 217 |
| Kagera | 0 | 0 | 5 | 21 |
| Iringa | 1 | 19 | 20 | 727 |
| Mbeya | 10 597 | 11 582 | 5 043 | 11 200 |
| Ruvuma | 75 | 10 | 20 | 483 |
| Total | 12 134 | 15 933 | 11 433 | 43 172 |

[a] 1987-88 Purchases include purchases of paddy converted to rice equivalent.
Source: MDB (1988).

## Appendix 3
## Regional NMC purchases of wheat grains
### (tonnes)

| Region | 1984-85 | 1985-86 | 1986-87 | 1987-88 |
|---|---|---|---|---|
| Coast | - | - | - | - |
| Morogoro | - | - | - | - |
| Tanga | - | - | - | - |
| Mtwara | - | - | - | - |
| Lindi | - | - | - | - |
| Arusha | 32 686 | 48 858 | 32 688 | 40 280 |
| Kilimanjaro | 35 | 146 | - | - |
| Dodoma | - | - | - | - |
| Singida | 63 | 289 | 379 | 2 134 |
| Tabora | - | - | - | - |
| Kigoma | - | - | - | - |
| Rukwa | - | 86 | - | - |
| Mwanza | - | - | - | - |
| Mara | - | - | - | - |
| Shinyanga | - | 66 | - | - |
| Kagera | - | - | - | - |
| Iringa | 405 | 844 | 443 | 337 |
| Mbeya | - | - | - | - |
| Ruvuma | - | - | - | - |
| Total | 33 198 | 50 289 | 33 510 | 42 789 |

Source: MDB (1988).

# 10

# Reform Of Maize Marketing In Kenya

*Mark O. Odhiambo*[1] *and David C. Wilcock*[2]

## INTRODUCTION

This paper discusses some of the current policy issues regarding grain marketing in Kenya. During most of the 1980s the Kenyan Government has been under constant pressure especially from the international donor community to liberalise trade in grains particularly maize (Schmidt, 1979; Booker and Githongo, 1983; Ackello-Ogutu and Odhiambo, 1986; Technosyneisis *et al.* 1988; and Odhiambo, 1988). For almost half a century, starting from colonial times and even after Kenya gained her political independence in 1963, the Government of Kenya has maintained rigid control over the marketing and pricing of the major cereals like maize, wheat and rice.

For the purposes of this paper, we will concentrate on the maize marketing system in Kenya and the reforms that have been proposed or implemented within the system. The paper is divided into four section. The introduction is followed by an overview of the maize production and marketing system in Kenya. The third section analyses maize marketing reforms while the final section presents conclusions.

## AN OVERVIEW OF MAIZE PRODUCTION AND MARKETING IN KENYA

### Maize Production

Maize is the most important staple food crop in Kenya and is therefore widely grown in the country. Kenya's diverse agro-ecological zones offer unique opportunities for maize production and inter-regional trade. Altitude and climate influence the distribution and patterns of maize production. In most parts of Kenya, maize can be grown twice a year to coincide with the long and short rainy seasons. Maize is grown only once a year in the high altitude areas and other parts of the country with unimodal rainfall patterns.

---

[1]Lecturer, Department of Agricultural Economics, University of Nairobi, Kenya.

[2]Agricultural Economist, Agriculture and Natural Resources Division, Development Alternatives, Inc., Washington D.C.

About 95 percent of the small-scale farmers plant maize during the long rains. During the short rains, however, only 65 percent of these farmers grow maize. The large-scale farmers, on the other hand, grow virtually all their maize during the long rains.

The structure of production affects maize supply patterns and the marketing channels (World Bank, 1982). Over the years dualistic production systems have developed consisting of small-scale farmers who mainly produce maize as a subsistence crop, and the large-scale farmers who grow maize as a cash crop. Precise statistics on the area under maize and total production are hard to come by especially on the basis of small and large-scale farm sectors. Table 1 gives a summary of aggregate production in recent years.

### Table 1
### Maize production in Kenya, 1979-87.

| Year | Area ('000 ha) | Yield/Ha Bags | Yield/Ha MT | Production Million Bags | Production MT'000 |
|---|---|---|---|---|---|
| 1979-80 | 839 | 21 | 1,93 | 18,0 | 1 620 |
| 1980-81 | 989 | 18 | 1,62 | 17,8 | 1 604 |
| 1981-82 | 1 208 | 16 | 1.46 | 19,7 | 1 768 |
| 1983-84 | 1 200 | 19 | 1,73 | 26,0 | 2 070 |
| 1984-85 | 1 130 | 14 | 1,25 | 15,7 | 1 411 |
| 1985-86 | 1 240 | 18 | 1,67 | 29,0 | 2 074 |
| 1986-87 | 1 220 | 25 | 2,21 | 30,0 | 2 696 |

Source: Government of Kenya, MOA.

According to recent studies (Ackello-Ogutu and Odhiambo, 1986; Odhiambo, 1988), the small-scale farming sector, consisting of farmers with 20 hectares or less, account for about 70 to 90 percent of the total annual maize production in the country. About 75 percent of these smallholders have less than two hectares of land. The large farms therefore account for only 10 to 30 percent of the total production. The majority of the small-scale producers are subsistence farmers who, in most cases, retain 70 to 80 percent of their production for home consumption and sell the balance (World Bank, 1982; Ackello-Ogutu and Odhiambo, 1986).

Recent studies (Maritim 1982; Ackello-Ogutu and Odhiambo, 1986; and Odhiambo 1988) estimate that about 60 percent of the total smallholder maize production comes from the Western Region of Kenya in the Rift Valley, Western and Nyanza Province. The districts in Central Province have a high potential for maize production but most of the farmers concentrate on the growing of high-value cash crops like coffee and tea and a small amount of maize for subsistence. Eastern and Coast Provinces are mainly deficit regions. The map in Figure 1 shows the major maize producing districts of Kenya and the deficit districts.

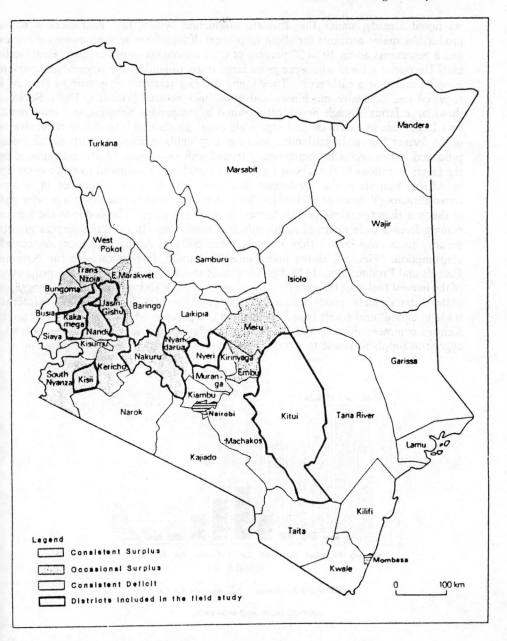

Figure 1: Map of Kenya's maize surplus and deficit districts.

As noted already, under the dualistic production system that characterises maiz
production, maize accounts for about 20 percent of total farm acreage under cultivatio
and it represents about 10 to 30 percent of total national crop production. Historicall
early European settlers who were given large tracts of land by the colonial governmer
adopted maize as a cash crop. They found maize a relatively easy crop to grow as :
required less expensive machinery and gave quick returns (Maritim, 1982). Some c
these large farms, though now mostly owned by indigenous Kenyans, still grow maiz
on a large scale as a cash crop. Large-scale maize production is therefore concentrate
in the former European settlement areas, mostly highland districts. Virtually all maiz
produced in this sector is commercially traded with only about 10 percent retained o
the farms as rations to the labour force or as stockfeed. Compared to other countrie
in Africa, Kenyan maize production and food security have a number of uniqu
characteristics (Wilcock *et al.* 1989). The maize harvest takes place over a greater pal
of the year than the staple cereals harvest in other countries. This is due to the harves
coming from a wide range of agro-ecological conditions. In turn, this implies greate
security from crop failure than in most other parts of Africa dependent on cerea
consumption. Figure 2 shows maize monthly harvest distribution with the Nationa
Cereals and Produce Board (NCPB) purchases superimposed to depict the proportio
of the harvest that goes through the official or formal marketing channel. The geograph
of the country's maize production and consumption provides ideal conditions for interna
trade in agricultural goods based on regional comparative advantage. The existence c
Kenya's commercially-oriented large-scale farm zones provides a key to the potentia
aggregate supply response to alternative scenarios under market reform programme.

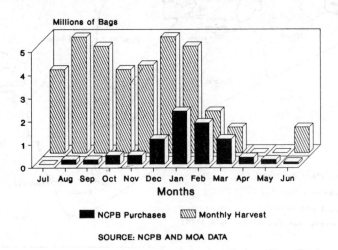

Figure 2:  Kenya maize monthly harvest and NCPB purchases.
Source: NCPB and MOA data.

## Maize Marketing

aize marketing in Kenya for a long time has been characterised by two distinct but mplementary sub-systems. The first sub-system is the "formal" or the "official" arketing channel which is monopolised by the National Cereals and Produce Board ICPB). The second sub-system is the "informal" or the unofficial marketing system - so referred to as the "parallel market". Although the two sub-systems are parallel in ay aspects (Figure 3), they are interdependent and complementary. Moreover, with e proposed changes embodied in the ongoing market reforms in the country, the rmal and informal maize marketing systems are bound to become increasingly inter- pendent.

### *The Formal Marketing System*

he NCPB, a parastatal organisation established under the Kenya Maize Marketing Act, empowered by the Government of Kenya (GOK) to handle all maize officially irchased or sold in the country. It is also the body that can import or export maize as e need may arise. Maize movement is regulated and limited by law. Until 1988 it was egal to move more than two 90 kilogram bags of maize across the district without a ovement permit issued by the Board or a government representative authorised to do . Since 1988 the restriction has now been relaxed to allow up to 10 bags to be moved ithin the country without obtaining a movement permit. Moving larger quantities of aize can only be done when accompanied by a permit issued by the NCPB.

istorically, government controls over maize marketing in Kenya were instituted during e colonial times in order to provide guaranteed export and local markets for the uropean settlers. During the Second World War, the colonial Government instituted e Maize Control Board requiring compulsory maize deliveries to increase marketed aize, ostensibly to support the war effort. After the war these regulations were aintained until 1959 when the Maize Marketing Board was formed. The new Board ontinued to provide European settlers guaranteed outlets and fixed prices while iscriminating against African producers by levying a tax on their maize to pay for export isses (Ley, 1975; Maritim, 1982).

t independence in 1963 a uniform maize pricing system for the whole country was itroduced. However, the new Kenyan Government inherited and retained most of the ontrol mechanisms in the maize marketing system. The bureaucratised marketing /stem has remained one of the greatest colonial legacies in Kenya. According to overnment stated policy the NCPB activities and other control mechanisms are designed (Ackello-Ogutu and Odhiambo, 1986):

o   ensure the availability of adequate food supplies to meet domestic demand and prevent malnutrition;

o   stabilise maize supplies in both surplus and deficit areas;

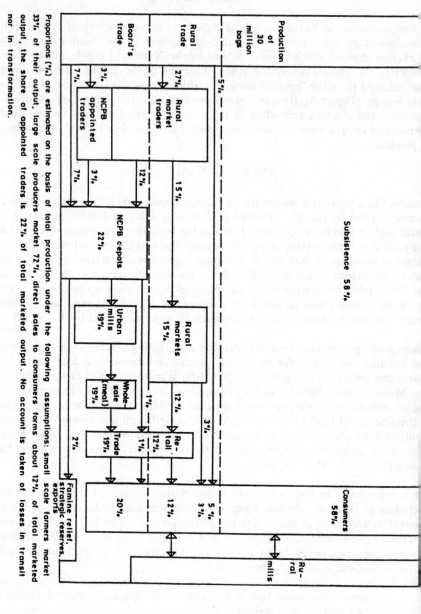

Figure 3: Maize marketing channels in Kenya, 1986-87.

SOURCE: Odhiambo, 1988.

Proportions (%) are estimated on the basis of total production under the following assumptions: small scale farmers market 72%, direct sales to consumers forms about 12% of total marketed output, the share of appointed traders is 22% of total marketed output. No account is taken of losses in transit nor in transformation. 33% of their output, large scale producers market 72%,

o   provide a secure outlet for smallholder production and prevent possible exploitation of smallholders by private trade;

o   maintain strategic reserves; and

o   control grain smuggling to neighbouring deficit countries.

ιe NCPB has a network of depots to facilitate its buying and selling functions. In the aize surplus areas, the Board buys maize through a system of Primary Marketing ιntres (PMCs), its appointed buying agents (ABA), cooperative societies and the Kenya ⸱ain Growers' Cooperative Union (KGGCU), or through farmers' and traders' direct liveries to the depots. A breakdown of maize deliveries to the Board through the ⸱ious channels is given in Table 2 below.

ιble 3 gives the recent NCPB maize transactions. The maize handled by the NCPB ⸱rough the official marketing system is sold to registered millers, traders and to ⸱nsumers at controlled pan-territorial and pan-seasonal prices. Most of the NCPB ιize goes to urban consumers and other maize deficit areas in the country. Except in ⸱nes of extreme shortage most maize surplus areas and other rural consumers depend ⸱ the informal marketing system for their maize.

### Table 2
### Sources of maize deliveries to the NCPB, 1988-89.

| ⸱rce | Percentage Purchased |
|---|---|
| ⸱mary marketing centres | 21 |
| ⸱ying agents | 3 |
| ⸱operatives | 20 |
| ⸱ect deliveries by farmers or traders | 53 |

⸱rce: NCPB

### The Informal Maize Marketing System

⸱e second marketing sub-system in maize trade is the informal marketing system which ⸱erates parallel to the official marketing system. According to Ministry of Agriculture ⸱OA) estimates, it handles 30 to 50 percent of the maize traded in the country and ⸱out 60 percent of the smallholder marketed maize surplus. The existence of the NCPB ⸱ a monopsony has not always guaranteed a secure outlet to all farmers and it is ⸱imated that about 30 to 50 percent of small-scale maize producers do not have access ⸱ the NCPB official marketing system (World Bank, 1982). Until 1988, the informal ⸱rketing system has been legally restricted. The volume of maize to be moved was ⸱tricted to two bags (90 kilograms each) or less, which had to be accompanied by the ⸱ner for inter-district transfers. Within a district the movement regulation allowed for ⸱ bags or less but such maize also had to be accompanied by the owner and declared

that it was intended for consumption by the owner and his family. All other mai
movement required a movement permit issued by the NCPB. Obtaining such moveme
permits always proved very difficult for traders.

### Table 3
### NCPB maize transactions 1984-89.
### ('000 bags)

|  | 1984-85 | 1985-86 | 1986-87 | 1987-88 | 1988-89 |
|---|---|---|---|---|---|
| **Opening Stock:** | | | | | |
| White maize | 3 977 | 1 812 | 7 470 | 11 180 | 9 572 |
| Yellow maize | 6 | 2 822 | 2 059 | 336 | 131 |
| **Purchases:** | | | | | |
| White maize | 4 036 | 9 323 | 7 693 | 5 369 | 6 866 |
| Yellow maize | 2 816 | 6 | 4 | 121 | 2 |
| **Sales:** | | | | | |
| White maize | 6 201 | 3 656 | 1 844 | 5 258 | 4 480 |
| Yellow maize | 0 | 494 | 656 | 347 | 1 |
| **Exports/Losses:** | | | | | |
| White maize | 0 | 9 | 2 139 | 1 719 | 1 690 |
| Yellow maize | 0 | 235 | 1 071 | (21) | 26 |
| **Closing Stock:** | | | | | |
| White maize | 1 812 | 7 470 | 11 180 | 9 572 | 10 268 |
| Yellow maize | 2 822 | 2 059 | 336 | 131 | 106 |

Source:  NCPB

Despite these restrictions, the informal marketing system evolved into a complex mai
marketing channel that has thrived through illegal inter-district and inter-provincial mai
trade. The system involves many stages and intermediaries between the farmers and tl
consumers (Figure 3). In its simplest form the system may involve such short chann
transactions as that between the maize farmer and a local consumer or trader. Howeve
the trade can become more complex whereby rural retail traders or larger scale inte
regional lorry traders buy maize directly from the farmers and either sell it locally
transport it to other markets within or across a given district boundary. Most of tl
large wholesale type of traders have devised ways and means of circumventing the leg
restrictions. However, these restrictions have made the informal system operate und
high overhead costs.

Unlike the formal marketing system which operates with fixed pan-territorial and pa
seasonal prices, the informal sector, because of its high costs and risks, operate wi
prices that vary regularly and consistently with seasons and across the country. Su
prices tend to be lower in the surplus regions and at harvest times than in deficit are
or seasons.

'he existence of movement control in the informal marketing channel together with the xed pricing system in the formal marketing system results in low market integration nd lack of price stabilisation in the informal system. The spatial price differentiation s far higher than would prevail in an open market. Operational efficiency is very low s reflected by high costs and an inability to achieve economies of scale in distribution Schmidt, 1979; World Bank, 1982; and Odhiambo, 1988).

## THE PROCESS OF MARKETING REFORM

### Previous Attempts at Marketing Reforms

Aany critics of the GOK's control of maize marketing have suggested liberalising the ystem and/or reducing the role of the NCPB (Heselmark and Lorenzl, 1976; Schmidt 979; World Bank, 1982; Booker and Githongo, 1983). The major issues in the iberalisation debate centre around:

o    the Government of Kenya policy or legal foundations of state participation in the maize trade through the NCPB;

o    the efficiency and cost implications of NCPB's involvement in marketing operations and the consequences of the monopoly powers of the NCPB;

o    efficiency and cost implications for other participants in the overall maize marketing system;

o    the movement controls in the informal marketing system and the pan-seasonal and pan-territorial price fixing regulations in the formal marketing system; and

o    the performance of the informal (free) marketing system in terms of market concentration, pricing efficiency, degree of market transparency and the extent of barriers to entry.

iome critics of the maize marketing system have pointed out that the GOK's objectives or controlling pricing and marketing have centred more on welfare than revenue •roducing considerations (World Bank, 1986). The GOK has had to defend its ntervention policies in the marketing system on the basis of protecting producers and :onsumers in an otherwise poorly developed marketing system where middlemen are ikely to exploit both producers and consumers (Odhiambo, 1988).

\s far back as 1974, the GOK had indicated a willingness to liberalise internal maize narketing by removing all legal restrictions (Kenya, 1974; Odhiambo 1988). Subsequent levelopment plans, including the current 1989-1993 Development Plan, have stated the ntention to reform the market, but implementation has been slow and cautious. Past :xperiments with maize market liberalisation have been short-lived. For example in the 1977-78 and 1986-87 seasons, farmers had a bumper harvest and the NCPB was unable o cope with maize deliveries from farmers. To ease pressure in the official marketing

channel the Government liberalised the market by allowing millers to procure maiz
directly from farmers and private traders. But experimental liberalisation in these tw
periods had devastating effects (Odhiambo, 1988). First, farmers received low price
from informal traders and became discouraged with maize production. The 1977-7
maize glut culminated in reduced production the next year which, together with drough
resulted in the maize shortage of 1979-80 in Kenya. Secondly, during the period of thes
liberalisation experiments, the NCPB was unable to sell its stocks as millers, who ar
the major customers of the NCPB, could now get cheaper maize directly from farmer
and traders. As a result, the Board experienced cash flow problems and were unable t
pay farmers in time, thereby reducing farmers' incentives to grow maize in subsequen
years. Following these problems, the experiments with market liberalisation in bot
1977-78 and 1986-87 had to be discontinued by the government.

Under the Structural Adjustment Programme (SAP) of the 1980s, the World Bank an
other donors laid increasing emphasis on the promotion of free markets, private secto
investment, and market reform. In the grain industry, the structural adjustment packag
emphasised a policy shift towards increased reliance on the private sector to carry ou
agricultural marketing functions previously monopolised by the NCPB. However, give
the long history of controls spanning over half a century, it is understandable that th
reform process advocated in the SAP package has taken time to be adopted. Again
given the bad experience with experiments on liberalisaton it seems the GOK neede
adequate time to study the proposals so as to weigh the costs and benefits of changin
from the familiar controlled system to a situation of being left at the mercy of fre
market forces especially with respect to maize, the staple food crop. A World Bank
sponsored study (Booker and Githongo, 1983) recommended reforms involving decontro
of maize movement, setting a price band within which the NCPB would intervene wit
the reduced role as buyer and seller of "last resort". However, the 1984 famine, followin
closely after the 1979-80 maize shortage, disrupted the Government's plans to implemen
these recommendations. The report submitted in 1983 was not finally accepted by GOF
until 1987. By this time, it was already overtaken by events as a new study sponsored b
the European Economic Community (EEC) was under way.

## THE EEC/GOK SPONSORED CEREAL SECTOR
## REFORM PROGRAMME (CSPR)

In 1987 the EEC and the GOK agreed to carry out a study on the reorganisation of the
NCPB. The study was done by a group of consultants (Technosynesis and Coopers &
Lybrand, 1988) with the financial support from the EEC. The study, like the others don
before it (*e.g.*, World Bank-sponsored Booker and Githonogo Report of 1983), conclude
in the findings that:

   o    The NCPB was inefficient and poorly managed. In particular the repor
        found that the Board had persistently made heavy losses in its pas
        operations to the extent that is was unable to cope with its financial an
        marketing obligations. It could not cope with crop purchases in years o

good harvest and neither was it capable of providing adequate maize supply to deficit areas in periods of severe shortages;

o   The Forward Planning Unit of the NCPB was underdeveloped and was incapable of providing information for precise policy decisions; and

o   The Board had inadequate and poorly planned storage facilities. Its transport system was also poorly organised and expensive.

The study recommended that the NCPB be reorganised and restructured to make it more efficient. It was also recommended that the Government of Kenya should write off the NCPB's bad debts accumulated over the years and provide budget subventions to the Board for market stabilisation and ensuring timely payment for crop purchases. A revolving fund to this effect was to be established.

The reorganised plan included modifying the role of NCPB in the maize market to one of buyer and seller of last resort to support floor and ceiling market prices. In this respect, a programme of phased decontrol of the maize market was to be launched, accompanied by liberalisation of the bean market and decontrol of minor crops handled by the board.

Following these recommendations the GOK entered into negotiation with the EEC for funding. The agreement establishing CSSP was signed in December 1987. The GOK approved a series of measures to introduce internal management reforms in the NCPB and improve efficiency in grain marketing channels. A detailed implementation timetable was designed to specify, in the form of a five-year action plan, the measures to be taken by NCPB, means of implementation, and how progress was to be monitored (Technosynsis/EEC Report, 1988). The phased partial maize market liberalisation was instituted in 1988 allowing some farmers, cooperatives and to a limited extent, traders to make direct deliveries to the mills until they accounted for 20 percent of the mills' requirements. The remaining 80 percent was to be supplied by the Board. Through annual review and monitoring the decontrol would be increased by allowing more private sector participation and reducing the share of the Board eventually to 25 percent. In addition, this agreement formally recognises the two cornerstones of the future reduced role of the Board (DAI, 1989):

o   to maintain a food security stock of maize; and

o   to be the maize buyer and seller of last resort stabilising the market within a defined floor and ceiling price band.[3]

---

[3]At the time of writing this paper there was an on going EEC-funded pricing study that was expected to come up with the formula for setting the band.

In the past two years the World Bank has largely ceded the leadership role on cereals policy reform to the EEC-sponsored CSRP programme, and is trying to support this effort with funding of complementary investments and studies. However, over the past 18 months, the CSRP has concentrated on internal restructuring and reorganisation of the NCPB. Less attention has been given to the detailed definition of the future reduced role of the Board, partly due to the political sensitivity and difficulty of decision-making in the latter.

## SUMMARY OF CURRENT SITUATION IN CEREALS MARKETING POLICY REFORM

There are many issues which need to be resolved in the process of developing an acceptable programme on cereals market reform. Some issues need immediate attention while others may be tackled over a period of time. In our assessment, after interviewing farmers, millers and GOK officials, the status of the reform process as of now can be summarised as follows:

o    In the cereals sector, Kenya is in the grey middle area between free markets and a totally controlled system, paying a high price for the inefficiency arising from the restricted private trade and the public budget support for the Government Grain Board.

o    The CSRP reform process is much further away from resolving key issues on the future reduced role of the NCPB than was initially believed. It is therefore unreasonable at this time to expect the GOK to be able to initiate an immediate and substantial reduction in the role of the Board since its role is still so operationally undefined.

o    The 1988-89 experience with partial liberalisation (80 percent NCPB and 20 percent private sector) showed that there is still some confusion arising from unresolved or undefined issues regarding private trade. Agreement on the objectives of the reduced role for the NCPB alone without detailed operational contingency plans for the reforms cannot guarantee the success of the cereals reform. The longer-term food security system and stabilisation roles for the NCPB must be defined with the modalities for their eventual implementation.

o    Addressing key issues such as relaxation of controls on grain movement (even if the positive effects on consumers can be shown clearly) will have to be able to alleviate two expressed fears: first, that informal channel liberalisation will further erode the tottering state of the NCPB and its continuing drain on GOK finances and second, that such changes would increase national food insecurity.

## USAID KENYA MARKET DEVELOPMENT PROPOSAL

The United States Agency for International Development (USAID) is one of the major donor agencies that has provided economic assistance to the GOK. As part of the Structural Adjustment Programme (SAP) in Kenya, USAID, like the World Bank, has advocated policies to strengthen public and private sector management capabilities with the goal of increasing participation of the private sector in a freer market environment (Odhiambo, 1989). Recently, USAID proposed to the GOK the idea of launching a Kenya Market Development Programme (KMDP) to complement the ongoing EEC-sponsored Cereals Sector Programme (CSRP).

The KMDP is still in the design and negotiation stage. The focus of attention of the proposed programme is on private trade especially involving the informal market of maize and beans. The KMDP is intended to combine support of reform measures with investments in the physical infrastructure and development of an information system that would facilitate efficiency in the marketing system.

In May/June 1989, USAID sponsored a study (DAI, 1989) to analyse the economic and social soundness of the proposed KMDP.[4] The study examined the relationship between existing formal and informal marketing channels for maize and beans through (a) extensive field work involving six districts representing both surplus and deficit areas; (b) interviews with Government and NCPB officials, farmers, traders and millers; and (c) a review of the literature on the subject. The DAI study found that there were striking contrasts between the formal and informal segments of the marketing system. The latter was characterised by low levels of operational efficiency because of legal restrictions and other barriers.

The main thrust of the policy measure recommended as a basis for KMDP is to incorporate reforms legitimising the informal maize trade in Kenya and eliminating movement controls. Other proposed aspects of reform in the programme include:

o    a decontrol of beans and other minor crops;

o    development of price and other market information systems;

o    contribution to food security; and

o    investment in infrastructure to enhance the marketing efficiency of maize and beans.

---

[4]The authors of this paper were part of the team constituted by Development Alternatives Inc. that did the study for USAID.

## THE ECONOMIC IMPACT OF
## ELIMINATING MOVEMENT CONTROL

In this section we present the analysis aimed at assessing in both quantitative and non-quantitative terms, the impact of the movement controls that currently restrict private commerce in maize. KMDP reforms can have the greatest impact in the informal marketing system if they can help to develop thriving private wholesaling activities that would be more efficient in terms of cost reductions and exploiting economies of scale in the informal vertical marketing channel. Spatial and temporal arbitrage would be greatly promoted in such an environment and it is estimated that there would be a general savings of 65 Kenya shillings(Ksh) per bag of maize going through such a system. These savings would be generated as follows:

o    the elimination of one or more (inefficient small-scale) market traders from the channel: Ksh45;

o    reduced handling charges due to fewer transactions and large volumes being handled in each transaction: Ksh5;

o    cheaper transport due to the use of larger lorries (economies of scale): Ksh15.

In other words, there would be a substantial reduction of marketing margins that would then be passed on to producers, consumers and the traders. A general model of the distribution of the potential benefits from this reduction in margins is illustrated in Figure 4. In order to derive the impacts on the various participants (producers, consumers and traders) in the system, a statistical model of Kenyan maize production and marketing was constructed (for details see Wilcock *et al.*, 1989). The model construction involved disaggregating data on maize production and marketing by provinces and by districts. Using secondary sources of data, the following parameters on maize production for each district and province were generated for the construction of the model: proportion of farms that fell into the small- and large-scale category; the average farm size in hectares; proportion of land under maize; number of maize farms; area under maize in the long and short rains; maize yields per hectare on small and large farms for both long and short rainy seasons; and total production also disaggregated by seasons (long and short rains) and by farm size categories.

The parameters on maize marketing were disaggregated by province because the district level data base was inadequate. The parameters included: proportion of harvest sold on small and large farms in both long and short rainy seasons; and the total number of bags sold by small and large farms in long and short rains.

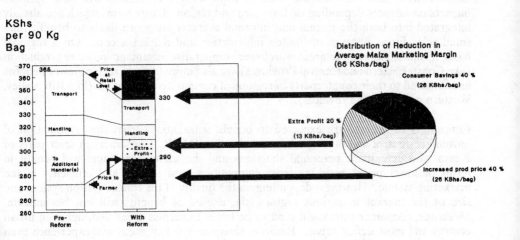

KShs
per 90 Kg
Bag

**Figure 4: Potential changes in marketing margins, consumer and producer prices due to elimination of movement controls in Kenya's informal maize market.**

On aggregate, the model reveals that in an average year Kenya has about 1,59 million hectares under maize and produces about 31 million bags (2,7 million tonnes) of which about 13 million bags (42 percent) are marketed. Table 4 gives a summary of the maize production and marketing parameters in an average year as derived from the statistical model.

Table 4
Maize production and marketing parameters.

| | |
|---|---|
| Total area in Maize | 1 588 000 hectares |
| Total farms growing maize | 1 388 000 |
| Total maize produced | 31 387 000 bags |
| Total maize marketed | 13 227 000 bags |
| Average area under maize per farm | 1,1 hectares |
| Average maize yield | 19,8 bags/ha |
| Average maize harvested per farm | 22,6 bags |
| Average percent market | 42,0 |
| Average Maize sold per farm | 9,5 bags |

Source: Calculated from GOK Economic Survey, 1989; GOK CBS Crop Forecast Survey 1981-82, and USAID Data Base.

Using the parameters from the model, it was found that elimination of movement control under KMDP and the resulting benefits from margin reductions will have variable impacts on farmers depending on farm size and region. Large farms which are already integrated into both the formal and informal markets are more likely to benefit than small scale farms because of limited information and market access. On a regional basis, farmers operating in areas with lower comparative advantage in maize production (like Coast, Eastern and Central Provinces) are also more likely to receive fewer benefits as compared to their counterparts in regions of comparative advantage (like Rift Valley, Western and Nyanza Provinces).

Consumers in general are expected to benefit substantially from the elimination of movement control and other packages under the KMDP. Consumers in drier parts of Kenya who experience perennial shortages and the urban consumers will benefit in terms of lower prices resulting from competition, cost savings and efficiency in the marketing system. However, depending on the quality of the transportation system and size of the market in various regions, the degree of benefits will not be uniform. Moreover, consumer prices will tend to be lower in surplus areas and higher in urban centres and most deficit areas. Remote, chronically deficit areas will experience even higher prices.

### The Implications of the Elimination of Movement Control for the NCPB

We have seen that under the Cereals Sector Reform Programme the NCPB is supposed to be strengthened to perform a reduced role. However, its reduced role as a buyer and seller of last resort and as the custodian of the strategic maize reserve still remains unclear and undefined. There is some perception that the elimination of movement control rapidly erodes the ability of the Board to compete cost-effectively in the Kenyan maize market. To address this problem requires analysis of the impacts of movement decontrol under three scenarios: bumper, average and deficit harvest conditions.

Under average or bumper harvest conditions, the elimination of movement control would not appreciably affect the NCPB as a buyer since its harvest price would generally be above prevailing market levels. The biggest question under bumper harvest conditions is one of how much price support the Board provides to farmers. The Board is also likely under this condition to accumulate large stocks far beyond security requirements and with no monopoly selling power, face greater cash flow problems.

Under mild deficit conditions, liberalisation clearly implies that the Board would have to compete for its needed stock acquisitions. This effect is very transitory, however, since under more severe deficit and drought conditions the Board would stop buying and begin releasing its security stock to the market and planning for food aid and commercial imports. Thus the elimination of movement controls would not have an appreciable impact on NCPB operation if the necessary logistics and mechanisms for its intervention in the market are properly defined.

## CONCLUSION

There are potentially sizable economic benefits to be derived from the decontrol of the informal maize trade sector. The GOK and the major donor agencies who have a keen interest in maize market reforms (EEC, World Bank, USAID) are in principle agreed on the need for reforms but seem to differ on the definition of what constitutes the reforms and the approach to take in the process. Indeed, the GOK 1989-1993 Development Plan (pp. 114-115) states that a major restructuring involving gradual liberalisation will be carried out over the next five years whereby the NCPB will (eventually) leave 75 percent of the market to private traders, millers, and cooperative societies. The Development Plan obviously echoes the EEC/GOK agreement on the CSRP. While recognising that the NCPB's proposed dual role of maintenance of national strategic reserves and acting as buyer and seller of last resort pose unique responsibilities to the board, neither the Development Plan nor the CSRP address this issue adequately. There is, for example, substantial debate on how an increased private sector role in the formal market might be accomplished without creating further financial problems for the Board during the transitional period (Wilcock *et al.* 1989). It must be recognised that partial market reforms are difficult to manage on a sustainable basis. There is therefore a need for longer range solutions to market liberalisation through a more complete GOK food security strategy. This will obviously take time to develop as there are practical difficulties for the GOK associated with the implementation of these proposals. For example, there are budgetary constraints which limit the size of food security stocks and the degree of producer price supports. Secondly, allowing consumer flour and maize grain to fluctuate freely within a band may be difficult to "sell" politically. Thirdly, it must be recognised that, in spite of the reform proposals, the Government must learn to have greater trust in the private sector, but this is a process that takes time, even in the comparatively liberal economic environment of Kenya.

In conclusion, it must be stressed that there is need for more applied research in generating practical and feasible food security policy options. Finally, the donor agencies and the GOK should coordinate their efforts in the policy arena and in the formulation and implementation of future reforms.

## REFERENCES

Ackello-Ogutu, C.A., and M.O. Odhiambo. 1986. *Maize Production in Kenya : A Study of Costs and Technological Constraints Associated with Output Expansion.* Report to USAID Kenya. Nairobi.

Booker Agricultural International and Githongo and Associated. 1983. *Grain Marketing Study.* Submitted to Ministry of Finance Government of Kenya.

Development Alternatives Inc. (DAI). 1989. *Economic and Social Soundness Analyses for the Kenya Market Development Programme.* Report USAID/Kenya.

Government of Kenya 1959. The Maize Marketing Ordinance. *Laws of Kenya.* Nairobi.

Government of Kenya. 1974. *Development Plans* (1974-1978). Nairobi.

Government of Kenya. 1982. *Crop Forecast Survey 1981-82.* Central Bureau of Statistics Ministry of Planning and Economic Development. Nairobi.

Government of Kenya. 1989. *Development Plans* (1989-1993). Nairobi.

Government of Kenya 1989. *Economic Survey*. Central Bureau of Statistics. Nairobi.

Gisanger, H. and G. Smith. 1977. *Decontrolling the Maize Marketing System in Kenya*. IDS Discussion Pape No. 254. University of Nairobi. Kenya.

Hesselmark, O. and G. Lorenzl. 1976. The Structure and Problems of Maize Marketing in Kenya *Zeitschri fur auslandische Landwirtschaft*. 15 (z) : 161-1971.

Ley, C. 1975. *Underdevelopment in Kenya : The Political Development of Neo-Colonialism*. Nairobi. London

Maritim, H.K. 1982. *Maize Marketing in Kenya : An Assessment of Interregional Commodity Flow Pattern* Ph.D. Thesis Technical University of Berlin. Berlin.

Ministry of Agriculture (MOA). *Annual Reports*. Various Issues. Government of Kenya (GOK) Nairob

National Cereal and Produce Board (NCPB). *Annual Reports*. Various Issues. Nairobi. Kenya.

Odhiambo, M.O. 1988. Grain Market Development. *Agricultural Policy Assessment Study*. Agriconsu Report to USAID/Kenya, Nairobi.

Schmidt, W.J. 1979. *Maize and Beans Marketing in Kenya*. Occasional Paper No 31 IDS. University Nairobi.

Technosynesis, S.P.A. and Coopers & Lybrand Associates. 1988. *National Cereals and Produce Board R organisation Study*. EEC Report/GOK Ministry of Finance. Nairobi.

Wilcock, D., M. Odhiambo, D. Hughes and F. Karuingi. 1989. Marketing Systems Analysis. In: *Econom and Social Soundness Analyses for the Kenya Market Development Programme*. DAI report USAID. Kenya.

World Bank. 1982. *Kenya Maize Marketing and Pricing Subsector Review Report No. 400-KE*. Washington, D.

World Bank. 1986. *Kenya Agricultural Sector Review Report of 1986*. Washington, D.C.

# 11

# Grain Market Reliability, Access And Growth In Low-Potential Areas Of Zimbabwe: Implications For National And Regional Supply Coordination In The SADCC Region

*Thomas S. Jayne[1], Munhamo Chisvo[2], Solomon Chigume2 and Charles Chopak[3]*

## INTRODUCTION

Many SADCC countries are currently on the horns of a dilemma: how to (a) stimulate smallholder food production and access, particularly in chronically food insecure areas; (b) stabilise national food supplies, and hopefully consumption, without; (c) inflicting intolerable costs on the government treasury. In the wake of recent market reform experiments, Malawi, Tanzania, Zambia, and Zimbabwe are each grappling with how to institute marketing, stockholding and trade policies to deal with this dilemma.[4] However, recent research on the subject to guide SADCC policymaking has focused primarily on issues (b) and (c), generally framing the research question in terms of finding the least-cost combination of stockholding and/or net imports to minimise the trade-off between budget costs and a given level of food supply stability -- holding market structure constant (see, for example, Pinckney, 1988). While such research is useful as a short-run supply management tool, more emphasis is needed on identifying critical changes in the organisation of the market that will, over the long run, reduce the magnitude of these trade-offs.

[1]Visiting Lecturer, Department of Agricultural Economics and Extension, University of Zimbabwe.

[2]Research Scholar, Department of Agricultural Economics and Extension, University of Zimbabwe.

[3]Research Associate, Department of Agricultural Economics, Michigan State University.

The authors would like to thank E.A. Nuppenau, M. Weber, D. Rohrbach, G. Mudimu, B. Kinsey and J. Govereh for comments on an earlier draft.

[4]These countries share the common predicament of being landlocked (with the exception of Tanzania), and subject to high transport costs, limited and uncertain transport capacity with lengthy time lags between order and delivery, high grain storage costs, and severe foreign exchange constraints. These factors complicate issues concerning the appropriate mix of trade and stockholding as mechanisms to meet objectives (a), (b) and (c).

For example, market restructuring that stimulates private incentives to invest in the production and marketing system in deficit areas may promote grain sales and access over the long run, reduce the quantity of stocks or imports required to stabilise supplies, *and* reduce marketing board operating costs.

The objective of this paper is to consider how market redesign may change the nature and magnitude of the trade-offs between objectives (a), (b) and (c). A thesis of the paper is that the incorporation of longer-run issues of investment, access, and growth into the design of grain stock, trade, and distribution policies may improve long-run food security and concomitantly strengthen the ability of low-resource households to withstand transitory production and income fluctuations.

## CONCEPTUAL FRAMEWORK: THE NATURE AND MAGNITUDE OF THE FOOD SECURITY PROBLEM

Several SADCC countries are grain self-sufficient in a normal year. This creates the illusion that the hunger problem is primarily a transitory rather than a chronic problem. Yet one is struck by the glaring contradictions of malnourished infants, children and mothers-at-risk standing right next to the mountains of food being piled up at the district and regional depots (Jackson and Collier, 1988). Even in a good rainfall year in a food self-sufficient country such as Zimbabwe, national supply stabilisation through trade or stock policies is insufficient to alleviate chronic food insecurity because a large proportion of rural households suffering from hunger are food inadequate on a continuous basis, not just in drought years (see, for example, Moyo *et al*, 1985. UNICEF, 1984). Field research in two communal areas situated in Natural Regions III, IV, and V indicate that 59 percent of farm households surveyed did not produce enough food for family requirements in a good harvest year (Chopak, 1988). The figure rose to 79 percent in the previous drought year. The distribution of cash income from coarse grain sales is equally skewed: over the last three years, *per capita* sales to the GMB from Natural Regions I and II have been seven times greater than those from Natural Regions IV and V (Table 1). Unfortunately, these low-resource areas contain 60 percent of the 5,2 million people living in Zimbabwe's communal areas, as well as 72 percent of the land area. Because of currently low agricultural productivity and limited scope for non-farm employment in these areas[5], cash income sources are frequently inadequate to meet household consumption requirements net of production (especially in drought years), and the Government must mount costly food aid programmes, as it has in four of the past seven years.

Even though *per eapita* coarse grain sales in regions IV and V averaged about 30 kilograms over the past three years, this masks severe chronic grain deficits among many communal areas situated in these regions. Table 2 presents the net grain sales of 244 rural households surveyed in 12 villages in Mutoko and Buhera communal areas over the 1988-89 marketing year.

---

[5]Jackson and Collier (1988) found that, over the 1984-85 marketing year, *per capita* income in rural areas spanning all Natural Regions averaged Z$227; the median *per capita* income was Z$138. The bottom 10 percent had a *per capita* income of Z$33 or less. Mudimu *et al*. (1989) found that *per capita* incomes among a sample of 234 households in Mutoko and Buhera communal areas averaged Z$140 and Z$153 during the 1988-89 marketing year.

## Table 1
## Per capita coarse grain sales to the GMB by Natural Region, 1986-7 to 1988-9

| | ----------Marketing Year---------- | | | % of estimated communal sector: | |
|---|---|---|---|---|---|
| Natural Region | 1986-7 | 1987-8[a] | 1988-9 | Population | Area |
| | ---kilograms per capita--- | | | | |
| I, II | 289 | 85 | 323 | 19,7 | 9,9 |
| III | 161 | 28 | 167 | 20,2 | 18,0 |
| IV, V | 39 | 7 | 36 | 60,1 | 72,1 |

[a] drought year
Source: computed from Food Security database, Department of Agricultural Economics and Extension, University of Zimbabwe.

## Table 2
## Grain marketing profile of survey villages[a]

| Location | Household Net Sales (kgs) | Net Grain Purchases (% of households) |
|---|---|---|
| 1 | 669 | 58 |
| 2 | -325 | 62 |
| 3 | 507 | 45 |
| 4 | -445 | 77 |
| 5 | 72 | 76 |
| 6 | 210 | 70 |
| Buhera C.A.[b] | 114 | 65 |
| 7 | 794 | 36 |
| 8 | 469 | 35 |
| 9 | 645 | 38 |
| 10 | 486 | 55 |
| 11 | -76 | 75 |
| 12 | 70 | 41 |
| Mutoko C.A.[c] | 291 | 38 |

[a] Data is preliminary only; data pertains to the 1988 harvest (1988-89 marketing year) which was above average in terms of rainfall and grain sales. Data also pertains to market transaction only (*i.e.*, grain sales to all sources minus grain/grain meal purchases from all sources; gifts and food aid are excluded).
[b] Average of villages 1 through 6.
[c] Average of villages 7 through 12.
Source: Chigume (forthcoming)

Sixty-five percent of the households surveyed in Buhera had to purchase grain and/or grain meal from the local market to meet their consumption needs. In Mutoko, 38 percent of households were dependent on the market to acquire needed grain, even though average net sales were positive. The distribution of household net sales shows that a small segment of relatively well-endowed farmers accounted for a disproportionately large share of grain sales, while the majority of households sold very little or relied on the market to procure grain for household food security (Chigume, forthcoming). It is therefore not a paradox that rural food insecurity persists despite a 300 percent increase in official grain sales in these communal areas since independence; the situation is due to substantial variation among households' command over productive resources (Mudimu *et al.*, 1989).

Three conclusions may be drawn from these results. First, market sales appear to be concentrated among a narrow segment of well-equipped farmers. Thus, the use of price policy to stimulate smallholder grain production, sales, and cash incomes may have highly concentrated benefits. Second, despite the fact that average net household sales was positive in both areas, a high proportion of these households are net grain deficit. Evidence suggests that these households lack the productive resources to respond to market incentives and increase market sales (Rohrbach, 1989; Govereh, forthcoming). Price policy designed to stimulate production incentives by raising grain prices would make these households worse off, at least in the short run. Third, "surplus" grain deliveries to the GMB (sometimes considered the residual between production and consumption within the communal area) may conceal structural grain deficits of great magnitude within that area.

The 244-household sample in this survey may be considered fairly representative of the population of rural households in Mutoko and Buhera communal areas.[6] Under this assumption, mean household net sales from the sample may be multiplied by the estimated household population in each communal area to obtain a rough estimate of net grain sales of the respective communal area -- prior to trade or distribution across area borders (Table 3, column c). This figure represents the sum total of surplus household grain sales and deficit household grain purchases within the communal area. If these surpluses and deficits were redistributed entirely within the area, Buhera would be grain surplus by about 3 200 tonnes, while Mutoko would be surplus by 2 900 tonnes. However, a substantial portion of sales by surplus households was directly or indirectly sold to the Grain Marketing Board (column d), which typically transports the grain to urban centres or exports it. Thus, once the grain of surplus households has been sold to the GMB, it is usually no longer available to meet the food needs of local deficit households within the district[7]. The grain outflow from these low-resource communal areas tightens the supply-demand situation for grain selling on local markets. The evidence suggests that grain outflows through the official distribution system would have turned both Buhera and Mutoko from largely self-sufficient areas into deficit areas.[8] Column (e) = (c-d) represents the amount of grain (in the form of grain meal and/or informal cross-district inflows) that must flow back into each communal area to achieve current levels of food intake.

---

[6] Household selection within villages was random. Village selection was purposive (see Chopak, 1988, for details on survey design and methodology). Survey villages in Buhera appear to be located in slightly drier areas than the communal area as a whole. Therefore, net grain sales measured in Buhera may be somewhat underestimated.

[7] An exception to this is during years of substantial drought relief aid.

[8] Further research will seek to clarify the exact percentage of GMB depot deliveries transported out of the area, since some of the grain had been reserved for drought relief.

It is clear, therefore, that grain "surpluses" delivered to the GMB are not necessarily an indicator of adequate food availability in low-resource communal areas. In fact, such deliveries may mask considerable grain deficits in these areas. These deficits appear to occur on a continuous basis, in both good and poor rainfall years. Consequently, large backflows of grain or grain meal into these communal areas are required to counteract the grain outflows through the official distribution system (as well as any deficits that may have existed before GMB redistribution). This not only increases the transport costs associated with this circuitous pattern of grain distribution, but also increases the demand for transport capacity, which currently is in short supply in Zimbabwe.

**Table 3**
**GMB grain purchases and communal area grain deficits[a]**

| Communal Area | (a) Mean household net sales (kgs) | (b) Estimated population (households) | (c) Grain Surplus before GMB distribution out of Communal Area (tonnes) (a x b) | (d) Grain deliveries to GMB (tonnes) | (e) Total grain surplus (tonnes) (c - d) |
|---|---|---|---|---|---|
| Buhera | 114 | 27 683 | 3 156 | 24 302 | -21 146 |
| Mutoko | 291 | 9 878 | 2 874 | 7 651 | -4 777 |

[a] These figures pertain to the 1988 harvest (1988-89 marketing year) which was above average in terms of weather and grain sales. Column (a) refers to market transactions only (*i.e.*, grain sales to all sources minus grain/grain meal purchases from all sources; gifts and food aid are excluded).
Source: Computed from Food Security database, Department of Agricultural Economics and Extension, University of Zimbabwe.

## FACTORS CONSTRAINING GRAIN MARKET ACCESS, STABILITY AND GROWTH IN RURAL DEFICIT AREAS

Before independence, the mandate of the Grain Marketing Board (GMB) was largely to buy grain in surplus (primarily commercial) farming areas and distribute the supplies to urban consumption centres and stockfeeders. The large private urban mills played a critical role in the distribution chain, since they converted the maize grain into edible meal[9], which was subsequently sold to private traders who distributed the meal locally.

Since independence, great strides have been made to improve market outlets for surplus grain production in communal areas. However, the structure of the market has changed little in terms of improving access to grain in deficit, low-resource areas. The GMB's relationship to communal areas is still primarily that of buyer only; the

---

[9]Maize meal accounts for about 70 percent of grain caloric intake in Zimbabwe.

vast majority of grain bought by the GMB is sold directly to the large urban mills and stockfeeders (Table 4).

Recently, however, the GMB has permitted individuals to buy small amounts of maize directly at local depots, at a mandated selling price. In 1988, the minimum buying volume was reduced from one tonne to one 91 kilogram bag. Maize meal is also distributed to rural areas under a prescribed pricing structure. During the 1988-89 marketing year, the official maize selling price was Z$22.30 per 91 kilogram bag. This is substantially below the official retail price of roller meal, which in Harare was Z$33.63 in 1988 and Z$42.35 in 1989.[10]

### Table 4.
### Composition of maize purchases from the GMB, 1980-81 to 1985-86

|  | Millers, Stockfeed Manuf'rs | Stock-feeders | Poultry Farmers | Brewers Services | Social | Other | Total GMB Sales |
|---|---|---|---|---|---|---|---|
| | ------------------------------'000 metric tons------------------------------ | | | | | | |
| 1980-81 | 593 | 36 | 22 | 50 | -- | 22 | 723 |
| 1981-82 | 596 | 8 | 13 | 48 | -- | -- | 665 |
| 1982-83 | 841 | 41 | 20 | 59 | 46 | 39 | 1 046 |
| 1983-84 | 828 | 95 | 36 | 55 | 224 | 34 | 1 273 |
| 1984-85 | 649 | 32 | 34 | 45 | 78 | 22 | 860 |
| 1985-86 | 444 | 18 | 19 | 47 | 10 | 22 | 560 |

Source: GMB annual reports.

To what extent have these official prices provided a ceiling for maize prices paid by households in local markets?[11]    Figures 1a and 1b compare these official and informal prices over the 1988-9 marketing year (Figures 1a and b). Prices followed the typical seasonal pattern with lowest prices occurring after harvest and rising during the several months preceding the following harvest. Because Buhera households appear to suffer from greater food insecurity on average (Table 2), it is not surprising that local market prices were significantly higher than in Mutoko. In neither area, however, was the GMB depot selling price able to restrain local market prices from rising considerably above it: during the four months preceding harvest, local prices exceeded the GMB selling price by 25 to 100 percent.

---

[10]Maize meal is normally sold in 5, 10, 20 and 50kg bags. The value is expressed in 91kg bags here to facilitate comparison with maize grain, which is normally exchanged in this unit of volume. At a subsidised transport cost of $0,02/bag/kilometre this would translate into a retail roller meal price of $45,20 and $47,35 per 91 kilogram bag at Mutoko and Buhera in 1989.

[11]We use the term "local markets" loosely, since most grain transactions in rural areas were from one household to another. Markets in the typical sense of public gathering places where numerous buyers and sellers interact appear to be conspicuously absent in Zimbabwe's communal areas.

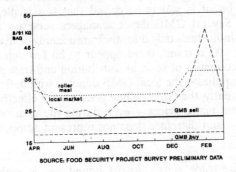

**Fig.1a. Structure of maize prices, Buhera District 1988-89 marketing year. (preliminary data)**

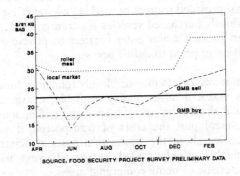

**Fig.1b. Structure of maize prices, Mutoko District 1988-89 marketing year. (preliminary data)**

Several factors account for the disassociation between local maize market prices and the official pan-seasonal selling prices. First, it is both inconvenient and costly for individuals to travel significant distances to buy a bag or two of grain. Traders could provide this function more efficiently by buying in bulk at the depots to resell in deficit rural areas, but it is widely perceived that this is illegal, even though it apparently is not. Several GMB depot managers surveyed reported they were authorised to sell to individuals only if for their own family or livestock consumption; resale is prohibited. As a result, there appear to be few actors in the marketing system to provide economies of scale in distribution and transport to link together a source of known supplies -- the local GMB depot -- with deficit households in the hinterland. Consequently, the GMB selling price cannot effectively restrain upward movementsin informal maize prices -- even during the relatively good production year under analysis -- and therefore does not represent an opportunity cost ceiling to acquire grain.

Second, private maize trade across district boundaries is prohibited. Therefore, private maize deliveries from grain-surplus to grain-deficit communal areas experiencing relatively higher local market prices are discouraged.

Third, even if surplus grain were available and accessible in town centres, its distribution to village areas is impeded by high transport costs, and often by no available transport at all.

Finally, there are a limited number of entrepreneurs possessing the necessary resources and capital to engage in grain trading. A survey of traders in Mutoko and Buhera indicates that almost all of them already operated businesses prior to entry into grain trading that provided sources of working capital (Chigume, forthcoming). Many had also previously purchased vehicles for transport. The high capital costs and lack of transport present major entry barriers to private grain trading, which hamper the distribution of grain to deficit areas.

The upper ceiling on maize prices may be closely related to local retail maize meal prices. As long as maize meal is readily available, consumers would have an incentive to purchase it should the cost of buying and milling maize grain rise above the price of mealie-meal plus the costs of transporting it back to the village. However, little is known about the transaction costs associated with purchasing maize grain and meal in thinly traded, dispersed areas with poor transport infrastructure characteristic of many communal areas.

## IMPLICATIONS FOR GRAIN PRICE, STOCKHOLDING AND TRADE POLICIES

### Promoting Reliable Availability of and Access to Grain in Low-resource Communal Areas

The subsequent discussion indicates that more reliable access to grain for purchase is necessary to enhance food security for a large proportion of households in low-rainfall areas of Zimbabwe. Previous research has stressed the trade-offs between stabilising grain supplies and government budget costs (Pinckney, 1988; Gray, 1986). A thesis of this paper is that selected restructuring of the grain marketing system may simultaneously promote income growth and reliable access to food in rural deficit areas and reduce government budget costs. Such potential reforms, the viability of which are contingent upon further research, may include the following:

1) strengthen the role of the GMB as seller of grain at local depots to facilitate grain access in deficit communal areas;

2) legalise cross-district grain trade;

3) identify and alleviate the constraints under which private traders, cooperative groups, and rural millers operate; and

4) improve local storage.

The essential feature of these policy changes are as follows: rather than transporting grain out of grain-deficit areas to urban centers, only to increase the required flow back into such areas, a certain proportion of grain accumulated in GMB depots in grain-deficit areas would be retained for local redistribution. The amount to be retained locally would depend on the supply demand conditions of the communal area in question, which would vary with the quality of the harvest. Private traders or cooperative buying groups could buy at the depots and resell in outlying areas, thereby increasing grain supplies in rural villages and presumably exerting downward pressure on local prices. The ability of traders to charge high mark-ups on grain would be impeded to the extent that the market were competitive and maize meal were available locally, since its price would put an upward ceiling on the price of maize grain plus milling charges. Policy (1) would entail streamlined and more widely articulated GMB selling procedures (since there appears to be substantial confusion in several rural survey areas about the movement restrictions on grain bought from the GMB, and whether it can be legally resold), facilitation of bulk sales to promote scale economies in exchange and subsequent distribution, and perhaps periodic selling days at the depot to concentrate exchange activities on certain days. A necessary complement to this is policy (3), since the efficient distribution of grain from the depot to outlying areas depends on a viable, competitive private trade and/or cooperative distribution network. Critical public sector investments may be required to induce the necessary private investments in the marketing system that would promote grain availability in deficit rural areas.

To be viable from the point of view of local traders, two critical conditions must hold regarding pricing structure: (1) the GMB selling price + transport charge to location i < local market prices for maize at location i; and (2) the GMB selling price + transport charge to location i + local milling charges < prevailing maize meal price at location area i. Condition (1) is necessary to provide traders with profit incentives to engage in spatial arbitrage. Condition (2) is necessary in order for grain-deficit households to demand maize grain rather than maize meal from the market.

Reference to Figures 1a and b show that these conditions held for significant portions of the 1988-89 marketing year, especially in Buhera. However, it is not clear that such margins would be sufficient to induce substantial private investment in grain distribution. Greater returns to investment in transport may be possible in other sectors (Amin, personal communication), which would mean that substantial increases in the supply of transport might be necessary before much of it would be used for private grain marketing. On the other hand, it should be mentioned that the 1988 harvest in both areas was relatively good, exerting a moderating influence on local maize market prices. A sub-normal harvest would only increase the differential between the mandated GMB selling price and prevailing rural market prices.

Cooperative organisation of grain purchasing from local GMB depots may also be a promising alternative to improve the availability of and access to grain in outlying deficit rural areas. Economies of scale in distribution could be promoted without the threat of monopoly profits often attributed to private trade.

Such changes in the organisation of the maize market would appear to have four major advantages:

(1) Improved grain access and supplies in deficit communal areas; (2) it would shift demand for processing from large urban mills to local rural mills, thus stimulating investment, employment, and farm/non-farm linkages in communal areas; (3) reduced GMB operating costs associated with transport from communal area depots to urban centres, as well as the cost of redistribution of maize meal back to deficit areas, thus generating the potential for cost savings to the consumer; and (4) it would free-up considerable transport capacity to provide other needed services such as fertilizer distribution from Harare manufactures to rural regions, collection of rural grain surpluses for delivery to GMB silos. A significant proportion of commercial transport is tied up in GMB contracts between depots and central silos (Financial Gazette, 8/25/89). Policies that rely more on decentralised storage and delivery of grain from the nearest surplus areas rather than delivery of mealie-meal from distant urban mills would significantly reduce the demands on transport and could therefore provide greater supply for external exports and other needed services.[12]

A further benefit of promoting reliable grain access in low-rainfall areas is the potential for increased income generation from production of higher-value cash crops agronomically suited to such areas. Research in Malawi and Tanzania indicates that smallholder diversification into crops such as cotton and tobacco is impeded by poor access to grain from the market (Lele, 1988). Improved access to grain at tolerable prices may reduce the risks of relying on the market for a portion of staple food requirements, and thus provide incentives to diversify somewhat into higher-value crops, enhancing both farm incomes and national foreign exchange earnings.

---

[12]Rough indicators of the savings in transport costs and capacity can be determined as follows. According to the SADCC Regional Early Warning Unit (1989), only two of the seven provinces in Zimbabwe are estimated as grain surplus during the 1989-90 marketing year, which seems fairly indicative of normal circumstances. On average, about one-half of national marketed grain sales (180 000 tonnes) come from the five provinces which are currently grain deficit (Stanning, 1989). Given that approximately 90 percent of this is transported to urban centres or exported, this would tie up the equivalent of 3 200 hauls in 50-tonne trucks and Z$3,8 million, based on transport charge estimates of Z$.30/tonne/km (Financial Gazette, August 25, 1989) and an average haul of 80 kilometres. This figure is probably higher in actuality since average hauling distance is probably much greater than 80 kilometres. One must then add to this the cost of transporting maize meal back to the deficit areas from urban mills, on a magnitude large enough to substitute for the GMB grain outflow.

Several disadvantages of these changes in the marketing system must also be considered. They may (1) increase GMB overhead costs associated with depot sales, since the agency is minimally involved in this function at present; (2) require greater analytical capacity to set selling prices at various GMB depots[13]; (3) create political difficulties in rationalising spatial price differences -- a major departure from current pan-territorial official price setting. However, it must be pointed out that under existing policies, such pan-prices are not maintained in communal areas.

The potential viability of such market restructuring critically depends on one's view of the efficacy of private markets. Proponents of market liberalisation have too often assumed that the sanctioning of private trade would be sufficient to induce a vibrant, competitive market in which traders immediately fill the void left by state decontrol of the market. This "vacuum theory of privatisation" is not supported by ongoing research findings elsewhere in Africa (Weber et al., 1988; Dione and Staatz, 1988; Goetz et al., 1988). The number of approved buyers in Zimbabwe has actually decreased since 1980 (Stanning, 1989). Unlike consumers in most African countries, who purchase their grain from the local market, most grain purchases in Zimbabwe's communal areas are from a neighbour. In grain-deficit areas however, neighbours' surpluses are insufficient to fulfil deficit households' requirements (by definition of a grain-deficit area), and the need for an organised market with low search costs becomes apparent. Therefore, the marketing changes described above should be accompanied by policies that alleviate major factors constraining entry and operation of private and cooperative buyers as well as rural hammer millers. Research is needed on how such policies should be structured and what critical public sector investments are needed to facilitate private investment in the system, while still allowing the Government to retain its influence over supplies and prices.

On the other side of the philosophical spectrum, proponents of the need for controlled markets may be concerned that traders might reap large windfalls by buying at GMB selling prices and reselling at exorbitant prices on local markets. However, the ability of traders to reap such windfalls comes largely from a lack of competition. This would suggest that the solution is not necessarily to restrict the operation of private traders, but rather to induce a greater number of them to invest in the system to promote competition among them. This also suggests the need for research and policy mechanisms that identify and remove the barriers impeding private trade.

## Implications for Grain Pricing and Stock Policies

It is becoming increasingly evident throughout Sub-Saharan Africa that the image of "urban consumers" and "rural producers" of food grains is an oversimplification. Ongoing research in Zimbabwe and elsewhere has consistently found many farm households (the majority in many cases) to be net consumers of coarse grains (Rohrbach, 1989; Mbwanda and Rohrbach, 1989; Chopak, 1988; Lele, 1988; Dione and Staatz, 1989; Goetz, 1989; Loveridge, 1988). Even with higher prices, these farm households lack the ability to produce a grain surplus because of insufficient labour

---

[13]One suggestion to alleviate this problem would be to develop a price structure by which cost differentials between GMB depots are determined by transport charges from grain surplus centres. This matrix of prices may be scaled up or down depending on size of estimated annual harvest.

or land, poor access to inputs, or inability to afford animal traction or other technologies to increase productivity. The concentration of marketed surplus among large, relatively well-equipped producers suggests that price supports for coarse grains may have highly concentrated benefits, and may exacerbate food insecurity in both urban and rural areas, at least in the short run.

It is also increasingly evident that "national grain surpluses" defined as stocks held by the GMB may be a misleading indicator of potential exportable surplus (Takavarasha, 1988). Ongoing micro-level research indicates that communal area grain deliveries to the GMB cannot be assumed to be the residual of on-farm supplies minus consumption requirements, since large marketed surpluses from a small segment of well-equipped farmers may mask considerable grain deficits among a large proportion of households in an area. A particularly erroneous perception of exportable surplus may emerge under the following scenario. After planting, the Ministry of Agriculture announces considerable producer price increases as an incentive to farmers, and a corresponding increase in official grain selling prices to avoid large GMB operating deficits. National maize deliveries to the GMB increase; most of this come from the more productive natural regions. Yet a portion of these deliveries come from surplus producers in grain deficit communal areas, which is extracted out of these areas and sent to centralised urban storage silos. Reduced local surpluses and the higher official selling price tend to push up local selling prices (the opportunity cost of selling grain in the local market increases). Therefore, consumption declines, especially among low-income households whose demand is more elastic (Mellor, 1978). The build-up of national maize stocks and increased sales gives the appearance of national food self-sufficiency and exportable surpluses when in fact food insecurity in deficit areas may be exacerbated because a large proportion of supplies have been delivered to the GMB and distributed to urban areas, rather than being retained in the communal area to meet the needs of deficit households. Greater inflows of maize meal are then required to make up the deficit. Consumption, on the other hand, is constrained by the fact that official retail maize meal prices plus transport charges usually exceed average local maize market prices (Figures 1a and b). To the extent that households are forced to purchase maize meal rather than maize grain because of limited supply of the latter, the price of staple food increases, reducing food security. Therefore, the existence of massive grain stocks in urban centres is unable to assure food security in grain-deficit rural areas because the distribution system is not adequately geared for grain backflows into such rural areas.

What are the implications for the design of grain trade and stockholding policies? Rather than conceptualise the problem in terms of stabilising national supplies in response to production fluctuations, food security may be more meaningfully enhanced by concomitant attention to the chronic constraints to more reliable access to grain in low-rainfall communal areas, which account for a large bulk of Zimbabwe's population. This may bring into focus issues of location, access to, and internal distribution of grain stocks, not just optimal amounts to be stored nationally to meet transitory production shortfalls. Policies designed to alleviate the chronic root causes of low investment and growth in the food system may simultaneously improve the ability of deficit households to cope with transitory production and income shortfalls.

## AREAS FOR FURTHER RESEARCH

1. What would be the effect of allowing private traders to buy in bulk from rural GMB depots to resell locally. What measures might be taken to ensure that monopoly profits are not earned? Would private traders service remote areas, or are cooperative or government distribution networks required to service these areas?

2. What effect would legalised cross-district trade have on supplies, prices, and access in surplus and deficit communal areas? What is the magnitude of informal cross-district grain flows into grain deficit areas?

3. What factors prevent the development of local "public" markets? How do deficit households identify surplus households with grain to sell? Why do surplus households sell a large proportion of their grain to the GMB, approved buyers, and non-approved buyers instead of their deficit neighbours, since local market prices usually exceed the GMB buying price?

4. What effect would more reliable market access to grain have on smallholder incentives to diversify somewhat into higher-value cash crops, thus enhancing farm income and national foreign exchange earnings?

5. What strategic public sector investments in the marketing system are necessary to promote reliable market access to food in deficit communal areas, in order to convert the potential of national supply stabilisation schemes into the reality of consumption stability nationwide?

6. Identification of strategic changes in market organisation -- including stock, pricing, and trade management -- to promote food production growth and access over the long run.

## REFERENCES

Chigume, S. Forthcoming. *Unpublished M.Phil Thesis.* Department of Agricultural Economics and Extension. University of Zimbabwe. Harare.

Chigume, S. and J. Shaffer. 1989. Farmer Marketing Strategies to Improve Food Security. In G. Mudimu and R. Bernsten (eds) *Household and National Food Security in Southern Africa.* Proceedings of the Fourth Annual Conference on Food Security Research in Southern Africa, October 31-November 3 1988. University of Zimbabwe/Michigan State University Food Security Research Project. Department of Agricultural Economics and Extension. Harare.

Chopak, C. 1989. Family Income Sources and Food Security. In: G. Mudimu and R. Bernsten (eds) *Household and National Food Security in Southern Africa.* Proceedings of the Fourth Annual Conference on Food Security Research in Southern Africa. October 31-November 3 1988. University of Zimbabwe/Michigan State University Food Security Research Project. Department of Agricultural Economics and Extension. Harare.

Dione, J. and J. Staatz. 1987. *Market Liberalisation and Food Security in Mali.* Staff Working Paper No. 87-73. Department of Agricultural Economics. Michigan State University.

*Financial Gazette.* 1989. AFC Attempt to Reduce Farmers' Transport Costs May Cause a Shortage. August 25. Harare.

Goetz, S. Forthcoming. *Unpublished Ph.D. Dissertation.* Department of Agricultural Economics. Michigan State University.

Govereh, J. Forthcoming. *Unpublished M.Phil Thesis.* Department of Agricultural Economics and Extension. University of Zimbabwe.

Gray, J.G. 1986. *The Role of Public Foodgrain Stocks in National Food Security in Tropical Developing Countries.* Paper presented at Tel Aviv Conference on Stored Product Protection. Food Studies Group. Queen Elizabeth House. Oxford.

Jackson, J. and P. Collier. 1988. *Incomes, Poverty and Food Security in the Communal Lands of Zimbabwe.* Rural and Urban Planning Occasional Paper 11. Department of Rural and Urban Planning. University of Zimbabwe.

Loveridge, S., S. Rwamasirabo and M. Weber. 1989. Selected research Findings from Rwanda that Inform Policy Themes in Southern Africa. In G. Mudimu and R. Bernsten (eds) *Household and National Food Security in Southern Africa.* Proceedings of the Fourth Annual Conference on Food Security Research in Southern Africa. October 31-November 3. 1988. University of Zimbabwe/Michigan State University Food Security Research Project, Department of Agricultural Economics and Extension. Harare.

Masters, W. Forthcoming. *Economic Efficiency and Comparative Advantage in Zimbabwean Agriculture.* Ph.D. dissertation. Food Research Institute. Stanford University. Stanford. California.

Mbwanda, C. and D. Rohrbach. 1989. Small Grain Markets in Zimbabwe: The Food Security Implications of National Market Policy. In G. Mudimu and R. Bernsten (eds) *Household and National Food Security in Southern Africa.* Proceedings of the Fourth Annual Conference on Food Security Research in Southern Africa. October 31-November 3, 1988. University of Zimbabwe/Michigan State University Food Security Research Project. Department of Agricultural Economics and Extension. Harare.

Mellor, J. 1978. Food Price Policy and Income Distribution in Low-Income Countries. *Economic Development and Cultural Change.* Vol. 27. No. 1. : 1-26.

Moyo, S., N. Moyo and R. Lowenson. 1985. *Drought Food Shortages and Women's Groups as a Development Strategy in Zimbabwe.* Paper presented to the Churches drought action for Africa Workshop, Arusha. Tanzania. 10-14 July.

Mudimu, G., C. Chopak, S. Chigume, J. Govereh, and R. Bernsten. 1989. In M. Rukuni, T. Jayne and G. Mudimu (eds) Forthcoming. *Household and National Food Security in Southern Africa.* Proceedings of the Fifth Annual Conference on Food Security Research in Southern Africa, October 16-18, 1989. University of Zimbabwe/Michigan State University Food Security Research Project. Department of Agricultural Economics and Extension. Harare.

Muir, K. and T. Takavarasha. 1989. Pan-Territorial and Pan-Seasonal Pricing for Maize in Zimbabwe. In G. Mudimu and R. Bernsten (eds) *Household and National Food Security in Southern Africa.* Proceedings of the Fourth Annual Conference on Food Security Research in Southern Africa. October 31-November 3, 1988. University of Zimbabwe/Michigan State University Food Security Research Project. Department of Agricultural Economics and Extension. Harare.

Pinckney, T.C. 1988. Storage, Trade, and Price Policy under Production Instability: Maize in Kenya. *International Food Policy Research Institute Research Report 71.* Washington, D.C.

Rohrbach, D. 1989. *The Economics of Smallholder Maize Production in Zimbabwe: Implications for Food Security.* Michigan State University International Development Paper 11. Department of Agricultural Economics. East Lansing. Michigan.

SADCC Regional Early Warning Unit for Food Security. 1989. *SADCC Food Security Bulletin.* May.

Stanning, J. 1989. Smallholder Maize Production and Sales in Zimbabwe. *Food Policy.* August 1989. : 260-67.

Stanning, J. Department of Agricultural Economics and Extension. University of Zimbabwe. *Personal communication,* 1989.

Takavarasha, T. 1988. Grain Trade, Barter, and Triangular Trade: Proposed Research and Policy Issues with Specific Reference to Zimbabwe's Experience. In: M. Rukuni and R. Bernsten, (eds) *Southern Africa: Food Security Policy Options.* Proceedings of the Third Annual Conference on Food Security Research in Southern Africa. November 1-5, 1987. University of Zimbabwe/ Michigan State University Food Security Research Project. Department of Agricultural Economics and Extension. Harare.

UNICEF. 1984. *Situation Analysis of Women and Children in Zimbabwe.* UNICEF and Government of Zimbabwe.

Weber, M., J. Staatz, J. Holtzman, E. Crawford, and R. Bernsten. 1988. Informing Food Security Decisions in Africa: Empirical Analysis and Policy Dialogue. *American Journal of Agricultural Economics.* Vol. 70. No. 5.

Wright, N. and T. Takavarasha. 1989. *The Evolution of Agricultural Pricing Policies in Zimbabwe.* Working Paper AEE 4/89, Department of Agricultural Economics and Extension. Faculty of Agriculture. University of Zimbabwe.

# 12

# The Impact Of The Economic Rehabilitation Programme On The Grain Markets In Maputo

*Firmino G. Mucavele*[1]

## INTRODUCTION

The Government of Mozambique introduced the Economic Rehabilitation Programme (ERP) in 1986 attempting to rehabilitate the national Economy. The economic and social structure suffered changes which are important to follow and analyse. After two years of the ERP, it is important to measure its impact on food security in Mozambique. Grain crops constitute the basis of staple foods for the majority of people in Mozambique. Food security is directly related to the grain supply. It is therefore of primary importance to study the impact of the ERP on grain production and markets. This study covers Maputo only.

### Objectives of the Study

The general objective of this study is to measure the impact of the ERP on the grain production, markets and households' grain consumption. It is also intended to study grain food accessibility for the households in Maputo. It is expected that the study will continue during Autumn 1989 and through 1990, to assess the impact of the ERP as well as the economic structural changes on food security in Mozambique.

This study is a part of the general research on patterns of efficiency of the smallholder farmers in Mozambique.

### Data and Methods

The sample of households was selected randomly among those living in Albasine, Hulene and Sabie. The sample comprises 30 households from Albazine, 30 households from Hulene, and 10 households from Sabie.

The major staple food grains considered in the study are maize, rice, sorghum, millet, groundnut and cowpea. Minor grain crops were not considered in the study.

---

[1]Assistant Professor, Head of Agricultural Economics Department (in formation) at the Faculty of Agronomy and Forestry Engineering, Eduardo Mondlane University, Maputo, Mozambique.

# THE IMPACT OF
# THE ECONOMIC REHABILITATION PROGRAMME (ERP)
# ON GRAIN MARKETS IN MAPUTO

The survey showed that in Maputo there was an increase of 13,3 percent of the population growing grain crops. Table 1 shows the number of farmers in the sample who grew grain crop from 1984-85 to 1988-89.

**Table 1**
**Number of farmers growing grain crops**

| Years | Albazine | Hulene | Total |
|---|---|---|---|
| 1984-85 | 26 | 24 | 50 |
| 1985-86 | 26 | 28 | 54 |
| 1986-87 | 28 | 28 | 56 |
| 1987-88 | 29 | 30 | 59 |
| 1988-89 | 30 | 30 | 60 |

Source: Mucavele (1989).

The major increase of the farmers growing grain crops was between 1986 and 1989, the period when ERP was introduced. These years followed the years of chronic food insecurity all over the country. Food grains were not available in the markets. Many farmers migrated from the rural areas to the capital city. The prices of staple foods increased from 1980 to 1984. The access to food decreased in many families. As a way to minimise the shortages of food, families that were not involved in crop production started to look for land to farm. On the other hand, families that were growing vegetables only, started to grow grain crops.

Table 2 shows that farmers were diversifying into other crops from 1984-85 to 1988-89. Groundnut enterprises increased from 11 to 55. Cowpea enterprises increased from 15 to 58. Maize did not vary so much, increasing from 43 enterprises to 56 enterprises. Maize, cowpea and groundnut are the major grain crops for the farmers in the sample. Sorghum and millet are the minor crops for the sample. The study shows that the households are retaining more quantities of grain crops than before ERP.

Table 3 presents the estimated grain crops retention for family consumption. Grain retention may be viewed as a way that families secure their consumption requirements. A family is likely to sell the grain they produce only if they are sure that they will have an opportunity to buy in the market. Therefore, the retention may indicate the scarcity of grain foods in the market. It is also possible to hypothesise an increase in grain crop production. However this hypothesis has yet to be confirmed. This hypothesis can be substantiated by evidence of grain shortages in the market and by the increase of robberies on the farms. This phenomenon does not occur in Ligongolo which is 90 kilometres from Maputo.

## Table 2
### Number of farmers in sample growing various crops

| Crop | 1984-85 | 1985-86 | 1986-87 | 1987-88 | 1988-89 |
|------|---------|---------|---------|---------|---------|
| Maize | 43 | 45 | 43 | 53 | 56 |
| Rice | 1 | 0 | 4 | 9 | 11 |
| Sorghum | 0 | 0 | 0 | 1 | 8 |
| Millet | 0 | 0 | 0 | 0 | 0 |
| Groundnut | 11 | 19 | 31 | 44 | 55 |
| Beans | 3 | 15 | 7 | 17 | 8 |
| Cowpea | 15 | 7 | 10 | 42 | 58 |
| Others | 3 | 1 | 7 | 2 | 6 |

Source: Mucavele, (1989).

## Table 3
### Estimated grain crop retention for family consumption
### (Kilograms)

| Crop | 1984-85 | 1985-86 | 1986-87 | 1987-88 | 1988-89 |
|------|---------|---------|---------|---------|---------|
| Maize | 7 200 | 7 920 | 8 280 | 10 860 | 12 950 |
| Rice | 3 600 | 3 600 | 2 640 | 1 200 | 730 |
| Sorghum | 720 | 720 | 160 | 0 | 0 |
| Millet | 0 | 0 | 0 | 0 | 0 |
| Groundnut | 7 200 | 5 760 | 5 040 | 8 720 | 10 720 |
| Beans | 7 200 | 1 440 | 1 630 | 1 510 | 1 800 |
| Cowpea | 2 880 | 2 160 | 2 950 | 3 800 | 4 830 |
| Others | 1 440 | 1 080 | 780 | 0 | 0 |
| Total | 30 240 | 22 680 | 21 480 | 26 090 | 31 030 |

Source: Mucavele, (1989).

The rules governing the exchange of grain foods have changed. For instance in 1984, one could exchange one kilogram of groundnut seed for two kilograms of cowpeas. Currently in Albazine one kilogram of groundnut seed is exchanged for four kilograms of cowpeas. Products which were not sold in 1984, such as sugar-cane, are now sold. The relative price among grain crops changed between 1985 and 1989. In 1985, in the parallel market in Hulene, one kilogram of maize cost 150,00 Mozambique Meticais and one kilogram of groundnuts cost 250,00 Mozambique Meticais. Currently, a kilogram of maize in the same market costs 500,00 Mozambique Meticais and a kilogram of groundnuts costs 2000,00 Mozambique Meticais. Therefore, the 1985 maize/groundnut ratio was 0,6 and currently it is 0,25. This means that the crop mix would change if farmers reacted to price changes. On the other hand, the consumers would shift from groundnuts to a possible substitute. Yet, this behaviour is not yet clear. More global commodity studies should be done. Even though, it can be accepted that there is a relative increase of production costs and returns. The relative prices among grain crops changed. Consequently, a change in consumption and in crop mixes is likely.

The survey indicates that food accessibility to households in Maputo decreased. Table 4 shows the average annual nominal income of families in Albazine and Hulene.

**Table 4**
**Average annual nominal family income**
(Mozambique Meticais)

| Year | Albazine | Hulene |
|------|----------|--------|
| 1980 | 42 800 | 60 000 |
| 1985 | 85 000 | 86 000 |
| 1989 | 360 000 | 394 000 |

Source: Mucavele, (1989).

Assuming that a family uses all their income to buy maize, this means that a farmer living in Albazine could have bought 556,6 kilograms of maize during the year 1985. Another family living in Hulene could have bought 400 kilograms of maize in the same year. The same families in 1989 could buy 720 kilograms of maize in Albazine or 788 kilograms of maize in Hulene. These quantities are higher than what was possible to buy in 1985.

Assuming that a family in Albazine used all their income to buy groundnuts in 1985, the family would have bought 340 kilograms of groundnuts. and a family living in Hulene 344 kilograms. For 1989 the family in Albazine can buy 180 kilograms of groundnuts and in Hulene 197 kilograms. These quantities are less than what was possible to buy in 1985.

Informal interviews pointed out that accessibility to grain food is decreasing. These studies should be continued in order to generate a clearer picture of the impact of ERP on grain food accessibility.

## POSSIBLE NATIONAL POLICY OPTIONS AND MEASURES TO REDUCE FOOD INSECURITY

Grain crops constitute the basis of staple foods for the majority of the people in Mozambique. Food security is directly related to grain supply. Solutions for chronic food insecurity in Mozambique fall into three categories:

o    income;

o    domestic production or grain importation; and

o    market reforms.

In Mozambique, where 80 percent of the population is in agriculture and 90 percent of those are smallholder farmers, policies must reallocate resources to the smallholders. In other words, the policies must shift resources from capital-intensive activities to labour-intensive activities. Along with the resource reallocation, the improvement of conditions should be speeded up for the worst affected groups, such as displaced people and refugees. The increase of grain food supply is possible if the policies are better designed to address the needs of smallholders who produce many non-traded grain foods. The price of non-traded grain foods are determined by the amounts produced domestically and by the effective demand. The supply of traded foods can be increased only by deliberate measures to increase imports or to restrict exports. Increasing the supply of traded foods will tend, in the long run, to lower its domestic price and decrease domestic production.

Changes in price will depend whether farmers are net buyers or net sellers of food. For net buyers, a fall in price will permit them to buy more of the food. For net sellers of food, a fall in the food price will mean a fall in their real incomes. Since many small-scale farmers in Mozambique are low-income farmers, they will suffer greater food insecurity. The poor people are mainly subsistence farmers who are neither net buyers nor net sellers. They do not benefit from an increase in the supply of traded food.

Price subsidies of food to consumers seem not to be the proper type of incentive at this moment in the rehabilitation programme. It looks as though the transfer of income in cash and in kind would be a more efficient way to increase the families' real incomes. The problem with this type of policy is high transaction costs.

Currently, one of the tasks is to assist the most vulnerable groups directly. These groups must be given agricultural tools to begin farming while, at the same time, providing them with some food to maintain adequate nutrition.

## CONCLUSIONS AND RECOMMENDATIONS

The major conclusions of the study are:

o   In Albazine and Hulene, the number of grain producers increased between 1985 and 1989;

o   Households are retaining more quantities of grains to meet the family consumption requirements and they tend to sell more of the surpluses than before ERP;

o   There are more robberies among the smallholder farm communities than before ERP;

o   The market institutions are changing. The input/product market is expanding but it cannot be determined whether there is a rise in grain production as yet;

o   The results suggest that the food accessibility has been decreasing for the households in Maputo. Currently, it is not clear if the households have enough resources to obtain food. However, informal interviews suggest that there has been a deterioration in food accessibility. More empirical work is necessary to further explore this issue.

# REFERENCES

Mucavele, F.G. 1989. *Inquerito Sobre o Sector Familiar.* Universidade Eduardo Mondlane. Faculdade de Agronomia. Maputo. Mozambique.

# 13

# Policy Dialogue, Market Reform And Food Security In Mali And The Sahel

*Josue Dione*[1]

## INTRODUCTION

The food crisis has been particularly severe in the semi-arid Sahelian countries of West Africa, a region encompassing nine countries and some 38 million people.[2] To combat the crisis, donors have poured an unprecedented US$15 billion of aid into the region over the past 13 years (1975-88) (de Lattre, 1988).

Many analysts have concluded that, besides the lingering effects of the prolonged drought of the early 1970s, poorly designed pricing and marketing policies have distorted agricultural incentives and failed to address the major causes of the food production gap in the Sahel. In the late 1970s, many donors pressed for policy reforms to restore farmers' and private traders' incentives to invest, in order to increase the production and improve the distribution of food. For example, under strong pressure from donors, the Government of Mali agreed in March 1981 to carry out a policy reform aimed at increasing official producer and consumer prices, liberalising grain trade and improving the efficiency of OPAM, the state grain board. Moreover, the scope of the policy debate has been broadened since 1986 to include concerns about food-grain trade liberalisation in the Sahel or the entire region of West Africa (Club du Sahel, 1987).

This paper analyses the impact of the process of market liberalisation on food security in Mali in particular and the Sahel in general. Based on the central thesis

---

[1]Visiting assistant professor, Department of Agricultural Economics, Michigan State University, and former Director of the CESA/MSU/USAID Food Security Research Project in Mali.

This paper is a revised version of an invited paper presented at the 9th World Congress of the International Economic Association, Athens, Greece, August 28 - September 1, 1989. It draws on research conducted under the Food Security in Africa Cooperative Agreement DAN-1190-A-00-4092-00 between the U.S. Agency for International Development (USAID) and Michigan State University (MSU) and under the CESA/MSU/USAID bilateral Food Security Project in Mali. The author gratefully acknowledges contributions and support from colleagues and staff of these institutions, as well as the helpful comments of Carl K. Eicher, John M. Staatz and Michael T. Weber on an earlier draft of this paper. The final content of the paper is, of course, the sole responsibility of the author and does not reflect official positions of either CESA or USAID.

[2]The Sahelian countries include Burkina Faso, Cape Verde, the Gambia, Guinea-Bissau, Mali, Mauritania, Niger, Senegal, and Chad.

hat output market liberalisation is a necessary but not a sufficient condition to mproving food security in the Sahel, the paper focusses on the interactive effects of echnology, institutions and policy reforms on food availability and access to food.

The remainder of the paper is divided in five sections. The first section highlights he food security problems in the Sahel in general. The second section presents an overview of the evolution of food and agricultural policy in Mali from 1928 to date. The third section discusses the objectives, implementation and achievements of the cereal market liberalisation process in Mali, and some of the major issues for the 1990s. The fourth section examines some of the major issues of regional cereal rade liberalisation. The last section draws some policy implications for food security n the Sahel.

## FOOD SECURITY PROBLEMS IN THE SAHEL

The attention of the entire world was captivated by news of hundreds of thousands people dying from hunger and suffering from starvation during the prolonged drought of the early 1970s in the Sahel, which was stricken again by a severe drought in the early 1980s. The international donor community responded generously, yet the food production gap continued to widen. The bulk of donors' aid was not directed at improving domestic productivity in the major food crops, for which *per capita* production declined.[3]

Following the disappointing performance of crop-production projects and integrated rural development projects of the 1960s and 1970s, donors' attention has shifted in the 1980s to policy reforms in the general framework of structural adjustment lending programmes throughout Sub-Saharan Africa. Pricing and marketing policies, which traditionally subsidised consumers by depressing producer prices and accumulating budget deficits of the state grain boards, were perceived as major impediments to food security. Output price and market liberalisation have therefore been selected as means to restore farmers' and traders' incentives to invest and increase the production and improve the distribution of the basic food staples, particularly cereals.

Food insecurity in the Sahel, however, stems from a complex set of problems which cannot be solved by price and marketing reforms alone (Eicher, 1982; Eicher, 1988). There are five fundamental causes of food insecurity in the Sahel.

First, the overarching cause of food insecurity in the Sahel is poverty (Sen, 1981). With *per capita* GNPs ranging between US$160 and US$260, five Sahelian countries were among the 16 poorest nations in the world in 1987. All Sahelian countries were among the world's 43 poorest countries (World Bank, 1989). Between 1965 and 1986, the average annual growth rate of *per capita* GNP was positive but less than 1,5 percent in four of the nine countries and negative in the other five

---

[3]For instance, de Lattre (1988) reports that of the total aid received by the Sahel, not much more than 25 percent was allocated to productive investment, and only 4 percent was devoted to improving productivity in rainfed food crops. Delgado and Mellor (1984) estimate that *per capita* production of foodgrain in the Sahel declined annually between 1961-65 and 1976-80 by 2 percent for millet, 1.3 percent for sorghum, 3 percent for maize and 1.4 percent for rice.

countries. Although the bulk of the population still lives in the rural area and is engaged in agriculture, over one-fourth of the Sahelians experience what Sen (1988) calls a "pull failure" in their food entitlement, *i.e.*, inadequate access to food because of the low level of their real incomes. Failures in effective demand affect both the urban poor and food-deficit rural people (non-farmers as well as farmers), thus compounding constraints on the supply-side of the Sahelian food-security equation.

Second, most Sahelian countries lack appropriate agricultural technology that farmers can readily adopt to expand and stabilise the production of rainfed cereals (millet, sorghum and maize), which account for about 80 percent of total foodgrain consumption in the sub-region. As a result of a heavy concentration on export crops (groundnuts and cotton), neither during the colonial period nor over the nearly thirty years of independence have strong national research institutions evolved to improve yields and stabilise the output of rainfed cereals in the Sahel. Today, there are no widespread high-yielding, drought and disease-resistant varieties for rainfed cereals.[4] Growth in aggregate food supply from domestic production will most likely be limited as long as there are no viable technological options to increase and sustain productivity in the major rainfed cereals.

Third, the capacity of farmers in the Sahel to finance investments in agriculture is undermined by various agricultural surplus extraction strategies, including taxation of crop and livestock production and exports, overvaluation of exchange rates, and head taxes that are levied on some categories of the rural population. The composite effect of the tax burden is not offset by subsidised government credit programmes. Hence, the supply response to higher grain prices is low.

Fourth, of course, severe imperfections in labour markets, farm input supply markets, financial markets and foodgrain markets are serious impediments to both improved availability of, and access to, food in the Sahel. Given the interactions among these different markets, their imperfections also have interactive effects on food availability (through production) and accessibility (through real income). Without a comprehensive view of market-related problems, the scope of actions undertaken to improve the efficiency in only one type of market (*e.g.*, cereal markets) will be constrained by prevailing imperfections in the other markets.

Fifth, rapid urbanisation is contributing to a shift in consumption patterns away from domestic production structures, hence to developing an unsustainable food-consumption profile throughout West Africa and the Sahel. Both price and non-price factors stimulate an orientation of urban-consumption preferences towards relatively cheap imports of two "fast-food type" commodities: rice (mainly from Asia) and wheat. With an annual urban population growth rate of about 7 percent, *per capita* consumption of rice and wheat products in the Sahel rose by 29 percent between 1966-70 and 1976-80, while that of coarse grains (millet, sorghum and maize) fell by 12 percent (Delgado and Mellor, 1984). Such a consumption profile is unsustainable because there is little hope in the medium term that domestic supply will respond adequately to the growing demand for rice and wheat. Moreover, the

---

[4]In a few cases, some of the research on export crops has benefited food crops. For instance, since cotton and sorghum are often grown in rotation, the fertilizer residual from cotton is of benefit to sorghum the following year.

Sahelian countries' capacity to earn foreign exchange for grain imports is restricted by their declining competitiveness, particularly in the world oilseed-product markets.[5]

## EVOLUTION OF FOOD AND
## AGRICULTURAL POLICY IN MALI

With an estimated *per capita* GNP of US$210 in 1987, Mali ranked as the twelfth poorest nation in the world (World Bank, 1989). Mali is landlocked in the semi-arid Sahel and Sahara desert in West Africa. About 80 percent of the population live in rural areas, subsisting essentially from rainfed agriculture and livestock production. The entire economy of the country rests on the rural sector, which provides the bulk of employment, food (essentially cereals), and foreign exchange (cotton, livestock and fish). Cereals provide approximately 70 percent of the total caloric consumption of Malians, and coarse grains (millet, sorghum and maize) account for 85 percent of this proportion. Mali appears as the Sahelian country with the best endowment in land suited for both rainfed and irrigated agriculture. In spite of this relative abundance in land, Mali's agriculture has, just as in other Sahelian countries, progressively failed to produce enough food-grain for a population growing at 2,5 percent per year.

The agricultural and food policy options followed by Mali after independence in 1960 were strongly determined by the 1928-1959 colonial policy legacy in French Sudan. The French colonial policy in this country aimed at expanding the production of export crops needed by the French industry (Jones, 1976, : 20-23). Groundnut production was successfully spread mainly because of the similarity of this crop to the local varieties of groundnuts grown for centuries in the region. Success in developing cotton production was much slower, as the first attempt to grow cotton under irrigation failed (Amin, 1965; de Wilde, 1967; Jones, 1976).[6] Cotton production took off in Mali only after 1949, with the interventions of the Compagnie Francaise de Developpement des Textiles (CFDT) in high-potential rainfed areas of the country.

Agricultural research efforts were consequently concentrated on developing improved seeds, fertilizers, pesticides and farming techniques for cash crops. The production of these crops grew particularly from the extension of cultivated land through the spread of animal traction and from the introduction of crop rotations, which included cotton, coarse grains (especially sorghum), and groundnuts. No significant research programme was undertaken to improve food production *per se*. Instead of market incentives, head taxes and village-level quotas of cash-crop delivery

---

[5]There are no heat-tolerant wheat varieties and no improved rainfed rice varieties in the Sahel. Moreover, Berg (1989) shows that in spite of a 50 percent increase in world rice prices in 1988, the cost of rice produced under irrigation in the largest rice-consuming country of the Sahel (Senegal) amounted to 2,3 to 3,6 times the average landed price of broken rice imported from Thailand. While the Sahel's imports of rice and wheat products continue to grow by nearly 8 percent per year, FAO trade data indicate that its exports of groundnut products fell by 67 percent in quantity and 69 percent in value between 1976 and 1986 (Delgado and Mellor, 1984).

[6]The *Office du Niger* project had the objective of irrigating 1,2 million hectares in the central delta of the Niger River in order to create the "bread basket" of French colonial West Africa and to substitute for U.S. sources in supplying raw cotton to the French textile industry.

were established as means to increase market surplus. All important marketing activities were entrusted to French commercial companies holding monopoly rights and to Lebanese traders, leaving only subsidiary assembly roles to domestic merchants.

Guided by an inherited anti-market/anti-merchant bias, misconception of the agricultural incentive system, and a high propensity for state interventionism and monopoly, the leaders of Mali opted at independence for a ·radical socialist development path, which lasted from 1960 to 1968. Central planning was adopted and initiated with French technical assistance, as the best way to achieve economic independence through rapid development of agriculture, industrialisation for agricultural input manufacturing and product processing, the systematic search for oil and mineral resources, and the implementation of mass-oriented social policies in education, health, administration, *etc.* (Amin, 1965; Jones, 1976; Bingen, 1985). A total of 33 state enterprises were created between 1960 and 1968 to undertake or control virtually all the major economic activities, including agricultural input and credit distribution, product processing, domestic marketing, and exports.

Agricultural and food policy was dominated by attempts to develop rice production under irrigation, implementation of crash-production projects in rainfed areas, collectivisation of production, and compulsory marketing through the *Office des Produits Agricoles du Mali* (OPAM), a state grain board created in 1964, with legal monopoly in agricultural product marketing. Yet merchants continued to trade grain clandestinely on the private parallel market. Official consumer and producer prices for all major commodities were fixed by the state with the three conflicting objectives of (1) increasing rural incomes; (2) providing cheap food (cereals) to urban consumers; and (3) extracting a surplus from agriculture to finance state investment in other economic sectors (Dione and Staatz, 1988). In reality, the last two objectives took priority, resulting in depressed official producer prices, the imposition on farmers of delivery quotas of cereals to OPAM, and subsidisation of consumers through urban consumer cooperatives, at the expense of accumulating OPAM deficits.

The philosophy underlying agricultural development and food policy remained essentially unchanged over the first two decades of Mali's independence. But there was a shift in the 1970s, with strong donor support, from commodity-based projects to integrated rural development programmes. By 1981, these programmes were managed by 26 public-sector agencies called *Operations de Developpement Rural* (ODRs), in charge of agricultural extension, input and credit distribution, and output marketing (SATEC, 1982). Except for cotton, basic investment in agricultural research and rural infrastructure remained insignificant.

In summary, aggregate food production in Mali stagnated in the 1960s and 1970s. The relative stagnation of food production resulted in Mali shifting from being a net cereal exporter in the 1950s and early 1960s to becoming a net importer of increasing quantities of food-grain after 1965. This deterioration in the country's food situation and the prolonged Sahelian drought of the late 1960s and early 1970s led to Mali's food crisis.

## THE CEREAL MARKET LIBERALISATION

Official producer prices of cereals were raised after the end of the 1968-74 drought to stimulate domestic production. OPAM was mandated to sell food-grain from both domestic supply and commercial imports at official consumer prices set below the full cost of the cereals. The resulting consumer subsidies translated into increasing OPAM budget deficit, which accumulated to about US$80 million by 1976-77 (Humphreys, 1986 : 7). Donor concerns grew in the 1970s about OPAM's mismanagement and accumulating deficits, and the perception that OPAM's legal monopoly in grain marketing and the official price system acted as major disincentives to domestic cereal production (de Meel, 1978). The resulting donor pressure led to the Cereal Market Restructuring Programme (PRMC by its French acronym), to which the government of Mali agreed in March 1981. A group of 10 major donors entered collectively into a policy dialogue with the government of Mali and pledged multi-year shipments of food aid in exchange for a major overhaul of cereals marketing policy.[7]

### Objectives

Initially designed for the six-year period of 1981-82 to 1986-87, the PRMC aimed explicitly at:

o   raising farmers' income through a gradual increase in official producer prices of cereals;

o   liberalising cereal trade through the elimination of OPAM's official monopoly and increased private trader participation; and

o   improving OPAM's operating efficiency through the restructuring of this marketing parastatal (Dione and Dembele, 1987 : 8-9).

The programme was to be financed by reflow money from sales of PRMC-related food aid.

The PRMC objectives and funding mechanisms proceeded, in the absence of adequate empirical information about the structure and conduct of domestic cereal production and marketing, from the implicit assumptions that:[8]

o   actual prices received by farmers were highly correlated with official producer prices, which significantly affected coarse grain production;

o   farmers constituted an homogenous group of net sellers of cereals, who would benefit from higher foodgrain prices;

---

[7]These donors were the World Food Programme (which acted as secretariat of the programme), Austria, Belgium, Canada, the European Community, France, Great Britain, the Netherlands, the United States, and West Germany

[8]Dione and Staatz (1988), Staatz, Dione and Dembele (1989) and Dione (1989) give more details on the objectives and the implicit assumptions of the cereal market liberalisation programme in Mali.

o    no major constraints other than price disincentives hindered farmers' marginal propensity to invest in cereal production;

o    private traders had the capacity and propensity to invest in response to new opportunities opened up by market liberalisation;

o    Mali would continue to experience cereal deficits, and to thus need food aid to support market liberalisation;

o    OPAM should continue to exist to channel food aid and protect its politically influential clientele from higher grain prices.

Because most of these assumptions were found by research to be inaccurate, several adjustments were made in the cereal market liberalisation programme, which was extended for three additional years in 1987.

### Implementation of the Cereal Market Liberalisation : 1981-89

This section assesses the achievements of the programme with respect to food-grain production, private grain marketing, and the state grain board (OPAM).

#### *Food-grain Production*

One of the major goals of the cereal market liberalisation programme was to raise farmers' incomes and incentives to produce more cereals for the market. Yet food-grain production in Mali has continued to be influenced more by rainfall than any other factor. An empirical study of farmers from 1985 to 1987 reveals that neither "getting prices right" nor producer floor prices are simple solutions to food insecurity problems in Mali (Dione, 1989a). First, severe liquidity problems restricted the ability of the government to sustain producer price supports through buffer-stock operations of the state grain board, as will be discussed later.

Second, research has raised serious concerns about the equity implications of increased cereal prices, even at the farmers' level.[9] Even following the two relatively abundant harvests of 1985 and 1986, up to 43 percent of the farm households of two of the best agricultural zones of Mali (CMDT and OHV) were net grain buyers (Table 1). These results are striking in that Mali is generally perceived as having a fairly egalitarian distribution of land. Only 53 percent of the survey farms were net grain sellers, and 90 percent of the total quantity of net sales came from only 28 percent of the sample farms. These were essentially farm households located in the more humid southern part of the CMDT zone, with good access to improved farming techniques through relatively efficient systems of agricultural research, extension, input supply and credit, and heavily engaged in cotton production.

This clearly illustrates the equity issue of what Timmer *et al.* (1983) have termed "the food-price dilemma". In the short run, higher cereal prices would mainly benefit

---

[9]Because of the lack of data on the clandestine private system which, in most years, handled over 70 percent of the estimated total quantity of coarse grains traded prior to cereal market liberalisation, it is impossible to quantify rigorously the effect of the PRMC on actual producer prices.

fewer than a third of the farm households, while depressing the real income of at least 40 percent of them which are net food-grain buyers. In fact, market demand for grain other than rice in Mali is essentially located in the rural areas (among non-farmers as well as a large number of food-deficit farmers), since millet, sorghum and maize account for less than 45 percent of the total cereal consumption of the 20 percent of Mali's total population living in urban areas (Rogers and Lowdermilk, 1988). Given the generally low supply elasticity for food in the context of poor technology, infrastructure and institutions in developing countries such as Mali, higher producer prices need a long gestation period and substantial complementary investment in research, extension and other supporting services before they induce any significant effect on food-grain availability and the real incomes of the rural poor.[10]

## Table 1
### Farmers' production, market-transactions and net per capita availability of coarse grains by rural development zone, agro-climatic subzone, and level of animal traction equipment, CMDT and OHV, Mali (1985-86 to 1986-87)

| Zones/Subzones and level of Animal traction Equipment | Production | | Percent of Farms | | Net Sales | | Net Grain Available per capita (kg) |
|---|---|---|---|---|---|---|---|
| | kg per Capita | Over 188kg per capita (% Farms) | Net Sellers | Net Buyers | kg per Farm | kg per Capita | |
| South CMDT[a] | 405 | 86 | 75 | 18 | 502 | 44 | 341 |
| North CMDT | 299 | 81 | 59 | 38 | -9 | -1 | 286 |
| South OHV[a] | 149 | 25 | 36 | 59 | -103 | -8 | 151 |
| North OHV | 108 | 27 | 15 | 83 | -510 | -42 | 146 |
| | | | | | | | |
| Total CMDT | 345 | 84 | 67 | 28 | 244 | 19 | 310 |
| Total OHV | 128 | 26 | 25 | 72 | -319 | -25 | 148 |
| | | | | | | | |
| Total South[b] | 314 | 66 | 62 | 31 | 306 | 26 | 273 |
| Total North[b] | 238 | 62 | 44 | 54 | -184 | -14 | 241 |
| | | | | | | | |
| Total Sample Equipped Farms | 322 | 83 | 77 | 19 | 290 | 16 | 290 |
| Semi-equipped | 240 | 63 | 45 | 52 | -11 | -1 | 230 |
| Non-equipped | 186 | 44 | 32 | 62 | -153 | -21 | 201 |
| | | | | | | | |
| Total | 273 | 64 | 53 | 43 | 54 | 4 | 256 |

[a] CMDT is the largest cotton-producing zone; OHV is a zone with a similar agricultural potential but without significant cotton production.
[b] The south of each zone has higher rainfall and better agricultural land than the north.
Source: Dione (1989a, 1989c).

---

[10]Various authors' report estimates of the price elasticity of agricultural supply, which typically range from 0,2 to 0,7 in most developing countries, including Sub-Saharan Africa (Berg (1989) : 13-18).

Third, adequate attention has yet to be paid to interactions between pricing and marketing policies and policies in other areas (especially fiscal policies), which jeopardise farmers' food security in the short run and impede their capacity to invest and sustain capital formation in agriculture. For instance, in one of our 1985-87 survey zones (OHV), 37 percent of the farmer households in 1985-86 and 25 percent of them in 1986-87 sold coarse grains without producing any real surplus beyond home-consumption requirements (Table 2). In this zone, over half of the total grain sales were made at low prices during the first three months following harvest, and 71 percent of the grain sellers reported head tax payment as the most important motive for their sales (Table 3; Figure 1). About 72 percent of the farm households of the same region had to buy back cereals later in the year at higher prices than those at which they sold at harvest, often using very costly coping strategies (*e.g.*, cereal loans to be paid at next harvest, migration, and sale of family labour during the cropping season). Moreover, indirect farmer taxation through official cash-crop price schedules and head taxes compound farmers' weak self-financing capacity. Restricted access to official credit further limits farmers' capacity to maintain their investments.[11]   Thus, about two-thirds of the OHV survey-farmers who had historically invested in animal traction had also disinvested from it to generate cash to face both household food shortages and head tax payments in years of poor harvests (Dione, 1989).

Table 2

**Percentage of farm households selling coarse grains without surplus production,
CMDT and OHV (1985-1987)**

| Zones/Subzones and Level of Equipment | Percentage of Farm Households | | Percentage of Coarse Grain Sellers | |
|---|---|---|---|---|
| | 1985-86 | 1986-87 | 1985-86 | 1986-87 |
| CMDT | 24 | 4 | 36 | 6 |
| OHV | 37 | 25 | 74 | 72 |
| South | 27 | 14 | 41 | 27 |
| North | 33 | 19 | 55 | 29 |
| Equipped | 24 | 7 | 31 | 8 |
| Semi-Equipped | 30 | 18 | 49 | 35 |
| Non-Equipped | 31 | 18 | 67 | 43 |
| Total | 30 | 16 | 48 | 28 |

Source: Dione (1989c).

Fourth, the search for increased foodgrain production and accessibility in Mali has overlooked important synergies among cash crops and food crops. These synergies and differences in the performance of agricultural support institutions may lead to considerable gaps in productivity and growth between regions with similar

---

[11]Estimated rates of implicit farmer taxation through official price schedules in the 1970s range from 24 to 61 percent for cotton and 48 to 65 percent for groundnuts (SATEC (1982)).

agricultural potential. Our 1985-87 survey found that, relative to other zones, higher agricultural growth was achieved in the CMDT cotton-zone through a strategy centred on a vertically coordinated set of activities (research, extension, input and credit distribution, processing and marketing, and investment in road infrastructure) for the long-term growth of cotton production and income. Cotton income not only covered farmers' fixed cash liabilities (taxes and loans), but also gradually supported the development of food production and non-farm activities. The CMDT cotton-farmers also produced on average 2,7 times as much coarse grains *per capita* as those in OHV, a zone with similar agricultural potential (Table 1). After net outflows amounting to 10 percent of their own production, the farm households in the cotton zone still had enough coarse grains to meet their home-consumption needs (at 188 kilograms *per capita* per year) at least a full year beyond the two years of the survey. By contrast the farms in the non-cotton zone could barely meet their family food-grain needs in spite of purchasing the equivalent to 16 percent of their own production.

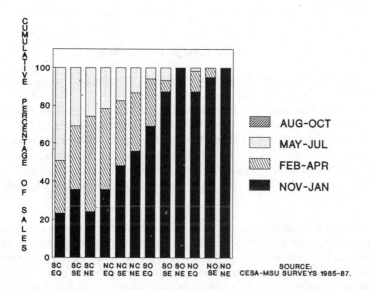

**Figure 1: Quarterly distribution of grain sales
CMDT and OHV (1985-86 to 1986-87)**

To summarise, there is more to improving food security at both the national and the farm-household levels in Mali than just improving grain pricing and marketing. In Professor Sen's terms, the endowment bundles and the *exchange entitlement mappings* are so interdependent in Mali that improving long-term access to food is almost synonymous with improving food and agricultural production. Mali still has to face the central issue of significantly raising the productivity of the agricultural sector. This requires that careful attention be paid to policies in other areas (agricultural **research, extension, financing, taxation,** employment generation, *etc.*), which have significant effects on farmers' opportunities and capacity to invest in agricultural production.  It also requires a comprehensive strategy aimed at real income growth in agriculture through the development of improved policies and institutions, technology adoption and capital formation.

### Table 3
**Percentage of coarse grain sellers by most important sales motive, CMDT and OHV, Mali (1985-86 to 1986-87)**

| Subzones | Food Condiments | Payment of Taxes | Payment of Debts | Equipment | Hired Labour | Social Events |
|---|---|---|---|---|---|---|
| South CMDT | 76,1 | 12,0 | 12,0 | 0,0 | 0,0 | 0,0 |
| North CMDT | 84,3 | 0,0 | 4,1 | 7,4 | 0,0 | 4,1 |
| South OHV | 30,7 | 51,3 | 18,0 | 0,0 | 0,0 | 0,0 |
| North OHV | 3,4 | 91,6 | 5,0 | 0,0 | 0,0 | 0,0 |

Source: Dione (1989a).

### Private Food-grain Marketing

From 1981 to 1986, the following Government measures were introduced to improve the capacity of firms to market cereals: the abolition of the monopoly position of the Government Grain Board (OPAM), the legalisation of the private grain trade, and the removal of restrictions on interregional cereal trade prior to 1981.  In fact, the abolition of OPAM's legal monopoly was more symbolic than real because the share of OPAM's grain marketing exceeded 5 percent of total domestic production and one-third of the estimated total quantities traded in only three of the eleven years prior to the beginning of the reform in 1981 (Dione and Dembele, 1987).

The legal action taken to promote private cereal trade nevertheless opened the door to new traders, who accounted for 39 percent of the 118 coarse grain wholesalers operating in four major cities in 1985.  This led to some increase in specialisation and scale of operations by longtime grain traders (Mehta, 1989).  Hence, most consumers, including food-deficit farmers (who previously had no access to OPAM's subsidised supplies), have benefited from cost-savings resulting from freer circulation of grain and larger-scale operations of grain merchants induced by the cereal market liberalisation (D'Agostino, 1988).

The inability to support producer prices through the buffer-stock operations of the government grain board led the market reform programme in 1987 to launch, with donor support, a seasonal grain-trade credit programme aimed at enabling private traders and farmer organisations to buy more food-grain in the post-harvest period and assume seasonal storage of cereals.  This programme has encountered several problems, including the complexity of loan procedures, the unwillingness of traders to keep large grain stocks as a loan guarantee, poor access to loans for those who lack political influence within the Chamber of Commerce, and poor loan repayment records of the politically influential members of the Chamber of Commerce.[12] In addition, several design problems remained to be solved to allow the credit programme to protect food-deficit rural households through the financing of cereals banks at the level of village associations, while safeguarding incentives for surplus grain-producer participation in the programme (D'Agostino, Staatz and Weber, 1989).

Even a significant improvement of this seasonal credit programme would leave several problems of the food-grain distribution system unsolved, however (Table 4).[13] First, private traders still lack access to bank financing for long-term investment in transportation and storage facilities. Second, very little basic investment has been made to improve road infrastructure and facilitate grain transfer between surplus and deficit areas. Third, the Government continues to show a high propensity to control private traders' operations tightly and food-grain exports even following good harvests. These controls and regulations apply to trader registration, minimum stock-levels, information about suppliers and clients, export authorisation, *etc*. Such restrictive conditions and high business taxes impede flexibility and overt competition in private grain trade.[14] Fourth, a generalised liquidity crisis, which grew worse under a continuous government fiscal crisis, results in an increasing reluctance of private traders -- who usually play also the role of informal bankers -- to extend additional credit in cereals to increasingly insolvent civil servants, whose food security is more and more at stake.

Finally, private grain traders are chronically subjected to unstable expectations caused by several risk factors (Table 4). In the context of the thin and volatile cereal markets in Mali,[15] these factors include:

o    Uncertainty about supply from domestic production which can be halved or doubled from one year to the next because of the vagaries of the weather;

o    Demand uncertainty resulting from the combination of unforseen interventions of the public marketing system (OPAM) and food aid distributors, and the weakness and instability of consumers' real income;

---

[12]Donors contribute funds to the seasonal credit programme, which is administered through commercial banks and the Chamber of Commerce.

[13]See Dione (1989a) and Mehta (1989) for details on the major constraints on the private grain trade.

[14]Since most traders are illiterate and do not hold formal accounts, business taxes are based on "guesstimates" of profits by agents of the Ministry of Finance. These estimated profits are taxed at 50 percent for companies and 30 percent for enterprises not set up as companies (Stryker *et al.* 1987).

[15]The coefficient of variation of both producer and wholesale prices of coarse grains ranged, depending on the region, from 18 percent to 27 percent between November 1985 and October 1987 (Dione, 1989 : 326).

o    Uncertainty about official cereal marketing and trade policies and regulations, which change constantly without prior consultation with, or notification to, private-sector participants; and

o    The absence of appropriate measures to induce the development of forward planning through enforceable contracting mechanisms.

These different kinds of risk contribute to inducing private traders to adopt short-run, small-scale, and diversified trading strategies, which do not allow the whole food production and distribution system to benefit from all potential economies of larger-scale operations.

### Table 4
### Wholesalers' perceptions of major constraints to private coarse grain trade
### (% of sample wholesalers)

| Constraints | Koutiala | Sikasso | Bamako | Mopti | Total |
|---|---|---|---|---|---|
| Limited Financing | 22,2 | 25,0 | 35,0 | 94,7 | 50,0 |
| High Business Taxes | 33,3 | 75,0 | 30,0 | 63,3 | 50,0 |
| Transport Costs/Means[a] | 33,3 | 8,3 | 10,0 | 5,3 | 11,7 |
| Supply Uncertainty | 77,8 | 60,0 | 7,6 | 47,0 | 41,1 |
| Demand Uncertainty | 0,0 | 10,0 | 30,7 | 82,4 | 38,3 |
| Licensing/Administrative Procedures | 0,0 | 0,0 | 15,4 | 0,0 | 5,1 |
| Public Inspection/Fines | 44,4 | 16,6 | 25,0 | 15,9 | 23,3 |
| Traders Reporting Fines | 55,6 | 58,3 | 70,0 | 84,2 | 70,0 |
| Contracting: | | | | | |
| Purchase Contracts | 88,9 | 30,0 | 34,6 | 52,8 | 46,8 |
| Oral contracts only | 50,0 | 100,0 | 77,8 | 44,4 | 62,1 |
| Violation of terms | 62,5 | 33,3 | 22,2 | 20,0 | 31,0 |
| Sales Contracts | 77,9 | 30,0 | 34,6 | 58,8 | 46,7 |
| Oral contracts only | 42,9 | 66,7 | 11,1 | 50,0 | 37,9 |
| Violation of terms | 57,1 | 0,0 | 11,1 | 40,0 | 31,0 |

[a] High transport costs or inadequate availability of trucks. Multiple responses are allowed.
   The percentage of traders by form of contract and the percentage of traders reporting violation of contract terms relate to the number of wholesalers operating contract transactions.
Source: Dione (1989a) : 320, 329.

### OPAM : The State Grain Board

The public sector received 92 percent of total PRMC food aid reflow funds (about US$41 million) used over the first six years of the cereal market reform programme (Table 6). OPAM alone received, in addition to considerable donor technical assistance, 72,5 percent of this share of the public sector. This paradoxical outcome of the food aid programme, which aimed primarily at increasing private-sector participation in foodgrain marketing, illustrates the political difficulty of this type of reform and the overriding concern of donors and the Government of Mali to improve OPAM's financial situation. Access to these funds, along with drastic cuts in personnel (60 percent) and truck fleet (about two-thirds), improvement in stock management, and reduced consumer subsidies, allowed OPAM to narrow its annual operating deficit by 68 percent between 1982 and 1986 (Dione and Staatz, 1988). OPAM's financial improvement was also facilitated by poor harvests, which kept market prices above official producer prices from 1982 through the harvest of 1985, thereby reducing the domestic supply of cereals handled by the public sector. Reflow funds from food aid (which increased by 229 percent, from an annual average of 38 000 tonnes in 1978-81 to 125 000 tonnes in 1982-85) served as an effective means to finance the PRMC activities between 1981-82 and 1984-85 (OSCE, 1988).

The sustainability of both supporting producer prices through direct public sector intervention in the market and financing the reform programme only with food-aid reflow funds was seriously challenged following two successive good harvests in 1985 and 1986. As a result of good rainfall, domestic coarse grain production rose by 44 percent in 1985 relative to 1984. OPAM was then authorised to use PRMC funds and bank credit to support producer prices (which fell in November 1985 to as low as 35 CFAF/kg for maize in major surplus zones) through buffer-stock purchases at the official producer price of 55 CFAF/kg. Notwithstanding record public-sector purchases of nearly 83 000 tonnes of millet, sorghum and maize between December 1985 and February 1986, actual producer prices of coarse grains merely stayed around 50 CFAF/kg until March 1986, then fell to 42-45 CFAF/kg for millet and 31 CFAF/kg for maize in March 1986, as soon as OPAM's funds ran out and it withdrew from the market. Unable to resell more than 43 percent of the total 103 000 tonnes of grain acquired through domestic purchases and food aid, OPAM was caught with most of its working capital tied up in cereal stocks in 1986, mainly because official selling prices were set too high above market prices (*Republique du Mali*, 1987).

The situation grew even worse with a second good harvest in 1986, which exceeded that of the previous year by 4 percent (OSCE, 1988). OPAM's intervention in 1986-87 was limited to purchasing 10 000 tonnes of domestic food-grains to replenish the national security stock, since the parastatal was ineligible for new bank credit because of its incapacity to pay the loans contracted the previous year. Producer prices of coarse grains in major assembly markets fell an average of 25-31 percent in 1986-87 relative to 1985-86, with bottom-levels of 24-25 CFAF/kg for millet and sorghum and 17-18 CFAF/kg for maize over the period of January-March 1987 (Dione and Staatz, 1988, p. 158; Dione, 1989 : 325).

These developments resulted in two major shifts in the policy reform package. First, several donors gradually agreed to replace some of their food aid contribution with cash to be injected in the private grain marketing channels to support producer prices in years of abundant production. Second, by the end of 1987, the Government of Mali abandoned the concept of official producer prices for coarse grains, and restricted OPAM's roles to: (i) managing the national security stock; (ii) managing and distributing food aid; (iii) assuring, in complementarity with the private sector, adequate food supplies in chronically food-deficit areas; (iv) developing and maintaining a market information system; and (v) providing other market facilitating services to private sector participants (Steffen, Dembele and Staatz, 1988 : 4-7).

The combination of a poor harvest in 1987 and a temporary ban on rice imports in early 1988 led prices to rise enough to allow OPAM to sell off most of its commercial stocks and thus improve its financial situation again. In addition, OPAM is clearly moving since 1988 toward a specialisation in producing and providing improved public-good type market services such as information and training fo different market participants. The sustainability of these new developments thus fa initiated and supported mainly by donors' financial and technical assistance is however, a major challenge that the Government of Mali will have to face in th 1990s.

### Table 5
### Allocation of PRMC food-aid reflow funds
### (CFA million, 1981-87)

| Allocation | 1981-82 | 1982-83 | 1983-84 | 1984-85 | 1985-86 | 1986-87 | Tota |
|---|---|---|---|---|---|---|---|
| OPAM deficit coverage | 452,0 | 195,0 | 408,0 | - | - | - | 1 055 |
| OPAM (miscellaneous) | - | - | - | - | 1 161,5 | - | 1 161, |
| Public sector imports | - | - | 425,0 | 1 211,0 | - | - | 1 636, |
| Nat'l security stocks | - | - | 725,0 | - | - | 726,0 | 1 451, |
| Price support through: | | | | | | | |
| - OPAM | - | - | 244,2 | 247,2 | 2 454,0 | - | 2 945, |
| - ON$^a$/OPAM | - | - | - | - | 896,0 | 539,2 | 1 435, |
| - ORS$^b$ & ORM$^c$/OPAM | - | - | - | - | - | 600,0 | 600, |
| Office du Niger | - | - | - | 152,0 | - | - | 152, |
| Price stabilisation through OSRP$^d$ | - | - | - | 397,0 | 550,0 | - | 947, |
| Studies & consulting | - | - | - | - | - | 8,0 | 8 |
| Private trader credit | - | - | - | - | - | 500,0 | 500 |
| Farmer coop. credit | - | - | - | - | - | 500,0 | 500 |
| Total funds used | 452,0 | 195,0 | 1 802,2 | 2 007,8 | 5 061,5 | 2 873,2 | 12 391 |
| Public sector share (%) | 100,0 | 100,0 | 100,0 | 100,0 | 100,0 | 64,9 | 91 |
| OPAM's direct share (%) | 100,0 | 100,0 | 100,0 | 72,6 | 71,4 | 25,3 | 66 |

$^a$ ON = Office du Niger,
$^b$ ORS = Operation Riz Segou,
$^c$ ORM = Operation Riz Mopti
$^d$ OSRP = Office de Stabilisation et de Regulation des Prix
Source: Mali, *Ministere de Tutelle des Societes et Entreprises d'Etat* (1987).

## ISSUES OF REGIONAL GRAIN TRADE LIBERALISATION

The scope of the dialogue for foodgrain market liberalisation has been broadene since 1986 from a national focus to a regional one, encompassing the entire Sah and West Africa. A general consensus seems to emerge about the need to promo free private grain trade among the Sahelian countries and their coastal neighbour though the idea of protecting such a regional cereals market from the rest of th world is still being strongly debated by policy-makers, donors and researchers. It hoped that the removal of national barriers to commercial flows of cereals amor these countries would expand demand beyond clandestine border-exports and redu food-grain price instability within the individual countries. This increase in deman in a more stable market would induce surplus-grain farmers with region comparative advantage to produce more for the global market.

Instability in coarse-grain markets in the Sahel and West Africa is mainly caused, however, by fluctuations in rainfall (therefore domestic production). Our Mali food security research findings show that surplus-grain producers tend to retain a significant proportion of their annual surpluses in household's security stocks to protect themselves against eventual production shortfalls.[16] The low productivity in rainfed cereals does not allow for the organisation of substantial inter-annual buffer stocks; one would therefore expect intra-regional grain trade to reduce only to some extent, but not eliminate, coarse-grain price instability. In addition, the lack of improved technology and institutional support for the production of these cereals will likely prevent the majority of farmers from responding to expanded food-grain demand opportunities in the short run.

A simulation exercise by D'Agostino and Staatz (1989) shows that, under assumptions of fluctuating production and inelastic supply and demand, a reduction of inter-annual grain price instability would hurt or benefit different categories of rural households depending on the level of annual harvests. Following an abundant harvest (1986-87) in our CMDT and OHV survey zones in Mali, a 30 percent reduction in the absolute deviation of grain prices from their mean would increase both the hypothetical net expenses of net cereals buyers (buyers and sellers/buyers) by 9 percent to 20 percent and the hypothetical revenue of net sellers by 13 percent to 29 percent (Table 6). Following a poor harvest (1987-88), the same reduction in coarse-grain price instability would reduce both net buyers' expenses by 6 to 12 percent and net sellers' revenue by 9 to 12 percent.

The results of this exercise clearly show that regional grain trade liberalisation, like national cereals market liberalisation, would not affect different categories of farmers uniformly. The same simulation can be expanded using alternative assumptions. First, one may safely assume that, in a multi-annual perspective, regional trade liberalisation would result in net coarse-grain exports from Mali, a country where relatively low income levels and restriction of cereals exports generally maintain grain prices at levels below those in neighbouring countries. Reduction in price instability caused by regional trade would therefore be accompanied in Mali by an increase in the average price level and the magnitude of the gains and losses discussed above. Second, the total available income that poor food-deficit households may spend as well as the borrowing capacity of these households are severely limited during any year. This would imply that the total expenses of food-deficit rural households on cereals -- rather than their demand for grain -- are inflexible to food-grain prices. For the same level of available annual income, lower prices would allow these households to buy greater quantities of cereals, while higher prices would constrain them to smaller purchases, thereby reducing their access to, and consumption of, food-grain. Third, fully-unrestricted food-grain trade (elastic supply of grain) would likely reduce both the relative gains and losses discussed above, and induce, depending on the degree of substitutability among different types of cereals, some changes in the consumption patterns of net grain buyers. These arguments clearly illustrate the need to carefully examine the distributional effects

---

[16] The estimated family security stocks of coarse grains built over 1985-86 and 1986-87 could meet home consumption needs for a period of 16 months for the sample farm households in the CMDT zone and 13 months for the group of fully-equipped households (Dione, 1989a).

of various policy reform packages on the food security of different segments of the population under different scenarios.

## Table 6
### Effect of reducing inter-annual price variability on average rural households' income.
### CMDT et OHV, Mali (1985-86 to 1987-88)

| Zones and Years | Buy Only[c] | | | Sell Only[d] | | | Buy And Sell[e] | | |
|---|---|---|---|---|---|---|---|---|---|
| | Ex-pense | Hypoth. Expense | Vari-ation | Rev-enue | Hypoth. Revenue | Vari-ation | Net Expense | Hypoth. Net | Vari-ation |
| | (1) | (2) | (2/1) | (1) | (2) | (2/1) | (1) | EXP(2) | (2/1) |
| CMDT [a] | | | | | | | | | |
| 1986-87 | 12 560 | 13 616 | 8% | 18 591 | 20 208 | 9% | 15 409 | 17 515 | 14% |
| 1987-88 | 44 726 | 41 845 | -6% | 29 503 | 27 807 | -6% | 15 198 | 14 374 | -5% |
| OHV [a] | | | | | | | | | |
| 1986-87 | 28 679 | 30 779 | 7% | 9 734 | 12 198 | 25% | 13 849 | 14 711 | 6% |
| 1987-88 | 51 462 | 49 377 | -4% | 11 687 | 10 451 | -11% | 23 369 | 21 498 | -8% |
| CMDT [b] | | | | | | | | | |
| 1986-87 | 12 560 | 14 144 | 13% | 18 591 | 21 017 | 13% | 15 409 | 18 567 | 20% |
| 1987-88 | 44 726 | 40 405 | -10% | 29 503 | 26 959 | -9% | 15 198 | 13 963 | -8% |
| OHV [b] | | | | | | | | | |
| 1986-87 | 28 679 | 31 829 | 11% | 9 734 | 12 566 | 29% | 13 849 | 15 142 | 9% |
| 1987-88 | 51 462 | 48 335 | -6% | 11 687 | 10 301 | -12% | 23 369 | 20 562 | -12% |

Note: Underlying assumptions:
[a] 20 percent reduction in the absolute deviation of prices from the mean.
[b] 30 percent reduction in the absolute deviation of prices from the mean.
[c] Perfectly inelastic demand for coarse grains.
[d] Perfectly inelastic supply of coarse grains.
[e] Perfectly inelastic demand for, and supply of, coarse grains.
Source: D'Agostino et Staatz (1989).

## CONCLUSIONS AND IMPLICATIONS FOR THE SAHEL

Structural adjustment lending programmes started in the 1980s and they are now underway in 32 out of the 45 countries of Sub-Saharan Africa. Mali, a poor and landlocked country in the Sahelian region of West Africa, was chosen by donors as a test case. Donors offered to provide multiyear food aid to help feed Mali's cities in exchange for food-grain pricing and marketing policy reforms. The cereal market liberalistion programme in Mali (PRMC) was launched on the basis of implicit assumptions about both farmers' and traders' capacity and propensity to respond to cereal market incentives. Because most of the initial assumptions were unsustainable, numerous changes have been made in the programme. As a result, some progress has been made since 1981: private grain trade has been legalised; cereals circulate more freely from suppliers to consumers; the roles of the public sector have been more appropriately redefined to some extent; and market facilitating services such as financing and information are improving.

Nevertheless, improved food-grain pricing and marketing, however important, address only one of the five fundamental causes of food insecurity in Mali and the Sahel. The Government of Mali and donors still have to address several additional crucial issues. On the production side, the weakness of the national agricultural research system results in the lack of appropriate agricultural technology that farmers can adopt to increase and stabilise productivity in food-grains. Farmers' capacity to respond to new market opportunities is severely undermined by heavy and rigid taxation and restricted access to more income-generating activities (such as cash-crop production), improved technologies, credit, input supplies, and efficient supporting institutions. These deficiencies critically hamper growth in food and agricultural production by impeding sustained capital formation through the adoption of more productive technologies in the rural area.

On the demand side, considerable instability in the cereal markets remains an unresolved issue for farmers, traders, as well as their clients. The rice production-consumption gap is also a major issue to address, since the demand for rice will continue to grow with urban population, while domestic production of rice under irrigation continues to be unable to compete with imported rice and no major prospect for expanding foreign exchange earnings is in immediate sight. Above all, the entire food-grain production-distribution system must cope with a persisting weakness of effective demand, which is characteristic of the general poverty and liquidity crisis of Malian consumers. The effects on food security of the cereal market liberalisation will remain modest as long as adequate attention is not also paid to these other major issues.

Notwithstanding some country-specificities, three major lessons emerge from Mali's experience with market liberalisation for the Sahel. First, because structural adjustment programmes involve tough political and institutional issues, and given the poor climatic, institutional and technological context of the Sahel, food security policy reform in Sahelian countries must be perceived as a medium- to long-term battle. It is clearly not a short-term undertaking as it was perceived by donors when the cereal market liberalisation programme was launched in 1981 in Mali. Second, the complexity of the food insecurity problems in the Sahel calls for a comprehensive approach to improving rural incomes across the board. Third, since severe resource limitations prevent Sahelian countries from simultaneously tackling all the major causes of their food insecurity, the prioritisation and the sequencing of the reforms become crucial. Focussing on the root cause of food insecurity, poverty should guide Sahelian governments' and donors' choice of actions. Since the bulk of the population of Mali and the Sahel are farmers, national food security policies must first deal with both sides of the food security equation -- increasing food availability and access to food -- at the household level. Such national policies would require substantial and long-term commitment to invest primarily to increase the productivity of food staples, recapture domestic markets through improved competitiveness, and generate new employment and income streams for the rural as well as the urban poor. In this sense, food security in the Sahel also involves improving cash-crop production and non-farm activities along with food crop production.

# REFERENCES

Amin, Samir. 1965. *Trois Experiences Africaines de Developpement:  Le Mali, la Guinee et le Ghana.* Presses Universitaires de France. Paris.

Berg, Elliot. 1989. The Competitiveness of Sahelian Agriculture. In:  Club du Sahel (ed). *Regional Cereals Markets in West Africa.* OECD. Paris. : 17-76.

Bingen, R. James. 1985. *Food Production and Rural Development: Lessons from Mali's Operation Riz-Segou.* Westview Press. Boulder. Colorado.

D'Agostino, Victoire C. 1988. *Coarse Grain Production and Transactions in Mali:  Farm Household Strategies and Government Policy.* Unpublished M.S. Thesis. Michigan State University. East Lansing.

D'Agostino, Victoire C., John M. Staatz and Michael T. Weber. 1989. *Notes on the Implications of Farm-Level Transactions Data for the PRMC Credit Programme.* Information Note No. 89-03, CESA/MSU/USAID Food Security Project.

D'Agostino, Victoire C. and John M. Staatz. 1989. *The Impact of Import and Export Policies on Malian Coarse Grain Producers.* Paper presented at the USAID Workshop on Food Security and Economic Growth in the Sahel. Washington, D.C. 6-8 September 1989.

De Lattre, Anne. 1988. What Future for the Sahel? *The OECD Observer* 153 : 19-21.

Delgado, C. and C. Mellor. 1984. Changing Food Patterns in West Africa: Implications for Policy Research. In: IFPRI (ed). *Compte-Rendu du Premier Atelier Interne du Project Conjoint sur la Substitution des Cereales Importees pour les Cereales Traditionnelles en Afrique de l'Ouest.* IFPRI. Washington D.C. 1-20.

De Meel, H. 1978. *La Politique Cerealiere au Mali.* FAO. Rome.

De Wilde, John C. 1967. *Experiences with Agricultural Development in Tropical Africa.* The Johns Hopkins University Press. Baltimore.

Dione, Josue. 1989a. *Informing Food Security Policy in Mali:  Interactions between Technology, Institutions and Market Reforms.* Unpublished Ph.D. Dissertation. Michigan State University. East Lansing.

Dione, Josue. 1989b. *Food Security Policy Reform in Mali and the Sahel.* Invited paper at the IXth World Congress of the International Economic Association. Athens. Greece. 28 August - 1 September 1989.

Dione, Josue.  1989c. *Comportement Commercial des Agriculteurs et Commerce Regional des Cereale. en Afrique de l'Ouest.* Invited paper prepared for the Regional Seminar sponsored by CILSS/Club du Sahel on Regional Cereals Markets in West Africa: Current Dynamics and Future Stakes. Lome. Togo. 6-10 November 1989. MSU Agricultural Economics Staff Paper No. 89-92.

Dione, Josue, and N. Nango Dembele. 1987. *Le Programme de Restructuration du Marche Cerealier au Mali (PRMC):  Une Analyse de ses Objectifs, son Fonctionnement et ses Performances,* Document de Travail No. 87-01. Project Securite Alimentaire MSU-CESA. Bamako.

Dione, Josue; and John M. Staatz. 1988. Market Liberalisation and Food Security in Mali. In:  M. Rukuni and Richard H. Bernsten (eds). *Southern Africa: Food Security Policy Options.* Proceedings of the Third Annual Conference on Food Security Research in Southern Africa. 1-5 November 1987. UZ/MSU Food Security Research Project. Department of Agricultural Economics and Extension. Harare. : 143-170.

Eicher, Carl K. 1982. Facing Up to Africa's Food Crisis. *Foreign Affairs.* 61 (1) : 154-174.

Eicher, Carl K. 1988. *Food Security Battles in Sub-Saharan Africa.* Revised version of a plenary address presented at the VII World Congress for Rural Sociology. June 26-July 2 1988. Bologna. Italy.

FAO, 1973-87. *FAO Trade Yearbook. Vols. 27-41* FAO. Rome.

Humphreys, Charles P. 1986. *Cereals Policy Reform in Mali.* Draft report. World Bank. Washington D.C.

Jones, William I. 1976. *Planning and Economic Policy: Socialist Mali and her Neighbors.* Three Continents Press. Washington D.C.

Mehta, Mona. 1989. *An Analysis of the Structure of the Wholesale Cereals Market in Mali.* Unpublished M.S. Thesis. Department of Agricultural Economics. Michigan State University. East Lansing.

Office Statistique des Communautes Europeennes (OSCE). 1988. *Statistiques de Base: Agriculture - Elevage.* OSCE. Bamako.

Republique du Mali. 1987. *Evolution de la Politique Cerealiere.* Paper prepared for the Seminaire National sur la Politique Cerealiere au Mali. 15-18 June 1987: Ministere de Tutelle des Societes et Entreprises d'Etat. Bamako.

Rogers, Beatrice L. and Melanee L. Lowdermilk. 1988. *Food Prices and Food Consumption in Urban Mali.* Final report of the Tufts/DNSI/USAID Food Price Project. School of Nutrition. Tufts University. Medford. Massachusetts.

SATEC, 1982. *Etude des Operations de Developpement Rural (ODR) et des Organismes Similaires: Premiere Phase - Analyse et Bilan.* SATEC. Paris.

Sen, Amartya. 1981. *Poverty and Famines: An Essay on Entitlement and Deprivation.* Clarendon Press. Oxford.

Sen, Amartya. 1988. Food Entitlement and Economic Chains. In: Brian W. J. LeMay (ed). *Science, Ethics, and Food.* Papers and Proceedings of a Colloquium Organized by the Smithsonian Institution. Smithsonian Institution Press. Washington D.C.: 58-70.

Staatz, John M., Josue Dione and N. Nango Dembele. 1989. Cereals Market Liberalization in Mali. *World Development.* 17, (5) : 703-718.

Steffen, Philip, N. Nango Dembele and John Staatz. 1988. *Une Critique des Roles Alternatifs pour l'OPAM sur le Marche Cerealier a Travers des Concepts de Biens Publics.* Document de Travail No. 88-02. Project Securite Alimentaire. MSU-CESA-USAID. Bamako.

Stryker, J. Dirck, Jean-Jacques Dethier, Ignatius Peprah and Donald Breen. 1987. *Incentive System and Economic Policy Reform in Mali.* AIRD. Washington D.C.

Timmer, C. Peter. Walter P. Falcon and Scott R. Pearson. 1983. *Food Policy Analysis.* The Johns Hopkins University Press. Baltimore.

Weber, Michael T., John M. Staatz. John H. Holtzman. Eric W. Crawford and Richard Bernsten. 1988. Informing Food Security Decisions in Africa: Empirical Analysis and Policy Dialogue. *American Journal of Agricultural Economics.* 70(5) : 1044-1051.

World Bank 1989. *World Development Report 1988.* Oxford University Press. New York.

## APPENDIX

## OVERVIEW OF THE CESA/MSU/USAID
## FOOD SECURITY RESEARCH PROJECT IN MALI

Empirical findings cited in this paper about food-grain producers and traders in Mali result from primary data generated between October 1985 and October 1988 by the on-going CESA/MSU/USAID Food Security Research Project. These data were collected at the level of a two-stage stratified sample of 990 farm households at the first stage and 190 farm households at the second stage, and a panel of 118 coarse-grain wholesalers in four of the major cities (Koutiala and Sikasso in the surplus-producing zones, and Bamako and Mopti in major marketed-cereal consumption zones). The sample farm-households came from 16 villages, which were equally distributed between the south (about 1 000 mm of annual rainfall) and the north (approximately 700 mm of annual rainfall) of two savannah zones with similar agricultural resource endowments: the CMDT, which produces the bulk of cotton and has the best agricultural support institutions in Mali, and the OHV, which has a weaker institutional base. The 190 farm-household panel was roughly distributed equally among three technological strata, *i.e.*, farmers owning (1) a full set of animal traction equipment; (2) an incomplete set of animal traction equipment, and (3) no such equipment.

Coarse-grain transaction (quantity and price) data were collected through repeated enumerator interviews, weekly in the major rural markets of the survey zones and monthly for farmers and wholesalers. These price data were complemented with PRMC-monitoring of time-series of cereal retail prices in the eight regional capitals of Mali. Less repetitive questionnaires and informal interviews were used to collect basic information on farm household production and farmer and trader characteristics and perceptions.

The primary data was processed for analysis using both tabular and econometric techniques. The results reported in this paper are essentially estimated group-averages for the 990 farm-household sample, where the estimates from the smaller 190 household sample are weighted by the respective proportions of the different farm strata among all the farms of the 16 survey-villages. The empirical findings of these analyses have been reported in numerous working papers and other documents, and continuously discussed with policy decision makers of the Government of Mali, members of the Technical Secretariat of CESA (the national monitoring and evaluation commission of the food strategy of Mali), and representatives of the PRMC donors. These frequent discussions have helped develop and maintain close interactions and feedback between policy makers and food security policy researchers in the course of the on-going policy dialogue between the Government of Mali and donors on food policy reforms. Weber *et al.* (1988) discuss the importance of this approach of simultaneously improving both the supply of, and demand for, policy-relevant empirical insights.

# IV

# Improving Household Food Security: Interaction Between Technology, Marketing And Trade

# 14

# Improving Household Food Security: Interactions Between Technology, Marketing And Trade

## THE MALAWI CASE:
## RECENT FINDINGS AND EMERGING
## POLICY AND RESEARCH ISSUES

*B.M. Kaluwa*[1], *B.F. Kandoole*[1], *G.Y. Mkamanga*[2]
*and P. Heisey*[3]

## INTRODUCTION

The central objectives of Malawi's agricultural policy objective are to attain food self-sufficiency and diversify its agricultural export base. This policy has been pursued since independence in 1964 and it was reiterated in the recent Statement of Development Policies (DEVPOL, 1987-1996). Malawi's agricultural sector comprises large scale or estate producers and smallholders. The latter dominate food production while the estates have concentrated on the main export crops: tobacco, tea and sugar.

Malawi's smallholder sector accounts for about 85 percent of all agricultural production and is the single largest source of income for the majority of the population. Although Malawi had previously achieved national food self-sufficiency, the overall food situation has become quite delicate over the past few years. After growing at an average annual growth rate of 3,2 percent between 1967 and 1979 smallholder food production declined in the 1980s because of numerous factors, including poor producer incentives (Christiansen and Southworth, 1988) and other factors. Kinsey (1975) argues that Malawi lost momentum in maize production between 1966 and 1975 as the nominal price for maize in Malawi fell significantly below the average price for the region.

[1]Department of Economics, University of Malawi

[2]Ministry of Agriculture, Malawi

[3]CIMMYT, Malawi

While the role of relative prices in changing cropping patterns has been demonstrated, nobody, including the Government is convinced that pricing policy alone can increase aggregate agricultural production. The two institutions that have played a dominant role in agricultural development are the National Rural Development Programme (NRDP) and the Agricultural Development and Marketing Corporation (ADMARC).

This paper reviews Malawi's experience with technology generation to improve household level food security, with emphasis on interactions between technology, marketing systems and trade regimes which might be exploited by policy makers.

## The Food Economy at the Household Level

The results of the two National Sample Surveys of Agriculture (NSSA) in 1979 and 1980-81, the Ministry of Agriculture's Annual Survey of Agriculture (ASA), and other independent surveys have generated some conventional wisdom about smallholders. At the household level, many smallholders face severe resource constraints. For example, the 1980-81 NSSA revealed that 37 percent of all smallholders cultivated less than 0,7 ha. and an additional 36 percent cultivated between 0,7 and 1,5 ha. Moreover, farmers with smaller land areas depend more on wage labour and local petty trading for family income relative to farm sales, than do large farmers (Centre for Social Research (CSR), 1988b). Because of high population density, land shortage is a critical factor in determining rural poverty. With present technology, the threshold farm size for meeting average household calorie requirements is around is one hectare. Analyses based on NSSA data (CSR, 1988; Kaluwa and Kandoole, 1988) and independent micro-surveys. *e.g.*, Peters (1989) confirm that land holding size is positively correlated with income and the ability to meet food requirements.

But even more worrying is the finding that households with large landholdings tend to be cash crop growers who are in a better position relative to the smaller farmers, in terms of access to credit and extension services. Smallholders are oriented to subsistence production because of risk aversion and the lack of technological packages (Blantyre Agricultural Development Division (BLADD), 1987). Msukwa (1984) calculates that, on average, farmers with less than 0,5 ha produce slightly over one-quarter of their annual food requirements and those with 0,5 and 1 hectare. produce about three-quarters. According to the NSSA, half of the rural households deplete their food stocks within five months after harvest.

The coping mechanisms of food insecure households include the reduction of the frequency of meals in the months before harvest with a resulting rise in the incidence of child malnutrition (Msukwa, 1989), local reciprocal labour/food exchange (Ettema, 1984; Peters, 1988; Kaluwa and Kandoole, 1988) and wage employment on larger farms, including estates. Improvement of land productivity is constrained by the agricultural extension and credit systems which are biased against the most vulnerable groups. And given variations in land and ecological constraints, the problem is more serious than one of merely balancing local food deficits from local surpluses. Some areas tend to specialise in cash crops and rely on the marketing system to secure family food supplies. For example, the low-lying areas specialise in irrigated crops such as rice, and other crops suited to semi-arid conditions (cotton, sorghum and millet) while the highland areas are better suited to tea growing. There is a heavy dependence on maize imports in some of these areas.

Maize dominates smallholder decision making. The percentage of calories coming from maize, as well as past levels of *per capita* maize availability are probably higher for Malawi than for any other country where maize forms a substantial portion of the human diet (NSSA, 1979; Blackie, 1989; CIMMYT, 1987). But despite this dominance, it would be unwise to ignore other food crops and cash crops. Alternative food crops dominate the diets in certain areas.

## TECHNOLOGY AND CROP MARKETING: THE INSTITUTIONAL FRAMEWORK

The major constraints on increasing smallholder production include small landholdings, low soil fertility, low wages and low income levels. Adoption of proven new technologies has been hindered by low producer prices, limited credit, and more recently, the high cost of inputs because of the removal of input subsidies and exchange rate devaluation.

### The National Rural Development Programme

The approach to smallholder development has been two-pronged. On the one hand, one approach aims at a gradual improvement in extension and farmer training throughout the country supported by a number of low-cost activities such as ox-training and dairy improvement. On the other hand, during the early years after independence, the Government adopted management-intensive rural development projects to develop and supply comprehensive packages of technology, services and infrastructure in selected areas. But this approach has proven to be too expensive and it was replaced by a new concept, the National Rural Development Programme (NRDP). The objective of the NRDP is to broaden geographical coverage and focus more directly on support services for production, extension, marketing, and credit. Under the NRDP, the country has been divided into eight Agricultural Development Divisions (ADDs) each covering areas sharing similar ecological characteristics.

### The Department of Agricultural Research

The Department of Agricultural Research (DAR), which is now within the NRDP, was already fairly established by 1940 with 21 experimental farms in the country. In 1954 it had 21 scientists in the main disciplines such as agronomy, soil science, entomology, pathology and ecology carrying out research on all of the crops currently grown by smallholders and others besides. The objective was to select and introduce suitable crop varieties for both local and export markets.

The technological implications of some of the consumer food preferences that exist today have been established by work during the 1950s and earlier. For example, consumer preference for "flint maize" (hard endosperm) over "dent maize" (soft endosperm) was based on its better storage and processing qualities. Flint maize also yields a higher proportion of white flour, *ufa* than does dent (DAR, 1956-57). A pounding experiment, for example, revealed that flint yields 12 percent more flour that was twice as rich in oil and 1,25 times as rich in protein as the dent varieties. But the preparation of *ufa*, as opposed to whole-meal flour *mgaiwa*, results in a loss of 37 percent of the protein, 84 percent of the oil in flint maize, compared to 55 percent and 91 percent respectively in dent maize. *Madeya*, the waste from dehulled maize before milling into *ufa* is fed to chicken and dairy animals or steers. *Ufa* is still preferred to *mgaiwa* because of its colour, texture and taste qualities. However, *mgaiwa* is a standard ration in institutions such as schools, hospitals, and it is widely consumed in urban areas.

The diet of Malawians is presently dominated by *mgaiwa*. Better technology in the grain milling industry has resulted in an intermediate flour, Gramil, between the traditional *ufa* and *mgaiwa*. Gramil, at present, is the most common flour in urban areas. Moreover, whereas in the past dehulling used to be done through pounding, it is now done by grain mills with special equipment. The Government is also stressing the value of *mgaiwa* and legumes (pulses and groundnuts) in human nutrition (DEVPOL, 1987-1996 : 29), and proposes the monitoring and evaluation of the adoption of *mgaiwa*.

There has been a shift in the orientation of maize research from what people historically preferred, "the flint" varieties (SV37, SV17, SV28, SV Mlonda, LH7 Mthenga and LH11 Bingo) of the 1950s and 1960s, to the semi-flint and dent hybrids (SR52, R200, R201, UCA and CCA) in the late 1960s and early 1970s. The reason for the shift in research orientation was the belief that high yielding green revolution varieties could be developed for Malawi. For example, the SR52 maize variety that was imported from Zimbabwe responded to high inputs of fertilizer, pesticides and improved agricultural practices, and replaced the low-yielding synthetic and flint hybrids LH7 (Mthenga) and LH11 (Bingo).

The Ministry of Agriculture encouraged the use of the high-yielding hybrid maize varieties starting in the 1960s in order to increase production and maintain self-sufficiency through the provision of credit for improved seed, fertilizer and the establishment of ADMARC markets within walking distance of smallholder farmers. At the same time the DAR dropped its flint maize breeding programme and embarked on maize population improvement programmes and the development of semi-flint and dent maize hybrids, *e.g.*, UCA, CCA, MH12, MH13, MH14, MH15.

The shift in maize research strategy was pursued in other programmes, *e.g.*, in vegetables, bigger cabbage varieties were selected and recommended -- drum-head *vs* the smaller variety Golden Acre; the groundnut variety, Mwitunde, was replaced with Chalimbana and Chitembana for the confectionery trade; and in the case of cattle, Malawi Zebu were replaced by Jersey and Frieseland dairy breeds and Malawi Zebu were crossed with Frieseland for milk production.

With the recent dramatic rise in the cost of transport, fertilizer and other inputs, farmers are reverting to low-input agriculture, including the lower-yield flint maize types. Now there is an outcry, particularly among donors who had previously supported development projects through the green revolution technologies, that the DAR should use on-farm research methods to bring a farming systems perspective to bear on technology generation. As a starting point, the Adaptive Research Programme was initiated in 1980 to gain an understanding of farming systems, and technical constraints, and to identify research opportunities likely to give a substantial pay-off in the near future. Adaptive Research was fully institutionalised by the DAR in 1985.

Parallel research is underway on crop storage and food processing technologies. In 1973 several Overseas Development Agency-funded projects carried out research on the reduction of post-harvest losses of maize, sorghum, pulses, and oilseeds; and pest control and storage practices. Insects are the major cause of weight and quality losses of stored grains in Malawi. The strategy for controlling post-harvest insect pests involves:

o     screening of new promising insecticides;

o     evaluating inherent susceptibilities of new and recommended maize/crop varieties;

o     testing for insecticidal activity in stored grain;

o     monitoring the outbreak of the Larger Grain Borer (*Prostephanus truncatus*) on the border with Tanzania; and

o     enforcement of strict quarantine regulation and inspection.

Most smallholders process their own food. The use of improved processing technologies would improve the availability of food at the household level, minimise waste and save women and children from time-consuming and energy-demanding activities. But many of the post-harvest processing technologies have not been adopted by smallholders because of the lack of information on available technologies, lack of credit, and the lack of funds for the researchers to import and assess the technologies.

## ADMARC and New Developments in Smallholder Crop Marketing

ADMARC was established in 1973 to replace the Farmers' Marketing Board as the official marketing channel for all smallholder food and export crops, the distribution of inputs (some of which have been subsidised, such as fertilizer) and starting from 1981, the management of Malawi's strategic grain reserve. ADMARC has been the major vehicle carrying out the Government's smallholder pricing policy which incorporates two basic elements: (1) pan-territorial pricing and (2) price stability through guaranteed floor prices. This policy has been supported by ADMARC's extensive network of some 1 200 marketing points throughout the country.

Under ADMARC's scheme, farmers organise themselves into credit groups of between 10-30 members. High repayment rates of about 90 percent have been achieved in most areas. The major factors believed to have influenced this success are the single purpose of the groups, their honorary management and the joint liability arrangement, and the credit recovery scheme which used ADMARC buying points for loan recovery at the time farmers sold their crops (Schaefer-Kehnert, 1980).

During the 1970s, price stabilisation played a subservient role to ADMARC's profitability (Christiansen and Southworth, 1988). But ADMARC modified its approach starting in 1982 and set prices for export crops (tobacco, cotton, and groundnuts) at export parity levels. At the same time, domestically traded crops,

mainly the food crops including maize, were priced according to the domestic foo
supply/demand situation. The result has been higher relative prices for maize whic
have led to reallocation of land away from groundnuts, a reversal of the trend durin
the early 1980s.

There have been two fundamental changes in smallholder marketing/pricing policy
The first was the phased removal of subsidies on fertilizer, which was to b
implemented as part of the structural adjustment programme embarked on in 198
The second was the liberalisation of private trade in food crops in 1987, whereb
private traders were allowed to compete with ADMARC. Both these changes hav
been marred by poor timing.

The fertilizer subsidy removal programme, which was designed to reduce th
Government deficit coincided with a period of unprecedented rise in transport cos
and the negative effects of devaluation. The Government has understandabl
resisted this measure and suspended fertilizer subsidies in 1987. But the move ha
nevertheless left fertilizer prices open to the other exogenous forces.

The market liberalisation move was implemented too hastily due to donor pressur
which left the Government no room for resistance or for planning and implementin
a phased approach. But more than this, it was pushed through within a few montl
of what turned out to be a particularly bad harvest year. Since one of the underlyin
motives was to improve ADMARC's operating efficiency and its financial positio
it was able to withdraw services from some of the remote and costly marketin
points. Marketing points were closed that were unable to attain an annua
throughput of 60 tonnes. Although only 125 (15 percent) of the markets wer
actually closed, the closures have far-reaching consequences for households in foo
deficit areas.

Although food marketing liberalisation is still quite recent, some evidence, thoug
limited, is available on both the private trader response and the consequer
behaviour of prices. Table 1 shows the number of licensed traders operating in eac
of the ADDs during the first and second years after liberalisation. Although th
figures do not include the vast number of unlicensed traders who are known to b
in operation, they may still be taken as fairly representative of the largest of th
private traders.

The total number of designated markets open to private traders, 1 200, is quite clos
to that of the original number of ADMARC markets. This is not surprisin
considering that private traders were supposed to compete with ADMARC in th
first instance. The next thing to note is that the pattern of entry by private trade
into the various ADDs is influenced more by remoteness than by the number o
designated markets. For example, the highest number of designated markets wa
in Mzuzu in the Northern Region and yet the number of licensed traders is amon
the smallest in both years. In sharp contrast, Blantyre, Lilongwe and Liwonde, hav
the largest urban concentrations and the highest numbers of traders.

## Table 1
## Number of private traders by ADD

|  | Marketing Season 1987-88 | Marketing Season 1988-89 | Number of Designated Markets |
|---|---|---|---|
| Blantyre | 99 | 417 | 134 |
| Mzuzu | 22 | 35 | 278 |
| Lilongwe | 113 | 128 | 189 |
| Liwonde | 109 | 224 | 139 |
| Karonga | - | 7 | 96 |
| Salima | 20 | 28 | 85 |
| N'gabu | 14 | 51 | 67 |
| Kasungu | 10 | 27 | 182 |
| Total | 387 | 917 | 1 120 |

Source: Mkwezalamba, 1989

Most licensed traders deal in more than one type of crop and typically buy and trade domestically, although some supply other persons who are licensed to handle export crops. The latter numbered 605 in 1987-88 but fell to 490 in 1988-89, partly because of a decline in the production of major crops in the 1987-88 cropping season. Private traders have been most activé in the exportation of pulses and this activity has preceded liberalisation. For example, between 1982 and 1984 private traders handled nearly all the exports of pulses which averaged 11 tonnes per annum. In 1987, private traders exported 59 percent of the much higher level of the exports (48,5 tonnes).

The outcome of licensed private trader activity in maize generally conforms to the inter-seasonal price trends observed in 1982 due to the activity of small unlicensed traders (Ministry of Agriculture, 1983). Soon after harvest, maize prices fall below ADMARC prices because private traders are more flexible than ADMARC in terms of their ability to start buying immediately after harvest, at prices considerably below ADMARC prices. When ADMARC purchases maize, prices move towards ADMARC prices. But due to relatively low agricultural production during the past two seasons, private trader prices have tended to exceed official prices. In 1978-79, for example, private trader prices for maize varied between 102 percent and 132 percent of ADMARC prices while in 1988-89 the range was between 109 percent and 120 percent (Mkwezalamba, 1989). Private traders are able to exercise this flexibility because they are better able to respond to scarcity and competing demand such as that from agro-processors in the food industry. There have been a number of consequences of this. First, earlier buying and higher prices later in the season have led to preference for selling to private traders. This in turn has led to a dramatic reduction in ADMARC purchases. For example, Blantyre ADD (1987) reports that ADMARC purchases were lower than seven-year averages in many markets.

Second, early buying (at low prices) and subsequent purchase at higher prices have also led to a rise in the incidence of "distress selling" by poor households in need of cash. Definitive evidence of this has come from Blantyre ADD (1987). If this generally holds, the adverse timing of selling and buying is increasing market dependence for a portion of households. Third, because private trader activity typically removes food from the producing areas, this can reduce local food availability. Even where ADMARC markets still exist, ADMARC will be constrained in redressing the situation by its own low stocks. Blantyre ADD, which has the worst land constraint problems and where 57 ADMARC markets have been closed, has felt the unfavourable impact of private trader activity. Whereas some of the Rural Development Project areas within the ADD, *e.g.*, the Mwanza and Phalombe areas, are surplus producers of maize, others like Thyolo are deficit producers and have been the worst affected (Blantyre ADD, 1987).

## TECHNOLOGICAL ISSUES

### Policy Options Related to Food Production Technology

The features of the Malawian food economy described above suggest that although pricing policy may play a large role in meeting national objectives such as aggregate maize supply, increased food production at the household level can be stimulated through a variety of instruments, including pricing, institutional development and improved technology. For maize, two technological options are now thought to be paramount. First is the development of high-yielding maize varieties that are acceptable to consumers. This is a key agricultural research issue, although there are a host of related factors, both of a research and institutional nature. Second, is the improvement of soil fertility. Again, this has institutional and research components. Some of the suggestions relate to improved delivery of inorganic fertilizer to small farmers, through innovative credit programmes (*e.g.*, fertilizer for work, fertilizer/commodity exchanges), or through the expansion of cash cropping opportunities, perhaps through the relaxation of constraints on the types of tobacco smallholders can grow and market. The underlying assumption of this latter strategy is that the marginal propensity to invest in food crop production out of cash crop income is relatively high. An alternative suggestion has been the improvement of food legume technology, particularly in the context of the traditional practice of intercropping, to enhance soil fertility and human nutrition.

The marketing/pricing features of various crops should be factored into policy approaches. For example, in the face of high input costs, producer margins are likely to be more positively affected by higher private trader prices than by the slower moving ADMARC price, which would effectively define minimum margins for most producers, barring the distress sellers. While this will be of benefit to both producers of the local maize and the hybrids, the latter would be encouraged to exploit the higher yields associated with the hybrids. The maize preference factor is not a serious constraint particularly for hybrid maize producers sufficiently close to urban areas with non-discriminating users (direct consumers and the milling firms). If hybrid maize production can rise to cater for much of the urban consumption, then local maize production would be freed to satisfy rural needs, at least until processing technology has diffused to the rural areas to satisfy the discerning tastes there.

The recent high prices of maize and the related withdrawal by private traders from deficit areas could likely have some effects on the land constraint. Proposed improvements in access to fertilizer by smallholders through smaller packages and improved access to credit are also likely to encourage hybrid maize adoption.

Farmers may conceivably even grow hybrids to fulfil much the same role as that played by the food reserve crops such as cassava. Due to the fact that some smallholders deplete their stocks early, the poorer storage qualities of hybrids may not pose as serious a constraint as would otherwise be the case. Still, the role of technology in reducing losses is as much a part of the food security problem as improvements in production.

## Processing and Trade Policies

We turn now to an issue which is of importance to smallholders who face ecological constraints in their areas, particularly in the low-rainfall area of the Lower Shire River Valley. Considerable attention has recently focussed on the need for SADCC countries to reduce their trade dependency on wheat imports. The solution lies in countries adopting appropriate trade policies for wheat imports, *e.g.*, import subsidy removal or some other way of raising import prices, in order to force the baking industry to adopt wheat/sorghum composite flour in baking. In Malawi the Government estimates that it is feasible to replace 25 percent of wheat with sorghum in bread without seriously compromising taste. The implementation of such a move will undoubtedly have a considerable impact on the people in the Lower Shire area where sorghum is grown for its drought-resistance qualities. At present sorghum is grown purely as a subsistence crop despite the fact that high yields are obtained, partly because ADMARC is not interested in buying the crop and therefore it offers a very low price (4t/kg).

An increase in the demand for sorghum in the agro-processing industries would raise producer prices and encourage production of marketed output. For Lower Shire farmers, this would diversify their sources of cash income beyond cotton, and in a few areas, irrigated rice. This new possibility will have an important impact on food security because maize is still the dominant staple despite the presence of millet and sorghum, and because the area is a maize deficit area. Any rise in the level of cash incomes will therefore also raise the ability of smallholders in the area to effectively compete in the market for the increasingly high-priced maize.

## Storage Technology, Marketing and Trade

Given the existing marketing and trade regimes, a number of technological issues emerge with respect to storage. At present, smallholders and ADMARC staff are aware of the recommended storage technologies. But private traders who can now trade in fairly large quantities of food grain have had no tradition of crop storage to minimise losses. They require exposure to recommended crop storage practices and, if need be, efforts must not be spared to establish intermediate technologies, which should soon be "on the shelf".

As long as storage problems prevent private traders from settling into their designated role of providing an alternative to ADMARC storage in some areas, the grain marketing system that will emerge and persist could undermine local and household food security. For example, in the case of private traders operating in an area where ADMARC has withdrawn, the attractive prices they offer could result in overselling as far as the local households are concerned. Now, if due to lack of available storage technology, traders remove crops for fast disposal elsewhere, food deficit households will not find local suppliers.

Serious problems like this are being experienced in a number of areas characterised by "distress sellers", *i.e.*, food deficit producers who sell food crops soon after harvest to alleviate immediate cash needs even if they will need to buy back some of the food at higher prices later on. But sometimes the food may simply not be available (Blantyre ADD, 1987, the example of Thyolo District).

Storage problems, like other constraints, can compromise the operations and success of the private sector by leading to uncompetitive marketing structures (Reusse, 1987). Displaced persons and natural disasters have opened the country to large inflows of food from different parts of the world. This has called for more resources for inspection, treatment and proper storage of food imports. Although problems with the traditional export/import routes through Mozambique led to the opening of the Northern Corridor, it also opened the country to the Larger Grain Borer in Tanzania. There is a need for stricter quarantine and produce inspection along the border in order to monitor the movement of the pest. Recent experience with the mealybug devastation of the cassava crop, which is a staple in some parts of the country, has resulted in such areas being treated as natural disaster areas, particularly the Lakeshore area in Nkhata-Bay District. Apart from the immediate impact on the food balance, such infestations have long-term consequences, which often requires reorienting the smallholders towards new cropping patterns, which may not be suited to the particular areas (Centre for Social Research, 1987).

There is need to maintain an active search for and screening of insecticides for crop storage and to identify the natural enemies of the important storage pests. Multinational chemical firms are an important source of "world technologies" for Malawi. The availability of the widest range of cost-effective and safe options would lead to the reduction of input costs as well as crop losses.

## CONCLUSION

Although there has recently been much discussion of household food security, most of the technological issues have received limited or no attention. The present study has sought to air some of these issues. We have highlighted some of the most important emerging issues which directly or indirectly influence household food security:

o    The shift in biological research away from flint maize varieties with desirable consumer, storage and processing qualities towards dent green revolution varieties has overlooked the now greater need for improved storage and processing technology.

o    The slow adoption of improved technology raises a number of policy options, including the use of innovative approaches to improve accessibility by poorer farmers, the new role of the marketing structure in providing incentive prices and the possibilities offered by relative maize/maize flour pricing.

o    The concern with improved production technology has tended to overshadow needed research on improved storage technology as a way to reduce crop losses at the household level. Storage technology can also contribute to the evolution of marketing systems that would not create a pattern of household grain sales after harvest only to be followed by grain purchases by the same households later in the season.

o    There are special cases where agro-processing can be influenced by trade policy. Also, domestic marketing responses can have positive trickle-down effects on sub-groups of farmers such as sorghum production for bread made with wheat (75 percent) and sorghum (25 percent).

o    Despite the fairly closed trade regime in grain, recent international developments have opened up Malawi to grain inflows which have increased the possibilities of crop infestations from new pests. There is a need for more active screening of pest control technologies.

## REFERENCES

Blantyre ADD. 1987. *Preliminary Assessment of the Food Situation and the Impact of the Agricultural (General Purposes) Act (No.11 of 1987).* Evaluation Working Paper 5/87.

Centre for Social Research (CSR). 1988. Report of the Workshop on Household Food Security and Nutrition, Zomba, 28 August to 31 August 1988 Vol. 1. Summary of Presentations, Discussions and Recommendations.

Centre for Social Research. Vol II Papers Presented. Centre for Social Research, 1988. *The Characteristics of Nutritionally Vulnerable Sub-Groups within the Smallholder Sector of Malawi: A Report from the 1980-81 NSSA.* University of Malawi.

Centre for Social Research. 1987. *Cropping Patterns in Lakeshore Areas of Nkhata-Bay District in 1986-87 and the Potentials and Requirements for Diversification.*

Christiansen, R.E. and V.R. Southworth. 1988. *Agricultural Pricing and Marketing Policy in Malawi: Implications for a Development Strategy.* Presented at the Symposium on Agricultural Policies for Growth and Development 31 October-4 November. Mangochi. Malawi.

Ettema, W. 1984. *Food Availability in Malawi.* Centre for Social Research.

Ettema, W. and L. Msukwa. 1988. *Food Production and Nutrition in Malawi.* University of Malawi. Centre for Social Research.

Hiwa, S.S. 1988. *Agricultural Development Policy and Food Production.* Presented at Workshop on Household Food Security and Nutrition 28-31 August. Zomba.

Kinsey, B.H. 1975. *Overcoming Impediments to the Effective Marketing of Staples.* Development Studies (University of East Anglia) Discussion Paper.

Lele, U. and R.E. Christiansen. 1988. *Markets, Marketing Boards and Cooperatives: Issues in Adjustment Policy.*

Lele, U. and A.A. Goldsmith. 1989. *The Development of National Agricultural Research Capacity: Indian Experience with the Rockefeller Foundation and its Significance for Africa.* Economic Development and Cultural Change Vol. 37. No. 2.

Livingstone, I. 1983. *Agricultural Development Strategy and Agricultural Price Policy in Malawi.* Presented at International Seminar on Marketing Boards in Tropical Africa. 19-23 September, Leiden, The Netherlands.

Malawi Government. Statement of Development Policies 1987-1996.

Mzwezalamba, M.M. 1989. *The Impact of the Liberalisation of Smallholder Agricultural Produce Pricing and Marketing in Malawi.* Ministry of Agriculture.

Msukwa, L.A.H. 1989. *Household Food Security and Nutrition: The Case of Malawi.* Presented at the UNICEF Regional Network Meeting on "Household Food Security and Nutrition" 6-6 April 1989.

Nankumba, J.S. 1989. *Food Requirement and Agricultural Production, Cropping Pattern and Land Ownership.* National Seminar on Population and Development in Malawi. 5-9 June. Chancellor College. Zomba.

Nankumba, J.S., B. Kaluwa and P. Kishindo. 1989. *Contract Farming and Outgrower Schemes in Malawi. The Case of Tea and Sugar Smallholder Authorities.* Centre for Social Research.

Reusse, E. 1987. Liberalization and Agricultural Marketing: Recent Cause and Effects in Third World Economies. *Food Policy* : 299-317.

Schaefer-Kehnert, W. 1980. Success with Group Lending in Malawi. *Quarterly Journal of International Agriculture* Vol.19 No.4. : 331-337.

# 15

# Household Income, Food Production And Marketing In Low-Rainfall Areas of Zimbabwe: Status, Constraints, And Opportunities[1]

*Godfrey Mudimu*[2], *Charles Chopak*[3], *Solomon Chigume*[4],
*Jones Govereh*[4], *Rick Bernsten*[5]

## INTRODUCTION

The Government of Zimbabwe is giving priority to improving national and household food security, as well as to improving the standard of living and incomes in rural areas. A major challenge facing the Government is how to enable communal farmers to increase their production so they can increase their participation in the market -- as well as stimulating the establishment of small rural enterprises.

Since Independence in 1980, the Government has undertaken numerous initiatives to meet these priorities, including the following:

o    strengthening institutions serving farmers; including credit, extension, agricultural marketing (crop collection) and agricultural research;

o    improving the physical infrastructure, particularly the road network;

o    guaranteeing incentive prices for food and cash crops;

[1] The authors wish to acknowledge the contribution of Michael Weber and Thomas Jayne in commenting on earlier drafts of this paper.

[2] Chairman, Department of Agricultural Economics and Extension, University of Zimbabwe.

[3] Research Associate, Department of Agricultural Economics, Michigan State University.

[4] Research Scholars, Food Security Research Project, Department of Agricultural Economics and Extension, University of Zimbabwe.

[5] Associate Professor, Department of Agricultural Economics, Michigan State University.

o    encouraging crop diversification from low- to high-value crops such as cotton and oilseeds (soybeans, sunflower, and groundnut) as a way to increase household cash income; and

o    encouraging crop diversification in low-rainfall areas by offering incentive prices for drought-tolerant crops such as sorghum, finger millet, and bulrush millet.

Both large- and small-scale farmers have responded to Government incentives as shown by the increase in marketed surplus of all major crops. Communal area production currently accounts for 55 percent of marketed cotton, 45-50 percent of marketed maize, over 90 percent of marketed sunflower, and 30-40 percent of marketed groundnut (Rohrbach, 1989; Stanning, 1985, 1988).

While the supply response in communal areas has been quite favourable, there is growing evidence that the response has not been evenly distributed across communal areas located in different agro-ecological zones; nor evenly shared by households within these zones.

A study by Jackson and Collier (1988) revealed that cereal production and marketing are highly skewed. About 40 percent of all cereal production was produced by the top 10 percent of farm households and 25 percent produced 64 percent of the output. In contrast, the bottom 25 percent of the households produced only 3,5 percent of the total cereal output. This study also reported that 83 percent of the cereals marketed through official channels (GMB) came from 10 percent of the households; while 40 percent did not market any cereals.

Rohrbach (1989) found that in Chivi and Mangwende Districts, the top 20 percent of producers accounted for over 50 percent of maize production in 1986 and 1987.

Research by Chigume and Shaffer (1989) and Chopak (1989) in Mutoko/Mudzi and Buhera Districts show similar highly-skewed patterns of income and crop marketings distributions.

Stanning (1988, 1989) showed that in Hurungwe District -- a high rainfall area -- 30 percent of the households accounted for approximately 75 percent of the marketed maize surplus. With respect to income, Stanning found that the top 25 percent of the households earned 60 percent of the income, with the lowest 25 percent earning only 7 percent.

A major factor contributing to skewness in production, marketings, and income distribution across communal areas is the differences in agro-ecological conditions. Approximately 74 percent of Zimbabwe's 16 350 000ha of communal land (supporting 60 percent of the communal population) lies in Natural Regions IV and V (Jayne et al., 1989; CSO, 1987). These NRs are considered marginal for agricultural production due to poor quality soils, low and unreliable rainfall, and a fragile ecology.

## Research Overview

In 1987 the Food Security Research Project at the University of Zimbabwe, Department of Agricultural Economics and Extension -- in conjunction with Michigan State University -- initiated a study to investigate the food security situation in representative districts in Natural Regions IV and V. The objective of this research was to assess the food security situation in the study areas, determine what factors explain interhousehold differences in food security and propose policy initiatives to improve household food security.

The results reported in this paper are based on preliminary analysis of data collected through a series of surveys conducted from December 1987 through August 1989. Specific survey modules include a monthly income and expenditure survey (18 months), and a number of focused surveys to collect information on household characteristics, livestock and equipment inventories, marketing activities, agricultural production, technology adoption, resources, and related topics.

The surveys were conducted in the lower potential areas of Mudzi/Mutoko and Buhera Districts. Mudzi/Mutoko District was selected to represent NR IV and Buhera District was selected to represent NR V. In each district, six villages were selected to represent varying distance to market -- with two selected in each location which were relatively close (<10 km), intermediate (11-30 km), and far (>30 km) from a GMB depot. In each village, approximately 30 households were randomly chosen as respondents.

## HOUSEHOLD INCOMES AND EXPENDITURES

The following analysis is based on monthly income and expenditures surveys for the period April 1988 through March 1989. This period was selected for analysis because it covers a 12-month period following the harvest up to the subsequent harvest.

### Income Patterns

Annual household *per capita* income, computed from the monthly surveys undertaken, is shown in Tables 1 and 2. The mean annual household *per capita* income for the Mudzi/Mutoko survey area (Natural Region IV) is Z$140, while for the Buhera study region (Natural Region V) it averages Z$153 per person in each household studied. These income levels are quite low compared to Government of Zimbabwe official estimates of nation-wide average *per capita* GNP of Z$1 010,00 in 1986 (CSO, 1988). However, rural incomes are significantly below those in urban areas, and within the rural population, households in Natural Regions IV and V are known to be considerably below the rural average. The study of 600 communal farmers (located in each of the natural regions of Zimbabwe) conducted by Jackson and Collier for the 1984-85 marketing year reports total *per capita* income from all sources (including the value of home production consumed) ranging from Z$28 to Z$771, with 50 percent of the households studied receiving less than Z$137 *per capita*, and 75 percent with less than Z$248 (Jackson and Collier, 1988). Thus, the estimates derived from the present study, while showing what appear to be very low incomes, are not out of line with this other recent study. These studies are most likely documenting the extremely difficult economic situation among many small holders in Natural Regions IV and V.

Since the sample wide averages hide considerable diversity, Tables 1 and 2 present household characteristics according to *per capita* income quartiles derived for the entire sample, rather than for each region separately. For example, households in the lowest *per capita* income quartile in both regions reported approximately Z$50 income per person, while those in the top quartile reported *per capita* income of Z$306. Yet only 18 percent of the subsample in Mudzi/Mutoko fall into the highest quartile, while some 31 percent fall into the upper middle quartile (Z$140). In Buhera District the highest income quartile has 28 percent of the sample while the upper middle quartile has only 21 percent. Overall, while there are slight differences in the quartile size grouping between the two study regions, these do not appear to be large, with about the same proportions of the sample in each Natural Region falling in the upper and lower half of the distributions.

When reviewing the household characteristics across the regions and income quartiles, household size and the number of workers do appear to vary significantly across *per capita* income quartiles. Given these differences, and the somewhat constant farm size across quartiles, there appears to be an increase in land *per capita* and per worker, as the household *per capita* income increases. The age of the household head is likewise lower for the higher income and smaller size households in both natural regions. Such results are consistent with the concept of younger households having fewer family members, for whatever reasons, and more land per family member and per worker, resulting in higher *per capita* income. The number of households that are totally equipped with animal traction, and equipment is significantly higher in Buhera, and this is consistent with the greater importance of large ruminant livestock in this area, compared to Natural Region IV (Mudzi/Mutoko). It is interesting to note that animal traction equipment ownership patterns do not appear to vary much across the *per capita* income quartiles.

Preliminary breakdowns of the principal sources of household income are also shown in Tables 1 and 2. Since we are working with a whole farm income concept, agricultural production that is retained for home consumption has been valued, and can be compared to the value of cash income derived from farm sales, non-agricultural sales and off-farm labour sales, as well as to the value of transfers (remittances). In general the estimated value of production for home consumption ranges from over 35 percent to never more than 50 percent of total household *per capita* income, with the lower income quartile households depending relatively more on home based consumption to determine income, compared to the highest income quartiles where cash income and transfers make up a larger proportion of household income. The lowest income quartile households in both regions derive approximately 70 percent of their total income from on-farm sources, including both the value of home production plus the value of all sales of agricultural products. This relationship changes slightly over the income quartiles, with the highest income groups deriving between 55 and 65 percent of their household income from these farm sources.

Farm sales are dominated by maize, small grains and the "other" category, which includes livestock. Later analysis will disaggregate this other category more carefully, but preliminary reviews indicate that livestock income will dominate. In both natural regions, households in the lower half of the income distribution derive very little income from the sale of cereals, or other crops for that matter. Maize is more important in Mudzi/Mutoko while small grains dominate in Buhera. Sunflowers appear as an important crop in both regions, with groundnut and roundnut appearing more important in Buhera. Only a small number of households grew cotton in one of the study villages in Mudzi/Mutoko, and little analysis has yet been done on this information.

## Table 1
### Reported annual household income (per capita) and expenditure (%) by income group, in Natural Region IV (Mudzi/Mutoko District, 1988-89)

| | Household per capita Income Quartiles[a] | | | |
|---|---|---|---|---|
| | Lower (x = $50) | Lower middle (x = $88) | Lower middle (x = $140) | Highest (x = $306) |
| **HH CHARACTERISTICS (N = 121)** | | | | |
| Households (#) | 32 (26%) | 30 (25%) | 37 (31%) | 22 (18%) |
| HH size (#) | 11 | 9 | 9 | 6 |
| Workers (#) | 5 | 4 | 4 | 3 |
| Dependency ratio[b] | 2,8 | 2,7 | 2,8 | 2,1 |
| HH head age (yrs) | 55 | 49 | 50 | 38 |
| Land/household (ha) | 3,8 | 3,2 | 2,9 | 3,3 |
| Land/capita (ha) | 0,3 | 0,3 | 0,3 | 0,6 |
| Land worker (ha) | 0,8 | 0,8 | 0,7 | 1,1 |
| ANTRAC:[c] | 50 | 57 | 51 | 55 |
| **INCOME per capita (Z$)** | | | | |
| Production for home consumption | 25 | 35 | 59 | 132 |
| Income generating activities | 19 | 37 | 59 | 113 |
| Farm sales | (10) | (19) | (29) | (70) |
| maize | 2 | 5 | 6 | 24 |
| sm grains | 1 | 1 | 4 | 21 |
| sunflower | 2 | 5 | 7 | 6 |
| groundnut | 0 | 1 | 0 | 3 |
| roundnut | 0 | 0 | 1 | 0 |
| other (including livestock) | 5 | 7 | 11 | 16 |
| Non-ag sales | (3) | (4) | (11) | (15) |
| Labour sales | (7) | (11) | (17) | (24) |
| Transfers | 7 | 16 | 22 | 64 |
| Total (sample mean = Z$140) | 51 | 91 | 140 | 309 |
| **EXPENDITURE (%)** | | | | |
| Consumption | 82 | 75 | 77 | 74 |
| Food/clothing | (74) | (67) | (69) | (69) |
| home produced | 45 | 35 | 38 | 48 |
| purchased | 30 | 32 | 30 | 20 |
| Travel | (1) | (2) | (2) | (1) |
| Milling | (6) | (3) | (3) | (3) |
| Other HH expenses | (1) | (3) | (4) | (2) |
| Intermediate goods | 7 | 7 | 7 | 10 |
| Agricultural inputs | (3) | (3) | (3) | (5) |
| Purchased labour | (4) | (4) | (4) | (5) |
| Investments | 10 | 16 | 14 | 15 |
| School | (6) | (9) | (7) | (8) |
| Animal/ag. equipment | (2) | (3) | (5) | (7) |
| House | (1) | (4) | (3) | (1) |
| Transfers | 1 | 2 | 2 | 1 |
| Total percentage | 100 | 100 | 100 | 100 |

[a] Income quartiles are for total sample.
[b] Dependency ratio   size of household/number of workers
[c] Percent of households fully equipped with animal traction equipment.

Table 2
**Reported annual household income (per capita) and expenditure (%)
by income group, in Natural Region V
(Buhera District, 1988-89)**

| | Household per capita Income Quartiles[a] | | | |
|---|---|---|---|---|
| | Lower (x=$50) | Lower middle (x=$88) | Lower middle (x=$140) | Highest (x=$306) |
| **HH CHARACTERISTICS (N=113)** | | | | |
| Households (#) | 26 (23%) | 31 (27%) | 24 (21%) | 32 (28%) |
| HH size | 12 | 9 | 9 | 7 |
| Workers (#) | 5 | 5 | 4 | 3 |
| Dependency ratio[b] | 2,6 | 2,3 | 2,6 | 2,3 |
| HH head age (yrs) | 49 | 48 | 45 | 38 |
| Land/household (ha) | 6,3 | 5,9 | 4,6 | 5,6 |
| Land/capita (ha) | 0,5 | 0,6 | 0,5 | 0,8 |
| Land/worker (ha) | 1,3 | 1,2 | 1,1 | 1,9 |
| ANTRAC: [c] | 73 | 74 | 71 | 75 |
| **INCOME per capita (Z$)** | | | | |
| Production for home consumption | 24 | 47 | 67 | 113 |
| Income generating activities | 21 | 31 | 60 | 171 |
| Farm sales | (11) | (14) | (29) | (61) |
| maize | 0 | 1 | 0 | 31 |
| sm grains | 7 | 6 | 15 | 3 |
| sunflower | 1 | 2 | 0 | 0 |
| groundnut | 0 | 1 | 3 | 9 |
| roundnut | 1 | 3 | 4 | 6 |
| other (including livestock) | 2 | 1 | 7 | 12 |
| Non-ag sales | (3) | (3) | (7) | (21) |
| Labour sales | (7) | (14) | (24) | (92) |
| Transfers | 6 | 11 | 13 | 21 |
| Total(sample mean = Z$153) | 51 | 89 | 140 | 305 |
| **EXPENDITURE (%)** | | | | |
| Consumption | 83 | 81 | 81 | 76 |
| Food/clothing | (68) | (71) | (67) | (64) |
| home produced | 33 | 41 | 39 | 32 |
| purchased | 35 | 30 | 29 | 32 |
| Travel | (4) | (3) | (2) | (4) |
| Milling | (3) | (2) | (2) | (2) |
| Other HH expenses | (3) | (2) | (2) | (2) |
| Intermediate goods | 1 | 5 | 5 | 5 |
| Agricultural inputs | (0) | (0) | (0) | (0) |
| Purchased labour | (1) | (5) | (5) | (4) |
| Investments | 14 | 11 | 14 | 17 |
| School | (5) | (4) | (4) | (7) |
| Animal/ag. equipment | (8) | (5) | (7) | (9) |
| House | (1) | (3) | (1) | (1) |
| Transfers | 1 | 3 | 2 | 2 |
| Total percentage | 100 | 100 | 100 | 100 |

[a] Income quartiles are for total sample.
[b] Dependency ratio = size of household/number of workers
[c] Percent of households fully equipped with animal traction equipment.

An important question is whether cotton, as well as other cash income crops such as sunflowers, groundnut and roundnut, as well as livestock can be intensified as one possible strategy to raise income levels in these regions. Given the importance of basic cereals to both home consumption, as well as cash sales, productivity improvements in these crops is also fundamental to improving household well being.

The cash income generation side of household behaviour is dominated in both natural regions by non-farm and off-farm income generating activities, compared to cash obtained from the sale of crop and animal products. In Buhera the sale of labour is the dominant non-farm cash income earning activity, while in Mudzi/Mtoko, transfers (remittances) are more important than either non-agricultural or labour sales. This is because there are more opportunities for households in the Mudzi/Mutoko region to send family members to the city to obtain permanent employment and remit earnings to the household, whereas it is more common in Buhera to sell labour to neighbouring farms and other enterprises.

As a final comment on household income, while the general level is quite low for both regions, the households in the lower 50 percent of the distribution have absolute incomes that are less than one-half of those in the upper income quartiles. And this relationship holds for both production for home consumption, as well as for cash income from various sources. The significance of this is that there are many rural households with absolute income levels, including home consumption, that are extremely low.

### Expenditure Patterns

Turning to expenditure information shown in Tables 1 and 2, two major themes emerge. First, food and clothing expenses dominate, with roughly 60 to 70 percent of household income being allocated to these items. And within this category, 40 to 50 percent of consumption is purchased across almost all of the income quartile groups (the one exception is the highest quartile group in Mudzi/Mutoko where purchases drop to about 30 percent of food and clothing expenditures). These findings destroy the often expressed image of households in the communal areas subsisting largely on what they produce and consume on their own farms. Clearly the purchased portion of food and clothing consumption is critical to household well being, especially at the lower end of the income quartiles where the absolute level of own farm production and consumption is so very low in absolute terms.

A second important feature revealed in this data is that agricultural input purchases are relatively low, especially in Buhera. Obviously with a large portion of cash income needed to satisfy basic food and clothing requirements, there is little left over to purchase agricultural inputs. There are investment expenditures on schooling and animal/agricultural equipment. In fact there appears to be a slight pattern of greater investments in schooling in Mudzi/Mutoko compared to Buhera where animal, and equipment investments are relatively higher.

## INCREASING HOUSEHOLD INCOME
## THROUGH CROP PRODUCTION

Crop production is the major source of income in both natural regions. Total crop production income may be increased through either an expansion in the area planted, increase in individual crop yields, or by farmers growing higher valued crops.

### Soil Fertility

Soil quality affects yield and, to some extent, determines what crop should be grown on the land. In general, Mudzi/Mutoko farmers rated their soils of higher fertility than Buhera farmers (Table 3). About 17 percent of the cropped land in Mudzi/Mutoko was rated poor, compared to 26 percent in Buhera. The data also suggest that cropped land and fallow land do not differ greatly in terms of fertility.

### Table 3
### Soil fertility characteristics of cultivated and fallow land,
### Mudzi/Mutoko and Buhera Districts, Zimbabwe, 1987-88

| | Mudzi/Mutoko | | Buhera | |
| | Cultivated (%) | Fallow (%) | Cultivated (%) | Fallow (%) |
|---|---|---|---|---|
| High | 21 | 16 | 14 | 10 |
| Average | 62 | 47 | 54 | 65 |
| Low | 17 | 37 | 32 | 26 |

Note: Cultivated refers to all cropped land; fallow refers to all uncropped land.
Source: Food Security Research Project surveys, 1987-89.

### Cropping Priorities

Bulrush millet and maize are the predominant crops grown in Mudzi/Mutoko and Buhera Districts (Table 4). In Mudzi/Mutoko, 97 percent of the households grow maize, compared to 85 percent in Buhera. In contrast, more households grow bulrush millet in Buhera (92 percent), than in Mudzi/Mutoko (83 percent). With regards to finger millet and sorghum, they are more widely grown in Buhera District. Groundnuts are the most widely-grown oilseed crop, cultivated by 50 percent of the households in Buhera and 39 percent in Mudzi Mutoko. The survey also revealed that roundnuts are an important food and cash crop in Buhera, where it is grown by 42 percent of the households.

Farmers' decisions regarding the location of crops, with respect to soil fertility also indicates farmers' priorities. In Mudzi/Mutoko, farmers prefer to grow maize on the most fertile soils (high and average), followed by groundnut and bulrush millet (Table 5). In Buhera, the greatest proportion of the sorghum and maize parcels tend to be planted on the high fertility land.

### Table 4
### Distribution of crop production
### (percent of farmers growing each crop),
### Mudzi/Mutoko Districts, Zimbabwe, 1988-89

| Crop | Mudzi/Mutoko (N=163) | Buhera (N=134) |
|------|------|------|
| Maize | 97 | 85 |
| Pearl millet | 83 | 92 |
| Sunflower | 45 | 13 |
| Groundnut | 39 | 50 |
| Sorghum | 24 | 40 |
| Finger millet | 13 | 25 |
| Roundnut | 13 | 42 |

Source: Food Security Research Project surveys, 1987-89.

### Table 5
### Distribution of crops by soil fertility,
### Mudzi/Mutoko and Buhera Districts, Zimbabwe, 1987-1988

| | Mudzi/Mutoko | | | Buhera | | |
| | High (%) | Average (%) | Low (%) | High (%) | Average (%) | Low (%) |
|------|------|------|------|------|------|------|
| Bulrush millet | 18 | 59 | 13 | 15 | 53 | 32 |
| Maize | 24 | 63 | 13 | 17 | 53 | 30 |
| Finger millet | na | na | na | 28 | 34 | 38 |
| Sorghum | 17 | 54 | 29 | 11 | 62 | 27 |
| Groundnut | 20 | 65 | 15 | 11 | 51 | 38 |

na = data not available
Source: Food Security Research Project surveys, 1987-89.

### Land Availability and Utilisation

Table 6 shows that the amount of land available and utilised for cropping (per household) is greater in Buhera than Mudzi/Mutoko. In 1987-88 farmers in both locations cropped about 85 percent of their arable land -- leaving the remainder in fallow. In Buhera, farmers planted 49 percent of the cropped land to bulrush-millet, 19 percent to maize, and 9 percent to sorghum

This is in sharp contrast to Mudzi/Mutoko where bulrush millet and maize were planted to an equal percent (32-33 percent) of their land. Small grains (sorghum, bulrush-millet and finger-millet) predominate in Buhera (61 percent of cropped acres) compared to Mudzi/Mutoko (37 percent of cropped area).

### Table 6
### Cropland use in Mudzi/Mutoko and Buhera Districts, Zimbabwe, 1988-89

|  | Mudzi/Mutoko (N = 163) | | Buhera (N = 134) | |
|  | Mean area/HH (hectares) | Percent of area cropped | Mean area/HH (hectares) | Percent of area cropped |
|---|---|---|---|---|
| Arable area | 3,22 | na | 5,63 | na |
| Cropped area | 2,72 | 100 | 4,86 | 100 |
| Fallow area | 0,50 | na | 0,77 | na |
|  |  |  |  |  |
| Bulrush millet | 0,90 | 33 | 2,36 | 49 |
| Maize | 0,88 | 32 | 0,91 | 19 |
| Sunflower | 0,32 | 12 | 0,14 | 3 |
| Groundnut | 0,10 | 4 | 0,34 | 7 |
| Sorghum |  |  |  |  |
| Red | 0,01 > 0,08 | 3 | 0,18 > 0,44 | 9 |
| White | 0,07 |  | 0,26 |  |
| Finger millet | 0,04 | 1 | 0,17 | 3 |
| Roundnut | 0,02 | <1 | 0,25 | 5 |
| Other crops[a] | 0,38 | 14 | 0,25 | 5 |

na indicates not applicable
[a] Other crops include intercropped parcels of land.
Source: Food Security Research Project surveys, 1987-89.

Summarising the land utilisation data, it is evident that:

o    bulrush millet is the predominant small grain in both locations, grown by at least 80 percent of the households;

o    sorghum is a minor crop in both locations;

o    white sorghum is significantly more important than red sorghum in both locations, probably indicating household preference for white sorghum for consumption;

o    Buhera is a more important small grain area;

o    Mudzi/Mutoko is a more important maize area;

o    Oilseeds are minor crops, in terms of land allocation, with sunflower more important in Mudzi/Mutoko and groundnut more important in Buhera; and

o    a sizeable amount of land (about 15 percent) in both areas is left fallow.

## Crop Output and Utilisation

Although in both survey areas, bulrush millet is allocated more land, its output is below maize. In Mudzi/Mutoko, the output of maize per household is approximately twice that of bulrush millet (Table 7). In Buhera, where the bulrush:maize land ratio is 2,5:1, the bulrush:maize output ratio is 1,08:1. The lower output of bulrush millet can be attributed to lower yields. In both survey areas, maize out-yielded bulrush millet; by a factor of 2,4 in Buhera and 2,0 in Mudzi/Mutoko. This is a reflection of the current state of available crop technology. Improved maize varieties are available to communal farmers. On the other hand, in both Mudzi/Mutoko and Buhera, farmers have available only traditional millet varieties.

In terms of total production, farmers in Mudzi/Mutoko produced twice as much maize as bulrush millet (Table 8). In contrast, about equal quantities of maize and bulrush millet were produced in Buhera. In Mudzi/Mutoko, farmers were self sufficient in bulrush-millet, but purchased substantial quantities of maize. However in Buhera, farmers purchased large amounts of both bulrush-millet and maize, with bulrush purchases double maize purchases. Regarding sales, in Mudzi/Mutoko, maize accounted for about 90 percent of grain sales; whereas in Buhera bulrush-millet accounted for over 90 percent of grain sales.

### Table 7
#### Total crop output, area, and yield by crop type
#### in Mudzi/Mutoko and Buhera Districts, 1987-88 production year

|  | Mudzi/Mutoko | | | Buhera | | |
|---|---|---|---|---|---|---|
|  | Output (kg) | Area (ha) | Yield (kg/ha) | Output (kg) | Area (ha) | Yield (kg/ha) |
| Bulrush millet | 570 | 0,90 | 633 | 1 011 | 2,36 | 428 |
| Maize | 1 124 | 0,88 | 1 277 | 936 | 0,91 | 1 029 |
| Finger millet | 102 | 0,04 | a | 53 | 0,17 | a |
| Sorghum |  |  |  |  |  |  |
| Red | 24 |  |  | 31 |  |  |
|  | } | 0,08 | a | } | 0,44 | a |
| White | 120 |  |  | 45 |  |  |
| Groundnut | 64 | 0,10 | 640 | 117 | 0,34 | 344 |
| Sunflowers | 128 | 0,32 | a | 11 | 0,14 | a |

a Data not available.
Source: Food Security Research Project surveys, 1987-89.

Table 8
Grain transactions in Mudzi/Mutoko and Buhera Districts, Zimbabwe,
1988-89 marketing season

|  | Mudzi/Mutoko | | Buhera | |
|---|---|---|---|---|
|  | B.Millet (kg) | Maize (kg) | B.Millet (kg) | Maize (kg) |
| Production | 92 910 | 183 212 | 135 414 | 125 424 |
| Purchases | 0 | 3 840 | 27 203 | 13 974 |
| Sales | 5 114 | 53 131 | 52 706 | 4 100 |

Source: Food Security Research Project surveys, 1987-89.

## Adoption of Recommended Cropping Practices

Agricultural extension (AGRITEX) provides technology recommendations for communal farmers. In low rainfall areas like Mudzi/Mutoko and Buhera, the recommended maize variety is short-duration R201. In both areas, a majority of farmers used the recommended hybrid, or another hybrid variety (Table 9). For bulrush millet, almost all farmers used the three or four most popular local varieties, as improved varieties are not generally available. Farmers planting groundnuts generally planted local cultivars. The most popular sunflower variety in Buhera was Masasa (67 percent), while in Mudzi/Mutoko farmers preferred to plant Perodovik.

Major recommended crop management practices include autumn ploughing, which enables farmers to plant with the early rains, basal fertilizer, and top-dressing fertilizer. Table 10 shows that in Mudzi/Mutoko, one-quarter to one-half of the farmers autumn-plough all of their crops. About half use basal fertilizer on maize and bulrush millet, while they only top-dress maize. In sharp contrast, Buhera farmers are significantly less likely to autumn-plough, with only a few (14 percent) using basal fertilizer on maize and almost none top-dress their maize.

These results indicate farmers give priority to maize, even in lower-rainfall Buhera which is considered unsuitable for the crop. Particularly in Buhera, there appears to be little adoption of potentially yield-increasing technology.

## Potential for Increasing Production

Production income may be increased by expanding the area under cultivation, increasing yields, or by diversifying to higher-value crops. Policies intended to stimulate supply response -- particularly price policy -- will be effective only if the necessary and sufficient conditions exist (ie., available land, labour, management know-how, and technology).

## Table 9
## Distribution of crop varieties planted
## Mudzi/Mutoko and Buhera Districts, Zimbabwe, 1987-88

| Variety | Frequency (#) | | Percentage (%) | |
|---|---|---|---|---|
| | M/M | Buhera | M/M | Buhera |
| **Maize** | | | | |
| Hybrid R200 | 11 | 25 | 8,8 | 22,3 |
| Hybrid R201 | 77 | 59 | 61,6 | 52,7 |
| Hybrid R215 | 34 | 26 | 27,2 | 23,2 |
| Local | 3 | 2 | 2,4 | 1,8 |
| **Bulrush millet** | | | | |
| Joni | 0 | 50 | 0 | 42,7 |
| Rujiri | 0 | 46 | 0 | 39,3 |
| Nyakashiri | 41 | 8 | 46,7 | 6,8 |
| Bandara | 16 | 0 | 18,6 | 0 |
| Maduni | 9 | 0 | 20,5 | 0 |
| Other | 20 | 13 | 23,3 | 11,2 |
| **Groundnut** | | | | |
| Chinzungwana | 7 | 32 | 20,5 | 52,5 |
| Blantyre | 1 | 20 | 0 | 32,8 |
| Other | 26 | 9 | 79,5 | 14,7 |
| **Sunflower** | | | | |
| Masasa | 7 | 8 | 13,4 | 66,7 |
| Perodovik | 33 | 0 | 63.5 | 0 |
| Pioneer | 7 | 0 | 13.4 | 0 |
| Other | 5 | 4 | 9.6 | 33.3 |

Source: Food Security Research Project surveys, 1987-89.

## Table 10
## Adoption of recommended practices (percent) by crop grown,
## Mudzi/ Mutoko and Buhera Districts, Zimbabwe, 1988-89

| | Autumn ploughing | | Basal fertilizer | | Top dressing | |
|---|---|---|---|---|---|---|
| | M/M | Buhera | M/M | Buhera | M/M | Buhera |
| Maize | 47 | 24 | 50 | 14 | 60 | 7 |
| Bulrush millet | 37 | 9 | 39 | 2 | 1 | 0 |
| Finger millet | 41 | 13 | 0 | 3 | 0 | 0 |
| White sorghum | 23 | 5 | 0 | 0 | 0 | 0 |
| Groundnut | 56 | 12 | 5 | 2 | 2 | 2 |
| Sunflowers | 40 | 0 | 5 | 5 | 3 | 0 |

Source: Food Security Research Project surveys, 1987-89.

## Area Expansion

While there appears to be about 15 percent of the land in fallow in both areas, it is not known why this land is not being cultivated. There are some indications that households have a shortage of labour as many households have male members working outside the area. With the expansion of primary and secondary education, fewer children are now available for farm work. Finally, any effort to expand area is likely to reduce grazing land, already in short supply.

## Availability of Labour

As noted above, farmers reported a shortage of labour at critical periods, particularly for land preparation, weeding, and harvesting. In addition, draft-power ownership is skewed, with many households having inadequate access to draft power. A further constraint on draft power is that animal health is often poor during the autumn and early-ploughing period of recurrent drought seasons.

## Technology Adoption

Currently, yields are relatively low in both Mudzi/Mutoko and Buhera. Except for maize, sunflower, and to some extent groundnut, farmers still use traditional varieties because new sorghum and millet cultivars are either not available or do not exist (Table 9). Other yield-increasing technologies such as fertilizer are currently used primarily on maize and applied at lower than recommended rates. Further analysis will evaluate the returns to fertilizer use and reasons for non-adoption of crop technology. Our working hypothesis is that given the frequency of drought, fertilizer application is quite risky -- particularly at high levels.

Furthermore, we will investigate the availability of credit. Fieldwork suggests that farmers growing crops like small grains do not qualify for credit from the Agricultural Finance Corporation. This is because the low yields make the crops unviable and risky for lending.

## Crop Diversification

Fieldwork suggests that constraints to crop diversification into such crops as cotton include the availability of seed, access to credit to purchase inputs (especially chemicals), lack of knowledge of husbandry practices, and unavailability of transport to market the harvest. Another possible constraint is the availability of appropriate soils and inadequate rainfall for high-value crops like cotton and tobacco.

## INCREASING HOUSEHOLD INCOMES THROUGH CROP MARKETING

Given the important contribution of agricultural production to household incomes, expanding crop sales is a potential strategy for increasing cash income.

## Concentration of Gross Sales

Mounting evidence indicates that the distribution of household grain sales is highly skewed -- not only between regions, but also within them (Stanning, 1988; Rohrbach, 1989; Chigume and Shaffer, 1989). Furthermore, the concentration of grain sales becomes even more skewed following a drought year because production declines most sharply in the low potential natural regions.

Data collected through the income and expenditure surveys show that in the 1988-89 marketing year (April 1988 through March 1989), grain sales in both Mutoko and Buhera Districts were highly concentrated among a small proportion of the farmers. In Mutoko, 16 percent of the households accounted for 87 percent of crop sales (Figure 1). In Buhera, 10 percent of the households accounted for 63 percent of total grain sales (Figure 2). In both areas, over 30 percent of the households market virtually none of their harvest.

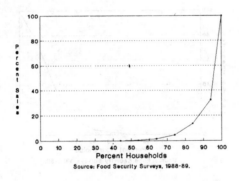

Source: Food Security Surveys, 1988-89.

**Figure 1: Concentration of grain sales : Mutoko/Mudzi District, Zimbabwe**

## Seasonality of Crop Sales and Purchases

Total income derived from crop sales depends on both the quantity sold and when the surplus is sold. In the research areas, sales were highly concentrated after harvest. In Mutoko District, 64 percent of the maize sales were made immediately after harvest (April through August), tapering off to almost no sales (2 percent) between December and March (Figure 3). On the other hand, maize purchases are low throughout the year, with most of the purchases made in August through October.

In contrast, farmers in Buhera District tended to delay maize sales -- with only one-half of their gross sales made between August and November (Figure 4). This delayed pattern may be explained by the fact that southern Buhera is a maize deficit area. Consequently, local market prices are higher than the controlled GMB price. Farmers who manage to produce a surplus, prefer to store their crop in anticipation of selling at higher prices on the local market, rather than selling to the GMB. In fact, the household transaction data shows that maize purchases greatly exceed maize sales during the latter part of the year, indicating that maize maybe flowing into the area from outside the immediate locality.

In Buhera District, the pattern of bulrush millet sales and purchases follow a similar pattern, with transactions concentrated in the early part of the marketing year. Generally, farmers sell bulrush millet to the GMB to obtain immediate cash soon after harvest (Figure 5). Furthermore, the fact that purchases are about 50 percent the level of sales indicates that about half the sales are made on the local market and the other half probably goes to the GMB.

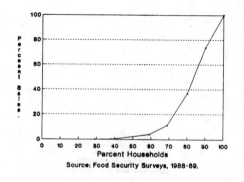

Source: Food Security Surveys, 1988-89.

**Figure 2: Concentration of grain sales : Buhera District, Zimbabwe**

### Factors Determining Gross Market Sales

In order to determine factors associated with interhousehold variability in gross market sales, correlation coefficients were estimated for total grain sales with several variables that characterise the households (Table 11). Several factors were significant. First, market access (approximated by distance to the nearest GMB depot) was significantly correlated with market sales (*ie.*, the nearer the market, the more households gear their production strategies to the market).

Second, in both locations draft-power ownership and gross sales were correlated, although the strength of the relationship was strongest in Mudzi/Mutoko ($r = 0,27$). This relationship may imply that farmers with better access to draft power can cultivate more land  and plant earlier with the onset of the early rains -- thereby obtaining higher yields.

Third, gross grain harvest was only significantly correlated with gross sales in Buhera (r=0,35). This suggests that once households in Buhera meet their consumption needs, they have a higher propensity to market the surplus.

Fourth, the correlation between gross sales and total land area per household member was significant (0,05 percent level), but relatively weak (r=approximately 0,15).

### Table 11
### Correlations between gross grain sales and several
### household characteristics, Mutoko/Mudzi and Buhera Districts,
### Zimbabwe, 1988-89

| Variable | Correlation coefficient[a] | |
|---|---|---|
| | Mudzi/Mutoko | Buhera |
| Distance from GMB depot (km) | -0,2112 (0,01) | -0,1390 (0,08) |
| Total number of draft oxen | 0,2771 (0,01) | 0,0798 (0,20) |
| Total grain harvest (tonnes) | 0,0375 (0,34) | 0,3507 (0,01) |
| Total land area/household (ha) | 0,0472 (0,30) | 0,2409 (0,01) |
| Land/household member (ha) | 0,1685 (0,03) | 0,1530 (0,06) |

[a] Level of significance is in parentheses.
Source: Food Security Research Project surveys, 1987-89.

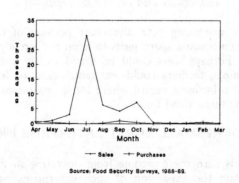

Month

— Sales  —+— Purchases

Source: Food Security Surveys, 1988-89.

**Figure 3: Zimbabwe : Seasonality of maize transactions; Mutoko/Mudzi Districts**

In summary, these results indicate that gross sales are normally higher for households who reside closest to the GMB depot, have better access to draft power, have higher gross production, and have more land/household members than those who participate less in the market.

## Marketing Problems Faced by Households

The problems encountered by farmers in marketing their produce last year (Chigume and Shaffer, 1989) persisted into the 1988-89 marketing year. In fact, they worsened because it was a good year, with marketings exceeding the previous year. However three crucial problems merit further analysis.

### Late Payment

Farmers complained of late payment of up to three months. Most farmers wanted to be paid cash on delivery. This is the most desirable solution, but should be viewed in terms of other constraints faced by the GMB. First, the manpower requirements are high. Second the GMB collects loans on behalf of the AFC, hence problems are bound to surface with some farmers disputing the amount of money they owe the AFC. As a result, the depot personnel may spend considerable time just on public relations. Only if the GMB is relieved of collecting loans on behalf of the AFC would this be a viable proposal.

### Payment on per Kilogram Basis

Most farmers insisted they should be paid on a kilogram basis as does the GMB for cotton. Given that the GMB accepts a bag weighing within the range 89-91 kilograms, and if a farmer is marketing large quantities of grain, the loss of income due to the unpaid kilograms becomes significant. For example, if a farmer sold 25 bags ranging from 89 to 93 kilograms, it means the farmer is losing about 100 kilograms -- almost a bag and a quarter. This amount, if translated in terms of lost income nationally, will show how much the GMB is implicitly "taxing" communal farmers.

### Inadequate and Unreliable Transport

These problems are worsening year after year because of the inability of the country to buy new trucks and spare parts to keep the already dwindled national fleet on the road. Perhaps ways could be found to use available trucks more efficiently. For example, farmers could use scotch-carts to ferry numerous and dispersed outputs to a business centre where lorries would come and collect the grain, thus increasing turnaround time.

## EXPANDING SMALL RURAL ENTERPRISE INCOMES

Currently, households earn some income from operating small rural enterprises. Policies that stimulate the expansion of such enterprises would contribute to improving household food security. Currently, we are analysing data collected from managers of various types of small enterprises found in the study area to identify the problems they face and what policies would relax existing constraints.

## EXPANDING TRANSFER INCOME

Transfer incomes result from both household members working away from home and sending back remittances (private transfers); and the provision of Government transfers such as food-for-work programme (public transfers). Future analysis will focus on analysing in greater detail the nature of transfer income, and identifying factors explaining interhousehold variability in transfer income.

## CONCLUSION AND POLICY IMPLICATIONS

These results have several policy implications for low-potential agricultural regions. First, they raise doubts about the merits of using price policy as a major tool to stimulate rural incomes. It appears that a price policy strategy would adversely affect the many households that increasing evidence suggests are net buyers of grain. Furthermore, given that only a small proportion of the households sell most of the grain marketed, the benefits of higher prices will accrue to a small proportion of the households -- leading to further rural income inequality.

Second, the results have implications for the existing pan-seasonal pricing policy. Pan-seasonal pricing reduces returns to storage, thereby concentrating grain sales in the months just after harvest. At the national level, this places heavy demands on the already over-stretched transport system during this period. In addition, it results in cash inflow in communal areas being highly concentrated during the few months after harvest. Also, pan-seasonal pricing encourages households to sell at harvest and decreases the incentive to home storage, leaving little grain surplus in the area for later in the year. This subsequently exacerbates informal market purchase price swings later in the year and requires transporting grain from national mills back into the communal areas to meet late-season consumption demand.

Third, farmers in the study areas use little high-yielding food crop technology -- except for maize. For other crops, particularly bulrush millet, sorghum and oilseeds, new technology is either not available, does not exist, or is risky. Future increases in low-rainfall production are unlikely to occur unless the research system develops improved varieties for small grains and oilseeds and/or existing improved varieties are better distributed in these areas. Once viable technology becomes available, significant effort will have to be made by the extension service to train farmers how to use it efficiently. Yet, since most new technology requires cash inputs, credit will have to be made available.

Given the diverse nature of constraints facing individual households, it will be necessary to develop a broad-based set of initiatives in order to improve the food security of rural producers, particularly the most food insecure.

## REFERENCES

Chigume, S. and J.D. Shaffer. 1989. Farm Marketing Strategies to Improve Food Security. In: G.D. Mudimu and R.H. Bernsten (eds) *Household and national Food Security in Southern Africa*. Food Security Research Project. Department of Agricultural Economics and Extension. University of Zimbabwe. Harare.

Chopak, C. 1989. Family Income Sources and Food Security. In: G.D. Mudimu and R.H. Bernsten (eds) *Household and National Food Security in Southern Africa*. Food Security Research Project. Department of Agricultural Economics and Extension. University of Zimbabwe. Harare.

Jackson, J.C. and P. Collier. 1988. *Income, Poverty and Food Security in the Communal Lands of Zimbabwe*. Department of Rural and Urban Planning. University of Zimbabwe. Harare.

Rohrbach, D. 1989. *The Economics of Smallholder Maize Production on Zimbabwe: Policy Implications for Food Security*. MSU International Development Paper No. 11. Department of Agricultural Economics and Extension. University of Zimbabwe. Harare and Department of Agricultural Economics. Michigan State University. East Lansing.

Stanning, J. 1989. Grain Retentions and Consumption Behaviour among Rural Zimbabwe Households. In: G.D. Mudimu and R.H. Bernsten (eds) *Household and National Food Security in Southern Africa*. Food Security Research Project. Department of Agricultural Economics and Extension. University of Zimbabwe. Harare.

Stanning, J. 1988. Policy Implications of Household Grain Marketing and Storage Decisions in Zimbabwe. In: M. Rukuni and R.H. Bernsten (eds) *Southern Africa Food Security Policy Options*. Food Security Research Project. Department of Agricultural Economics and Extension. University of Zimbabwe. Harare.

Zimbabwe Government, Central Statistics Office. 1987. *Statistical Yearbook*. Harare.

Zimbabwe Government, Central Statistics Office. *(undated) Quarterly Digest of Statistics*. Harare.

APPENDIX

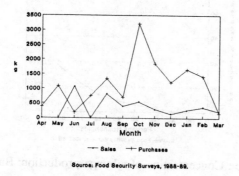

Figure 4: Zimbabwe: Seasonality of maize transactions; Buhera District

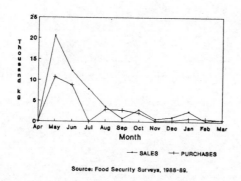

Figure 5: Zimbabwe : Seasonality of mhunga transactions; Buhera District

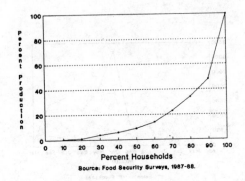

Figure 6:  Zimbabwe : Concentration of mhunga production: Buhera District

# 16

# Industrial Utilisation Of Sorghum And Millet In Zambia: An Approach To Food Security

*David D. Rohrbach[1] and Chungu Mwila[2]*

## INTRODUCTION

Sorghum and millet are broadly known as food security crops in the SADCC region because of their relative drought tolerance. Farmers in each SADCC country's semi-arid regions are commonly advised to plant these crops. Despite this, farmers in the drought-prone regions persist in growing maize. Land historically planted to sorghum or millet has been shifted into maize. This failure to exploit the genetic potential of sorghum and millet has ultimately worsened food security and reduced agricultural productivity in the SADCC region.

The justification for the maize preference can be found in the heavy bias of government support for this crop. National food strategies are preoccupied with maize. Investments in research, extension, credit, input markets, product market infrastructure and processing have heavily favoured maize. In contrast, sorghum and millet are still widely viewed as "traditional crops", "inferior foods" or "poor man's grains". Though efforts have recently been expanded to develop improved sorghum and millet technologies (with strong external assistance), sectoral development strategies encompassing extension, marketing, credit, processing and utilisation remain virtually non-existent.[3]

Strong government support for maize is a by-product of the demand for this crop in urban and industrial markets. Demand has similarly stimulated greater interest in the production of wheat, rice, cotton, oilseeds and other cash crops. Sorghum and millet, in contrast, are not perceived as industrially important. They are not viewed as urban foodstuffs. They are not perceived as strategically important crops.

Food security objectives alone will not justify the implementation of a coordinated programme of production and market support for sorghum and millet. This

---

[1]Principal Economist, SADCC/ICRISAT.

[2]Research Fellow, Rural Development Studies Bureau of the University of Zambia.

programme will only arise out of recognition of these crops as industrially important. It will be stimulated by an expansion of urban demand. In these circumstances, food security might best be viewed as a product of the recognition of these crops as important industrial inputs. A production and market development strategy derived from urban and industrial demand will provide a stronger basis for promoting sorghum and millet than the objective of food security *per se*.

This argument is set forth using Zambia as a case study.[4] Roughly half of this country's 7,5 million people live in urban areas. Population growth averages 3,7 percent with a 5,5 percent growth rate of urbanisation. Zambia is the most highly urbanised of the SADCC countries (GRZ, 1989a; World Bank, 1988). Yet many of the following observations and conclusions apply equally to the other SADCC countries.

## Sorghum and Millet in the Zambian Agroeconomy

### Government Support for Small Grain

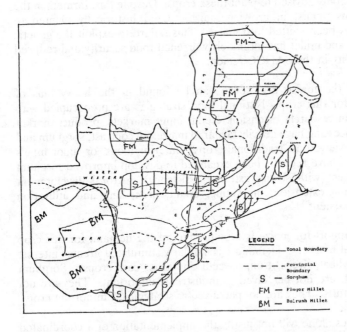

**Figure 1. Areas Most Suited to the Production of Sorghum and Millet in Zambia.**

Almost one-third of Zambia is agroecologically suited to the production of sorghum and millet (Figure 1). The Zambian agroeconomy is dominated, however, by maize. This crop accounts for 85 percent of cereal grain area and over 90 percent of cereal grain production. In comparison, sorghum and millet account for only 12 percent

---

[4]Much of the analysis underlying this paper was conducted in the context of a national traditional crops promotion study for the Government of Zambia.

of cereals area and less than 5 percent of cereal grain production. In 1989, maize, sorghum and millet harvests were respectively estimated to be 1,86 million, 37 000 and 26 000 metric tonnes (GRZ, 1989b).

Over 1,3 million metric tonnes of maize were purchased by the nation's cooperative marketing system after the 1988 harvests. This represented roughly 70 percent of total maize output and 90 percent of the total value of crops marketed through the national cooperative system.[5] In comparison, the Provincial Cooperative Unions (PCUs) purchased less than 700 metric tonnes of sorghum and less than 600 metric tonnes of millet. Small quantities of sorghum and millet were sold on local informal markets, largely for beer production. Most small grains were retained for home consumption.

Maize has dominated the Zambian cereal grains economy since the opening of the copper mines in the early 1950s. At this time, the expansion of maize production was sought as a means to provide cheap food for a burgeoning mine labour force. Rapid growth in copper revenues helped stimulate rapid urbanisation and the Government also used its copper wealth to provide cheap food to its urban population. Heavy investments were made in maize research and extension, credit, input delivery, marketing infrastructure and processing industries. These, in effect, lowered national wage costs. In comparison, sorghum and millet have been virtually ignored.

The magnitude of government support for maize is evident from the massive size of production and market subsidies in recent years. Fertilizer subsidies were established to promote the adoption and use of this input. In conjunction with a major expansion of credit (offered at negative real interest rates), these subsidies have facilitated the widespread adoption of improved maize technology packages. Though the fertilizer subsidy applies to all crops, roughly 90 percent of the subsidy has ended up in the hands of maize producers (GRZ, 1989c). Farmers were strongly encouraged to use subsidised fertilizer on maize. No similar encouragement was offered for the traditional crops.

Transport and handling cost subsidies covering the movement of grain from farm to cooperative depot to end user are a second set of major subsidies favouring maize. These subsidies legally apply only to the collection and assembly of maize. PCUs are fully reimbursed for the costs of maize marketing. This reimbursement applies to each bag of maize handled. No reimbursement is offered for the handling of traditional crops.

The maize transport and handling subsidy prompted NAMBOARD (the now defunct parastatal), and later the cooperatives, to expand market services for maize. Since the reimbursement was paid for each bag of maize handled, the incentive was to maximise the size of the maize intake. If other crops were available for delivery, these could be handled at a smaller marginal cost.[6] Yet the cooperatives had little

---

[5]Provincial cooperatives represent the only formal sector grain marketing channel in Zambia.

[6]In fact, evidence suggests the costs of small grains marketing was at least partially cross-subsidised. Even so, these crops did not offer the assured returns of maize.

incentive to actively seek out deliveries of other commodities such as sorghum and millet. Maize marketing could be viewed as a source of revenue. The marketing of sorghum and millet was viewed as a source of risk.

In addition, Government subsidies were offered to offset the costs of milling maize and the distribution of maize meal to the consumer. These aimed to promote the consumption of maize. Fashioned out of a concern to ensure that all Zambians could meet their basic food needs, these subsidies encouraged a shift in consumption patterns away from traditional crops and in favour of maize.

The heavily subsidised maize was equally available to the brewing and stockfeed industries. In effect, these companies could obtain maize at the farmgate price. In contrast, they had to pay at least a portion of the handling costs for small grains. The production and marketing subsidies aimed at improving national food security were also promoting the development of the beer and stockfeeds industries. As direct (as food) and indirect (as beer and feed) maize consumption grew, even greater priority was attached to the objective of expanding maize production.

By 1986, the burden of maize subsector subsidies had increased to K566 million or more than one-third of the total government budget deficit (Table 1). In 1989, national maize subsidies increased to an estimated K1,5 billion or twice the total budget deficit. Increased Government borrowing and the expansion of the money supply necessary to support this deficit, have contributed to an estimated inflation rate of over 80 percent. This has placed upward pressure on wages while increasing the concern to control food (principally maize meal) prices. Though macro-economic indicators (*e.g.* the debt structure, the foreign exchange deficit and inflation) justify a sharp reduction in subsidy levels, concerns about the welfare of poorer consumers justify the maintenance of maize supports.

**Table 1**
**Zambia maize subsidy payments, 1986-89**
**(K million)**

|  | Fertilizer | Maize | Budget Deficit | Subsidies as Percent of the Budget Deficit |
|---|---|---|---|---|
| 1986 | (a) | 566 | 1 570 | 36 |
| 1987 | (a) | 676 | 1 182 | 57 |
| 1988 (est) | 206 | 1 248 (b) | 1 919 | 76 |
| 1989 (est) | 357 | 1 133 (c) | 730 | 204 |

(a)   Fertilizer subsidy included in maize
(b)   Includes subsidies to millers of K478 million.
(c)   Includes coupon subsidy of K600 million
Source:   Government Budgets, Ministry of Finance and National Commission for Development Planning.

In late June of 1989, the Government announced its intention to end price control for all commodities except maize meal. Subsidy payments were to be reduced and eventually phased out, except for those on maize meal. Markets were to be liberalised (GRZ, 1989c). While the maize subsidies have since been reduced, th phasing and specific form of the entire set of market reforms are still being worked out.

## Production Potential for Sorghum and Millet

The strong Government support for maize has shifted the structure of national production away from a distribution of coarse grains more suited to its agro-ecological circumstances. Large portions of Zambia (indicated in Figure 1) are suited to sorghum and bulrush millet because they are drier, prone to drought and contain less fertile soils. Throughout the northern third of the country, acid soils favour the production of finger-millet. Yet maize production has been encouraged in each of these regions. Farmers have faced a choice of adopting improved maize technologies, with their complement of institutional support, or unimproved small grains technologies lacking extension or marketing assistance.

The impact of historical investments in maize research and extension becomes starkly apparent in a comparison of the relative growth and current levels of alternative coarse-grain yields. Average maize yields have roughly tripled over the past two decades (Figure 2). In comparison, sorghum and millet yields have remained constant. During this period, maize production has risen from 85 to almost 97 percent of total coarse-grains[7] output.

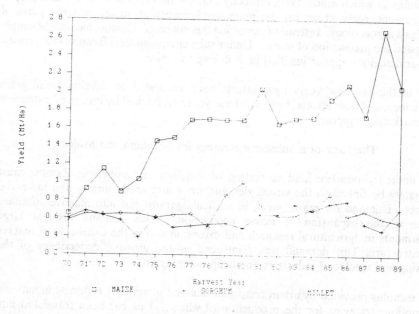

Figure 2: Zambia coarse grain yields, 1970-1989 (kg/ha)

---

[7] Sorghum, millet and maize

These trends are reflected in the relative yields of alternative coarse grains even in the nation's semi-arid areas. In the Gwembe Valley, one of the driest parts of the country, recent yield estimates show maize yields substantially better than sorghum in good rainfall years (Table 2). Maize yields appear only marginally worse in drought years. In the latter, however, average yields are so poor that alternative food sources are required regardless of cropping decisions. In response to such incentives, despite the previous year's drought, more land was planted to maize in 1987-88 than sorghum.

### Table 2
### Maize and sorghum yields in Gwembe District, Southern Province, 1987 to 1989

|  | Maize | Sorghum |
|---|---|---|
|  | - kg per hectare --- | |
| 1986-87 (drought year) | 22 | 108 |
| 1987-88 (high rainfall) | 1 800 | 450 |
| 1988-89 (high rainfall) | 900 | 360 |

Source: Provincial Crop Forecasts 1986-87, 1987-88 and 1988-89.

While sorghum and millets may have a genetic advantage over maize, they no longer have an economic advantage. Sorghum and millet ought to perform well under conditions in which maize faces difficulty. Given appropriate cultivars and proper management, these crops can be more productive than maize in large parts of Zambia's agroecology. Instead of exploiting this potential, Zambia has sought simply to expand the production of maize. Under such circumstances, farmers in Zambia's semi-arid regions appear justified in switching to maize.

Only in the last few years have efforts been expanded to develop small grain technologies. These efforts, however, have yet to be backed by improved extension and marketing support.

### The Lack of a Subsector Strategy for Sorghum and Millet

The limited production and marketing of sorghum and millets in Zambia must ultimately be linked to the strong demand for maize in the urban and industrial market. Demand for maize meal, in particular, translated into massive subsidies favouring the expansion of maize production. This demand brought large investments in agricultural research and extension and in the expansion of market infrastructure. This demand was reinforced by the growing dependence of the brewing and stockfeed industries on cheap maize grain.

The stimulus provided by urban consumer demand is similarly reflected in national promotion strategies for the production of wheat. This has been translated into priority attached to foreign exchange allocations for irrigation equipment, foreign exchange credits and major investments geared to the development of both irrigated and rainfed wheat technologies.

Promotional programmes for cotton, another industrially important crop, have encompassed the establishment of a new parastatal company to promote production and marketing, special training for extension agents, special seed multiplication through contract growers, interest-free credit and direct farmer-to-industry marketing links. Similar strategies have been pursued for the promotion of soyabeans, sunflower, groundnuts, cashewnut and coffee production and utilisation.

In comparison, sorghum and millet appear all but ignored. These may be viewed by some as food security crops, but they are not seen as commercially important. The lack of market demand for sorghum and millet translates into a lack of interest in expanding small grains production. Ultimately, this reduces the food security of small grains producers. The failure to take advantage of the biological advantages of alternative cereal grains also reduces national income, increases disparities in the distribution of national income and raises the nation's need for cereal grain imports.

Subsidies on small grain consumption on a magnitude similar to that historically given to maize makes little sense in the context of extreme government austerity. Relatively little new government investment will be required, however, if existing research, extension and market institutions and programmes are simply stimulated to expand their support for these crops. Such stimulation can most effectively be derived from an expansion of industrial demand.

### Options in the Baking, Brewing and Stockfeed Industries

#### Utilisation in the Baking Industry

One of the strongest justifications for promoting the expansion of sorghum production lies in the cost savings accruing from its use in composite flour. Zambia's wheat demand has been increasing rapidly as a result of urbanisation. For many years, the Zambian baking industry has heavily relied on concessionary wheat imports from the United States, Canada and Australia. These cheap wheat imports have reinforced the expansion of demand. While urban bread demand has prompted placement of a priority on the expansion of domestic wheat production, this remains less than 40 percent of the nation's wheat requirements.[8]

The donors have recently ended concessionary wheat sales to Zambia as a means to stimulate the Country's wheat production. Correspondingly, the National Milling Company (NMC)[9] decided earlier this year to begin adding 6 percent of maize to its wheat flour. The company had ready access to maize in its capacity as a major maize miller. Maize was also chosen because this technology is well tried. Maize composites are commonly employed in neighbouring Zimbabwe. In addition, no other grain was available on local markets in adequate quantities and grades for a composite flour programme. Historical efforts to promote maize production and utilisation had left the grain with little competition.

---

[8] Actual requirements are difficult to estimate in Zambia's rationed market. The domestic wheat milling capacity currently stands at about 100 000 metric tonnes of grain.

[9] Zambia's wheat importer and main miller.

Given the fact that Zambia is likely to remain with a wheat deficit for at least the next seven to ten years, the technical and economic viability of small grain composites ought to be considered. On technical terms, sorghum is, in fact, preferable as a composite with wheat. A range of investigations have shown that maize can be substituted for wheat flour at a concentration of 10-20 percent if both maize and wheat are of high quality. Sorghum can be substituted at rates up to 30 percent in bread flour and up to 50 percent in buns and biscuits (Dendy and Trotter, 1988). In each case, the resulting product should be comparable with a 100 percent wheat bread. Several new sorghum cultivars just released by the Zambian agricultural research service are believed to have good milling characteristics.[10]

The justification for using sorghum also lies in the relative cost savings offered by this input. The NMC must pay approximately K500[11] per 90 kilogram bag of wheat grain. In comparison, subsidised maize costs only K108 per bag and sorghum costs K103. At the current 6 percent level of maize blending, a bag of maize-wheat composite should cost K476,50. At a 15 percent level of blending, a bag of sorghum-wheat composite would cost only K440,50. The savings are even greater with the higher levels of blending feasible in the production of buns and biscuits (Table 3). Altogether, Zambia could save roughly K83 million (on a domestic wheat consumption of 100 000 Mt) by employing a sorghum-wheat composite.[12]

Table 3.
**Comparative cost savings from alternative flour inputs, 1989[a]**

| | Wheat Price (K/Bag) | | Wheat (%) | | Alternative Grain Price (K/Bag) | | Alternative Grain (%) | | Total Cost (K) |
|---|---|---|---|---|---|---|---|---|---|
| **Bread:** | | | | | | | | | |
| Wheat | (500) | x | (100,0) | + | (0) | x | (0) | = | 500,00 |
| Wheat-Maize | (500) | x | (94,0) | + | (108,0) | x | (6,0) | = | 476,48 |
| Wheat-Sorghum | (500) | x | (85,0) | + | 103,0) | x | (15,0) | = | 440,45 |
| | | | | | | | | | |
| **Buns:** | | | | | | | | | |
| Wheat | (500) | x | (100,0) | + | (0) | x | (0,0) | = | 500,00 |
| Wheat-Maize | (500) | x | (85,0) | + | (108,0) | x | (15,0) | = | 441,20 |
| Wheat-Sorghum | (500) | x | (75,0) | + | (103,0) | x | (25,0) | = | 400,75 |

[a] Based on domestic grain prices at mid-1989.

These savings are available despite the current production and marketing subsidies favouring maize. Even if sorghum were priced at double the cost of maize, this should be a preferred wheat substitute.

---

[10] WSV 187, WSV 387 and WSH 287 are hard white sorghums.

[11] K16 = US$1.00

[12] This assumes wheat, maize and sorghum are milled at similar extraction rates, that the milling costs of composite flours are not appreciably higher than pure wheat flour and that 60 percent of Zambia's wheat is allocated to bread.

The savings would not simply be in local currency, but also in foreign exchange. Approximately 73 percent of the costs of producing a bag of wheat in Zambia is in foreign exchange (Clements, 1988). While domestic production saves foreign exchange which might be allocated to wheat imports, it uses substantial quantities of foreign exchange for input imports. Larger savings could be obtained from sorghum blending while benefiting a larger number of farmers.

Further testing is required to examine the technical feasibility of using Zambian sorghums in composite flour. The quality of the grain input is extremely important for milling efficiency and baking quality. Poor quality grain can lead to low extraction rates, poor loaf texture and volume, discoloration, poor crumb structure and limited shelf-life. These milling and baking tests still need to be conducted on a commercial level.

In addition, major efforts are required to promote the adoption of improved technologies (particularly the new hard, white seed varieties) and expansion of market flows. At a 15 percent rate of blending, 15 000 metric tonnes of sorghum grain may be required. In comparison, sorghum sales on the formal market averaged less than 1 000 metric tonnes over the 1980-1988 period. At current average yield levels of only 600 kg/ha, a 50 percent increase in national sorghum hectarage would be required. This would bring total plantings back to the levels of the early 1970s. But if current yields were increased by 50 percent, no new sorghum land would be required.

Production promotion programmes would need to be coordinated with market development efforts. In particular, grain standards required by industry would need to be enforced in the market. Grading practices would need to consider grain colour and hardness as well as moisture content and purity. New mechanisms may be required for grade enforcement.

Given important concerns about grain quality, the NMC may initially choose to purchase most of its sorghum from larger-scale commercial producers situated closer to urban and industrial centres. Yet the stimulus created by the industrial demand for sorghum will ultimately benefit sorghum-growing households which are now food and income insecure. Technological advances alone will benefit these poorer farmers. More broadly, the development of a subsectoral strategy linking research, extension and market support for the small grains will ultimately increase incentives to produce and consume these crops. Investments in developing a sorghum-wheat composite flour can aid food security while yielding industrial profits.

## Utilisation in the Brewing Industry

### *Opaque Beer*

Sorghum and millets are commonly used in the brewing of traditional beers in Zambia. These grains provide an essential source of malt and an important flavouring agent. Correspondingly, they are widely sold in small quantities in localised, informal markets either as whole grains or in dried, germinated form. Maize meal provides the main adjunct ingredient because of its cheaper price. Maize meal subsidies reinforce this competitive position.

In contrast, the opaque beer produced by the monopoly National Breweries Limited (NBL), popularly known as "*Chibuku*", is made entirely from maize. Commercial enzymes are imported to replace the small grains malt. In 1987, the NBL was directed by the Zambian Government to completely substitute sorghum for maize by 1990. This policy was viewed as a means to save maize for direct food consumption and reduce occasional maize import requirements. The NBL set up a contract growers scheme in an effort to promote sorghum production. Participants were offered prices 50 percent greater than the gazetted floor price.

This scheme turned out to be poorly run. The national research service was not consulted about sorghum technologies and management practices. Extension support was limited. Inputs arrived late, if at all. Arrangements for transporting the contracted grain from farm to brewery were poorly coordinated. Further, the NBL had little idea of consumer preferences for sorghum beers. Questions arose in some breweries about whether consumers would accept a red sorghum-based beer. These problems reflect both poor management and the lack of historical support for the small grains subsector. If a framework of government support had been in place (as with maize), the scheme would undoubtedly have run more smoothly.

Regardless of the difficulties the NBL faced implementing the contract growers scheme, the company still had a strong financial incentive to continue using maize. Despite the recent moves to reduce maize subsidies the competitiveness of a sorghum malt is limited. There is no commercial malting capacity in the country.[13] The import price of enzymes is substantially lower than the estimated cost of a sorghum malt. In 1988-89, NBL spent roughly US$340 000 importing malting enzymes to produce 2,5 million hectolitres of beer. These enzymes could be replaced with domestically produced and malted sorghums. But the exchange rate would have to move from K16 to K45 to the US dollar for this option to become competitive (Table 4).

### Table 4
### Comparative costs of imported enzymes and sorghum malt, 1989

|  | Import Cost US$ | K16/US$1 | K45/US$1 |
| --- | --- | --- | --- |
| Enzymes cost | 0,34 million | K5,50 million | K15,3 million |
| Implied malting grain: |  |  |  |
| Cost per metric tonne |  | K 687,50 | K1 912,50 |
| Cost per bag |  | K 61,88 | K 172,13 |
| Sorghum floor price (per bag) |  | 103,00 |  |
| Transport and handling cost (per bag) |  | 43,50 |  |
| Malting production costs (per bag) |  | 15,00 |  |
| Total costs (per bag) |  | 161,50 |  |

[13]Though a feasibility study is nearing completion for a barley malting plant for the clear beer industry.

The economics of sorghum use in adjunct are inconclusive. The extra dehulling costs of producing a sorghum grit may be offset by the higher quality of this input. Maize grits tend to have a higher fat content, particularly if poorly milled. Ultimately, breweries situated in or near sorghum growing regions will face a stronger incentive to use sorghum grain. High transport costs may justify continued maize use in breweries situated in maize surplus regions. The extent of sorghum competitiveness will shift as sorghum-cropping technologies improve and maize subsidies are reduced.

## Clear Beer

As with wheat in composite flour, strong justification exists for the replacement of costly, imported barley with locally grown sorghum in clear beer malt. Zambia currently imports over US$4,0 million worth of barley malt for its clear beer industry. This expense has sparked Government directives to seek self-sufficiency in barley production within three years. Zambia Breweries Limited, in conjunction with a newly established malting company, Zambia Maltings Limited, correspondingly created a contract growers scheme for barley. This offered an incentive price set 20 percent above the NMC wheat price as well as a foreign exchange incentive for every bag in excess of 2 000 produced.

The prospects of achieving self-sufficiency in barley production within the next decade are limited. Few farmers participated in the barley scheme despite the price incentive. In effect, farmers with irrigation are being asked to take land out of winter wheat. At the same time, the NMC keeps raising its wheat buying prices to attract more resources to the production of wheat. Foreign exchange constraints severely limit the speed with which irrigated land can be expanded.

It is technically feasible for sorghum malt, with supplementary commercial enzymes, to replace imported barley. This substitution is already underway in Nigeria (Uche, 1985). Economic analysis reveals the use of sorghum could save US$3,9 million on imported malt inputs (barley malt costs minus the cost of enzymes necessary for use with sorghum). Sorghum could be priced up to K328 per bag and still be competitive. If the barley price continues to rise with the increases in wheat prices resulting from domestic wheat shortages, the incentive to switch to sorghum malt will grow further. Ultimately, Zambia can save the foreign exchange required for both barley malt and irrigation infrastructure.

The use of sorghum for clear beer adjunct is less competitive than its use as malt. Roughly the same parameters apply as in the consideration of sorghum for opaque beer adjunct, except the quality standards of the grain and grit must be higher. The industry needs a hard, white sorghum which is easily milled and has a low fat content. Again, the relative competitiveness of maize and sorghum will ultimately depend on their market prices and the value of the respective milling by-products. Hard white sorghums might initially be allocated to composite flour production. As supplies enlarge, substitution in clear beer adjunct can be initiated.

### Utilisation in the Stockfeed Industry

Zambia produces roughly 160 000 metric tonnes of stockfeeds per year. Virtually all of this uses maize as the principal energy component. This converts to roughly a 65 000 metric tonne maize requirement. While industry growth has been severely limited in recent years due to shortages of protein, mineral and vitamin supplements, the industry has strong growth potential. Coarse grain consumption in the developing world is growing fastest in the stockfeed industries.

It is technically feasible to fully replace maize with sorghum or millet in the production of stockfeeds. The actual level of substitution will depend on the relative prices of alternative energy and protein sources. The higher protein level of sorghum, compared to maize, is offset by the higher tannin content of most feed grain sorghums. This leads to roughly a 5 percent price differential on world coarse grain markets. Because low tannin white sorghums do not suffer this constraint, they will be employed at prices equal to or marginally higher than maize. Bulrush millet, with a higher fat content than maize, similarly will be used at a marginally higher price.

Table 5 indicates what Zambia grain prices would need to be to justify substitution of alternative energy inputs. Though white sorghum is priced below its feed value, virtually none is available on the market. This gazetted price does not attract white sorghum supplies. The competitiveness of red sorghum is offset by the transport and handling subsidies for maize. The millets are simply uncompetitive.

### Table 5
### Zambia: comparative feed grain prices, 1989
### (K per bag)

|  | Floor Price | Feed Value Price |
| --- | --- | --- |
| Maize (graded) | 108 | 108,0 |
| Sorghum (white) | 103 | 108,0 |
| Sorghum (red) | 103 | 102,6 |
| Bulrush Millets | 198 | 118,8 |
| Finger Millet | 198 | 108,0 |

The current low prices for maize on Zambian markets simply discourage the use of alternative inputs. Perhaps more seriously, maize marketing channels are well developed. These offer a consistent flow of a relatively consistent quality of grain. In contrast, small grains market flows are inconsistent and limited. If small grains, particularly sorghum, become more competitive as a result of concerted production and marketing support, they will first be used in stockfeed plants situated closer to the small grains growing areas. The stockfeeds industry may also benefit from access to milling and brewing industry small grain by-products.

### SUMMARY:
### THE NEED FOR A SMALL GRAINS ACTION PLAN

Maize has come to be recognised as Zambia's pre-eminent food security crop because of its importance as an industrial input and urban foodstuff. Wheat, for similar reasons, is increasingly being recognised as a strategic crop. Barley has become important out of a concern to reduce the brewing industry's demand for foreign exchange. In each case, demand pressure has stimulated the expansion of research, extension, credit and market support. In contrast, support for small grains languishes.

A sorghum and millet development strategy for Zambia cannot simply be based on a perception of their drought tolerance. While food security may be a significant political goal, this does not translate into the investment and policy setting required to promote the production and marketing of these crops. A small grains promotion strategy can be more effectively derived from a recognition of the industrial value of these crops. Urban and industrial demand should be mobilised to stimulate the demand for new technologies, improved extension support and expanded marketing assistance.

The Zambian economy has a clear and immediate need for a promotion programme favouring small grains, particularly sorghum. Wheat imports are being cut off. Sorghum-wheat composites will extend limited domestic supplies and reduce import requirements. Barley malt imports are increasingly expensive. Domestically-produced sorghum could fully offset this requirement. In both cases, foreign exchange required for the importation of irrigation equipment could be saved. The exact formula for composite mixtures and malts requires testing. Careful attention to grain standards and market grades is required. As maize subsidies are reduced and eventually eliminated, sorghum and millet will become increasingly competitive in the stockfeed industry.

Finally, it should be noted that these circumstances are not unique to Zambia. Sorghum and millet production has been declining through most of the SADCC region. Little sorghum and millet enters formal sector markets. Industrial demand for these commodities is extremely limited due to uncompetitive prices and variable market flows. This results in little interest in these crops in ministries of agriculture. Sorghum and millet are simply not viewed as strategic crops. An examination of their urban and industrial market potential holds the promise of reversing this bias.

## REFERENCES

Clements, D.J. 1988. *A Preliminary Economic Analysis of Rainfed Wheat Production in Zambia.* Report submitted to CIDA. June 1988.

Dendy, D.A. and B.W. Trotter. 1988. Wheatless and Composite Breads, Technologies Awaiting Adoption. *Lebensmittel Technologies* (6) : 13-18.

Government of the Republic of Zambia (GRZ). 1989a. *Fourth National Development Plan.* Republic of Zambia, Lusaka.

Government of the Republic of Zambia (GRZ). 1989b. *Provincial Crop Forecasts for 1986-1989.* Mimeo.

Government of the Republic of Zambia (GRZ). 1989c. *New Economic Recovery Programme Economic and Financial Policy Framework 1989-1993.* Republic of Zambia. Lusaka.

Uche, Nena. 1985. Wanted: A Brewer for Femos Beer *The Guardian.* Tuesday March 19 1985.

World Bank. 1988. *World Development Report 1988.* World Bank. Washington. D.C.

# 17

# Supply, Demand And Marketing Of Principal Food Grains In Lesotho

*Joseph Lefa Mokotjo*[1]

## INTRODUCTION

Most economic challenges faced by Lesotho in the process of attaining efficient economic growth, equitable distribution of income, nutritional well-being, and food security are common to those faced by many African countries and developing countries in the world. These challenges include a weak industrial base relative to Europe and North America, increasing pressures on land resources, inadequate infrastructure, insufficient transport and communication networks and a growing rural population. Lesotho's population of about 1,6 million is growing at rate of 2,6 percent *per annum*. Population growth is outpacing the growth of agriculture which provides a livelihood to the majority of the society.

Only 393 939 hectares, or 13 percent of total arable land is suitable for cropping. The remainder of the country is largely mountains with the highest peak of 3 482 metres. The highlands of Lesotho support the livestock industry.

The agricultural sector is characterised by declining production of staple grains, decreasing relative share of the sector in the gross national product because of a reduction in agricultural output, and decreasing arable land both in *per capita* and absolute terms due to urban sprawl and soil erosion. The climate is characteristic of high levels of variability and drought during the growing season.

The majority of the farmers are smallholders, some of which live at the margin of existence. All farmers grow staple grains under rainfed conditions. Risks associated with dry farming in Lesotho are compounded by drought during the growing season and early frosts in April. As a result, risk avoidance dominates economic considerations in decision-making. Having limited resources and low risk-bearing capacity, many farmers are reluctant to adopt new technological packages. Preference is for choices that reduce risks, even if these choices provide less potential for economic improvement than alternatives. In most cases, risk aversion influences farmers to adopt production packages and practices which do not maximise resource use.

---
[1]Chief Marketing Officer, Ministry of Agriculture, Cooperatives and Marketing (MOACM), Maseru, Lesotho

This paper addresses the supply and demand situation of the principal grains in Lesotho: maize, wheat and sorghum. Marketing issues are also addressed. First, the segmentation of the rural sector as it relates to supply and demand for staple grains is presented. Second, the supply and demand situation is discussed followed by an overview of marketing patterns and processing.

## DESCRIPTION OF RURAL HOUSEHOLDS AND FARMERS BY RESOURCE DIFFERENCES

A general consensus among planners and decision-makers is that resource differences among farmers dictate differences in management practices and potentials to produce a surplus and earn income from crop production. As such, government programmes and strategies for agricultural development should take into account differences of farmers in terms of resources. Unfortunately, farmers are, in most cases, treated as a homogeneous group.

The results of the 1979 Census of Agriculture reveals an inequitable distribution of arable land. For example, 50 percent of the arable land in Lesotho is held by 20 percent of the farm households. The majority of these large farmers produce a surplus for urban markets and generate the largest farm incomes. Also, the majority of this group own livestock and necessary resources such as farm machinery to exploit land to its optimal potential. Farmers in this group do not need group action to command confidence in the eyes of credit institutions so as to obtain capital. They are well versed about new technological packages and well informed of Government policy direction and support programmes. This group knows where to obtain both technical and policy advisory services. Consequently, it is a group that captures a large share of Government agricultural programmes.

The second category is resource-poor households who lack adequate support services (*e.g.* credit) to meet their family food needs. The resource-poor group represented 55 percent of the agricultural households in the 1979 agricultural census. Farmers in this category possess some arable land and/or livestock but unfortunately these resources are underutilised. As a result they depend on the market for food, starting a few months after harvest. From November through February when food stocks in most rural households are depleted, grain is purchased from the few "surplus grain" farmers, the depots of Co-op Lesotho (the largest grain buying institution in Lesotho) or is imported from the Republic of South Africa (RSA).

The majority of the farmers in the second category have inadequate support services to efficiently utilise their land resources. They rely on hired machinery or share-cropping. The little income generated from farming is supplemented by off-farm incomes by members of the families employed in urban areas or in the mines of South Africa.

According to the 1986 Population Census, 75 percent of the rural households possess arable land, down from 89 percent in 1970. The Census reveals that 47 percent of rural households possessed land and livestock and 17 percent had no land. The number of households who had no arable land and livestock was 20 000, 35 000 and 46 000 in 1970, 1980 and 1986, respectively. This is a third group of rural households.

The resource-poor households can benefit from lower food prices and employment generation programmes from agro-industries, and labour-intensive horticultural crops. Agricultural enterprises which require little land such as poultry, dairy and piggery can also provide income for the landless.

## SUPPLY SITUATION OF MAIZE, WHEAT AND SORGHUM

The total supply of grain in Lesotho is simply an aggregate of domestic production, commercial imports and food aid. Table 1 presents a ten-year trend of these three components of total supply. It can be deduced from the table that domestic production of wheat and maize has been declining since 1978-79. The index of maize self-sufficiency was 61 percent in 1978-79 but it dropped to 42 percent in 1983-84 and remained at this level through 1987-88. The share of wheat in domestic production dropped from 64 percent in 1978-79 to 18 percent in 1987-88. Self-sufficiency in sorghum has remained at 90 percent over the past decade.

### Table 1
### Total supply for five major crops 1978-79 to 1987-88
### (whole grain basis '000 tonnes)

| | --- MARKETING YEAR --- | | | | | | | | | |
| | 1978-79 | 1979-80 | 1980-81 | 1981-82 | 1982-83 | 1983-84 | 1984-85 | 1985-86 | 1986-87 | 1987-88 |
|---|---|---|---|---|---|---|---|---|---|---|
| **COMMERCIAL IMPORTS** | | | | | | | | | | |
| Maize | 85,3 | 83,0 | 95,7 | 102,0 | 87,2 | 94,9 | 99,8 | 102,3 | 97,9 | 110,5 |
| Wheat | 30,8 | 31,5 | 30,3 | 23,9 | 22,0 | 31,8 | 32,0 | 32,0 | 32,0 | 41,4 |
| Sorghum | 1,8 | 1,4 | 1,0 | 1,7 | 3,3 | 1,3 | 1,0 | 1,0 | 1,0 | 3,4 |
| Pulses | 0,5 | 0,2 | 0,5 | 0,5 | 0,6 | 0,7 | 0,7 | 0,7 | 0,7 | 3,4 |
| **DONATED IMPORTS** | | | | | | | | | | |
| Maize | 6,0 | 8,0 | 10,0 | 15,0 | 12,0 | 9,0 | 9,0 | 15,0 | 15,0 | 20,5 |
| Wheat | 1,3 | 6,9 | 7,4 | 6,4 | 11,8 | 20,6 | 26,6 | 30,7 | 31,0 | 42,9 |
| Sorghum | 0 | 0 | 0 | 0 | 0 | 0 | 0 | 0 | 0 | 0 |
| Pulses | 0,4 | 1,0 | 0,5 | 0,7 | 0,7 | 1,1 | 1,1 | 1,6 | 1,6 | - |
| **TOTAL IMPORTS** | | | | | | | | | | |
| Maize | 91,3 | 91,0 | 105,7 | 117,0 | 99,2 | 103,9 | 108,8 | 117,3 | 112,9 | 131,0 |
| Wheat | 32,1 | 38,4 | 37,7 | 30,3 | 33,8 | 52,4 | 58,6 | 62,7 | 63,0 | 84,3 |
| Sorghum | 1,8 | 1,4 | 1,0 | 1,7 | 3,3 | 1,3 | 1,0 | 1,0 | 1,0 | 3,4 |
| Pulses | 0,9 | 1,2 | 1,0 | 1,2 | 1,3 | 1,8 | 1,8 | 2,3 | 2,3 | 0,7 |
| **DOMESTIC PRODUCTION** | | | | | | | | | | |
| Maize | 143,2 | 124,9 | 105,6 | 105,7 | 83,0 | 76,2 | 79,4 | 92,4 | 86,5 | 94,9 |
| Wheat | 57,9 | 33,6 | 28,2 | 17,0 | 14,5 | 14,8 | 17,1 | 18,4 | 18,4 | 18,5 |
| Sorghum | 85,8 | 69,0 | 59,3 | 47,7 | 26,0 | 30,7 | 33,8 | 54,8 | 33,6 | 31,2 |
| Pulses | 15,2 | 15,3 | 8,1 | 6,7 | 7,1 | 4,0 | 5,0 | 5,8 | 5,3 | 4,8 |
| **TOTAL SUPPLY** | | | | | | | | | | |
| Maize | 234,5 | 215,9 | 211,3 | 222,7 | 182,2 | 180,1 | 188,2 | 209,7 | 199,7 | 225,9 |
| Wheat | 90,0 | 72,0 | 65,9 | 47,3 | 48,3 | 67,2 | 75,7 | 81,1 | 74,0 | 102,8 |
| Sorghum | 87,6 | 70,4 | 60,3 | 49,4 | 29,3 | 32,0 | 34,8 | 55,8 | 34,6 | 34,6 |
| Pulses | 16,1 | 16,5 | 9,1 | 7,9 | 8,4 | 5,8 | 6,8 | 8,1 | 7,6 | 5,5 |

Sources: BOS; Lesotho Flour Mills; Marketing Section. Planning Division. Ministry of Agriculture; Catholic Relief Services; World Food Programme; Food Management Unit.

As indicated earlier, a significant portion of national food grains is produced by resource-poor farmers who have limited land, agricultural equipment and capital resources. Increased production is dependent on access to sufficient land, capital, management, and modern inputs. In other words, the selection of appropriate crops and technology is guided by production resources to efficiently utilise land.

Table 2 presents the area planted to the five principal crops as a proportion of total arable land for the period 1977-78 to 1986-87. Maize ranks first. An average of 44 percent of total arable land allocated to five crops (maize, sorghum, wheat, beans and peas) is planted to maize. Sorghum ranks second followed by wheat. This ranking does not necessarily imply the relative profitability of these crops.

**Table 2**
**Land use by maize, sorghum and wheat as a percent of total arable land**
**1977-78 to 1986-87**

| Year | Maize | Sorghum | Wheat | Pulses |
|---|---|---|---|---|
| 1977-78 | 38 | 21 | 16 | 7 |
| 1978-79 | 40 | 18 | 12 | 6 |
| 1979-80 | 40 | 22 | 10 | 5 |
| 1980-81 | 46 | 21 | 8 | 5 |
| 1981-82 | 43 | 20 | 8 | 10 |
| 1982-83 | 43 | 19 | 11 | 6 |
| 1983-84 | 46 | 21 | 11 | 7 |
| 1984-85 | 48 | 27 | 14 | 6 |
| 1985-86 | 49 | 20 | 9 | 8 |
| 1986-87 | 49 | 24 | 9 | 8 |

Source: Bureau of Statistics, (1987).

Table 3 displays the trends in area planted and the production of maize, sorghum and wheat. Table 3 also shows that there is an upward trend in maize area and that the majority of landholders in Lesotho prefer to grow maize.

The production of maize, sorghum and wheat in Lesotho has been decreasing since 1978-79. The record yield and production levels have never been regained.

Aggregate staple grain production (maize, sorghum, and wheat) dropped by four percent over the period 1979-80 through 1986-87. However, it grew by 3,3 percent in the period 1981-82 to 1986-87. *Per capita* grain production over 1981-82 to 1986-87 fell by 7 percent. Unfavourable climatic conditions such as severe droughts that occurred during the period 1980-81 to 1983-84 are major causes of production decline.

Commercial imports of maize and wheat have been increasing steadily over the last seven years. The amount of donated maize and wheat in whole grain terms has remained steady. Most of commercial imports come from the Republic of South Africa. Commercial imports of sorghum are insignificant, partly because sorghum is less preferred to maize as a daily meal; it is mainly used for beer brewing. The indigenous sorghum variety is preferred to imported varieties for beer brewing.

**Table 3**
**Production trends for maize, sorghum and wheat**
**1977-78 to 1986-87**

| Year | Maize Area Planted (Ha) | Maize Production (Tonnes) | Sorghum Area Planted (Ha) | Sorghum Production (Tonnes) | Wheat Area Planted (Ha) | Wheat Production (Tonnes) |
|---|---|---|---|---|---|---|
| 1977-78 | 111 530 | 143 168 | 62 033 | 85 775 | 45 606 | 57 906 |
| 1978-79 | 122 338 | 124 856 | 54 102 | 68 952 | 37 977 | 33 629 |
| 1979-80 | 118 460 | 105 619 | 64 537 | 59 286 | 30 650 | 28 194 |
| 1980-81 | 136 521 | 105 674 | 63 735 | 47 729 | 23 539 | 16 993 |
| 1981-82 | 136 668 | 83 028 | 58 673 | 26 148 | 26 992 | 14 462 |
| 1982-83 | 126 824 | 76 180 | 56 947 | 30 687 | 31 846 | 14 810 |
| 1983-84 | 138 665 | 79 384 | 62 569 | 33 768 | 33 497 | 17 127 |
| 1984-85 | 144 903 | 92 350 | 81 594 | 54 823 | 43 132 | 18 434 |
| 1985-86 | 141 484 | 86 488 | 57 175 | 33 440 | 25 999 | 11 009 |
| 1986-87 | 166 683 | 94 912 | 78 670 | 31 232 | 29 395 | 18 520 |
| | | | | | | |
| 10 Year Average | 134 076 | | 640 035 | | 328 633 | |

Source:  Bureau of Statistics, (1987).

## DEMAND FOR MAIZE, SORGHUM AND WHEAT

Maize, sorghum and wheat are utilised for human and animal consumption. Demand for these cereals is affected by population growth, milling and processing capacity, changes in income, and the growth and development of intensive animal production. White maize is the most preferred food staple for human consumption. Sorghum is the least preferred for daily consumption but is used for weaning food, and soft porridge. It is mainly used in brewing traditional beer.

Substantially increased demand, particularly for maize and sorghum, is expected in the livestock industry.  This expansion will be induced by the new feed mill with a capacity of 12 000 tonnes of animal feed per year per single shift.  Yellow maize will be used as a major raw material because it is most suitable as an energy feed for chicken and pigs.

As it is well known, the food balance sheet is used to display average food consumption levels.  But the food balance sheet does not provide information about the consumption patterns by the poor and the rich or by rural and urban inhabitants. Household budget surveys can provide a clearer picture of food distribution patterns if data are collected on expenditures and quantities of individual commodities consumed.  The differences in prices among regions and seasonal price differences should also be taken into account.

Table 4 presents estimates of human consumption of cereals in Lesotho that have been calculated from the production data provided by the Bureau of Statistics (BOS) and imports statistics compiled by the Ministry of Agriculture, Cooperatives and Marketing.  The data on stocks were obtained from the major roller-mills and the Food Management Unit for 1979 through to 1988.  The coefficients for animal feed, seed, harvest and post-harvest losses were established by the Early Warning Unit of the Ministry of Agriculture.

### Table 4
### Per capita income of maize, sorghum and wheat in Lesotho
#### (average for 1977-78 to 1986-87)

| Item | Maize | Sorghum | Wheat | Total |
|---|---|---|---|---|
| Production (tonnes) | 99 000 | 47 000 | 23 100 | 169 100 |
| Harvest & post harvest loss & seed retention (%) | 15 | 15 | 15 | |
| Animal feed (%) | 10 | 10 | 10 | |
| Net Production (tonnes) | 74 250 | 35 250 | 17 325 | 126 825 |
| Change in stocks | 6 500 | 0 | 5 500 | 12 000 |
| Commercial imports (tonnes) | 94 231 | 1 500 | 29 586 | 125 317 |
| Donated imports (tonnes) | 11 000 | 0 | 15 855 | 26 855 |
| Total consumer supply (tonnes) | 185 981 | 36 750 | 68 266 | 290 997 |
| Milling and processing loss (%) | 10 | 15 | 12 | |
| Net for consumption (tonnes) | 167 383 | 27 563 | 60 074 | 255 030 |
| *De facto* population (middle period) | --- 1 364 998 --- | | | |
| Annual *per capita* consumption (kgs) | 123 | 20 | 44 | 187 |

Source: Compiles by the author

Estimates of the human consumption levels derived from Table 4 in annual *per capita* terms are 123kg for maize, 20kg for sorghum and 44kg for wheat. These estimates are comparable with those of 1983-85 Food Balance Sheet compiled by the FAO for Lesotho as follows, 126kg, 32kg and 47kg for maize, sorghum and wheat, respectively. Of course, these average figures mask food access issues.

The total demand for the three food grains derived from Table 4 and the present requirements of the feed-mill are 202 756 tonnes, 41 450 tonnes and 85 176 tonnes for maize, sorghum and wheat, respectively. A significant increase in demand is expected over time due to population growth and the expansion of intensive livestock production.

## MARKETING

Marketing issues discussed in this paper embrace distribution, storage, processing and pricing for maize, sorghum and wheat. The Government of Lesotho places highest priority on development of market infrastructure, improvement of storage and transportation logistics for efficient distribution of food commodities.

There are two types of marketing chains for staple grains in Lesotho. The first chain involves farmers, traders, and consumers. The transactions take place largely at the village level, where transport costs are minimal. The produce is sold in small quantities ranging from 18kg to 70kg. The second chain involves farmers, Co-op Lesotho, millers, retailers and consumers. Farmers in need of cash bring their produce after harvest to Co-op Lesotho depots where they obtain prices no less than minimum prices set and gazetted by Government. Co-op Lesotho grades and assembles small lots into 70kg bags for transportation to the roller mills.

## Pricing Policy

The pricing alternative adopted by Government is the principle of import parity pricing for importables and export parity pricing for exportables. This policy recognises that the country cannot afford potential losses to Government that may be incurred in the form of subsidies to support farm level prices above regional prices.

Prices of staple grains in the region are fixed for a year for many reasons. Setting prices for staple grains on parity with the cost of importing them into Lesotho minimises smuggling of the same products.

Though import parity pricing may not provide signals as to what are the economic and physical advantages to be exploited in production, it has an in-built mechanism to minimise smuggling across borders. Otherwise, Government regulatory work would need to be expanded and enforcement machinery would be required. Sales of Lesotho food grain products would be reduced in the case of lower prices in the markets of the RSA. There would be inefficiencies in the milling industry. In the case of retail prices in the RSA being lower, there would be untenable potential pressure on Government.

## Disparity of Prices Between the Formal and Informal Sector

Prices in the informal sector are higher than prices prevailing in the formal sector. Spot checks made by the Marketing Division of the Ministry of Agriculture indicate that prices for grains in the informal sector are between 10 and 50 percent higher than those paid by buyers in the formal sector (Co-op Lesotho and the roller-mills). Consumers in the informal sector relate the price of grains to the value of the products milled by the roller-mills and distributed by the retailers. The cost of milling in the informal sector is lower than the retail price for the unsifted meal processed by the roller-mills. Another reason for the higher value of grains in the informal sector is that grains keep better than meal.

## Processing and Storage

The available storage capacity in the country is 119 519 tonnes. The only storage facility that can receive grain in bulk are the 60 000 tonne silos in Maseru. The rest have no rail connections with the outside world.

Giant steps have been made by Government to establish agro-industries to capture value-added, generate employment and stimulate increased production in th country. The domestic milling capacity for maize is 128 000 tonnes *per annum* provided by three major roller-mills. The capacity for commercial milling for maize is currently sufficient to meet demand. The milling capacity for wheat is 50 000 tonnes *per annum*.

## REFERENCES

Ministry of Agriculture and Bureau of Statistics. 1987. *Agricultural Situation Report, 1977-78 to 1986-87.* Maseru.

Bureau of Statistics (BOS). 1987. *Household Budget Survey 1986-87.* Maseru.

Olson, R.E. 1985. *Marketing Patterns and Long-Term Demand for Maize Meal in Lesotho.* Maseru.

Timmer, C.P., W.P. Falcon and S.R. Pearson. 1983. *Food Policy Analysis.* The Johns Hopkins University Press. Baltimore.

# V

# The Potential Role Of Livestock And Cash Cropping In Food Security

V

# 18

# Cashcropping And Food Security In Swaziland : A Background To Further Research

*V.M. Sithole and J. Testerink*[1]

## INTRODUCTION

The world's food problem is nothing new. Satisfying man's food needs has always been a struggle for the majority of the world's population. Many have *frequently, if not continuously, suffered from, at best, an inadequate food supply and, at worst, from hunger if not starvation* (Dilon, 1984 :4). However today, hunger, actual or potential, is no longer seen as a natural part of the human condition because, with improved communication and technology, there is a general awareness of the problem, and science and technology are now seen as possibly capable of providing a solution to the problem.

In support of the latter point, the World Bank states that the world has ample food: *The growth of global food production has been faster than the unprecedented population growth of the past forty years* (World Bank, 1986a :1). Despite this, some 34 percent of the population of the developing world -- excluding China -- still does not eat well enough to lead an active working life and nearly half of these are barely subsisting on a minimum survival diet. This means that about 730 million people do not have enough food, and amongst those, there are some 340 million persons who are acutely undernourished (World Bank, 1986a).

In the global sense, and often in individual countries, inadequate food production is no longer the source of the problem. Problems with food security do not necessarily result from inadequate food production; they also arise from a lack of purchasing power on the part of nations and of households. Food security can be ensured in the long run by raising the real incomes of households so that they can afford to acquire enough food (World Bank, 1986b). The production of cashcrops can be regarded as one way to increase rural incomes.

The present paper will explore the impact of cashcropping on food security, focusing on the situation in Swaziland. As some of the cashcropping in Swaziland takes the form of contract-farming, due attention will be given to this concept. The first section of the paper will deal with the definitions of food security, cashcropping and contract-farming. This will be followed by a brief description of government policies pertaining to cashcropping, and an overview of cotton and tobacco production in

---

[1]Social Science Research Unit, University of Swaziland.

Swaziland.  We will then focus more specifically on the relationship between cashcropping and food security.  We will conclude with a number of research questions to be addressed in further investigations.

## DEFINITION OF TERMS

### Food Security

Food security can be defined as dependable access by all people (in a homestead, village, region or nation) at all times to enough food for an active and healthy life. Thus the food security issue can be analysed in terms of availability of food due to own production, and access to food, mainly through ability to purchase. An analysis of food security can be carried out at household level, village level, regional level and national level.

Two kinds of food insecurity exist.  There is chronic food insecurity if there exists a continuously inadequate diet caused by the inability to acquire food.  It affects the family, village, region, or nation that persistently lacks the ability either to buy enough food or to produce their own.  There is also transitory food insecurity if there is a temporary decline in a household's access to enough food.  It results from instability in food prices, food production, or people's incomes -- in its worst form, it produces famine (World Bank, 1986a).

Food security at the national level can be seen in terms of the country's ability to produce enough food for its population's requirement, or to have enough foreign exchange to be able to import from other countries either part or all of the food required.  At the regional (village) level, the analysis would involve investigations of the region's (village's) ability to produce enough food for itself, or the ability to import food from outside.  Food security analysis at the household level requires an understanding of the household's ability to either produce enough food or to generate enough effective demand to purchase food or to obtain food transfers.

### Cashcropping

Cashcropping, or commercial farming, can be defined as growing a crop[2] with the purpose of selling it.  A cashcrop then is a crop that is sold for cash or what Maxwell (1989 : 3) calls the common sense definition.  This definition easily applies to non-edible cashcrops.  For example, cotton produced on the farm and marketed is a cashcrop.  For edible crops, however, when high yields are achieved due to favourable rainfall, more farmers would be commercialised than in years with lower yields.  However, in both years the farmer would have used the same amount of resources with the aim to meet subsistance needs in a normal year.  In a good year, however, there would be a "windfall" marketable surplus.

In our view, any definition of cashcropping should take into consideration a deliberate goal of the farmer to produce marketable surplus (see Testerink, 1984 for an elaborate definition).  In the context of food security, or more specifically the

---

[2] It would also include raising livestock, but for the purpose of this paper, this aspect of commercial farming was excluded.

effect of cashcrops on food security, it may be argued that the production of edible cashcrops other than "luxury" crops like sugar (*i.e.*, the sale of a deliberately produced surplus), reflects a situation of farm level self-sufficiency. There may be exceptions however; the farmer who sells produce directly after harvest to satisfy short-term cash needs or due to storage problems, only to buy food (at a higher price) later. A further example would be the farmer who entered into a contract and is therefore under the obligation to sell all or part of his crop. For the purpose of this paper however, we exclude the production of edible crops as a cashcrop, and we will focus on those farmers growing cotton and tobacco, the major non-edible cashcrops on Swazi Nation Land[3].

Cashcroppers (cotton and/or tobacco growers) reallocate the factors of production, *i.e.* land, labour and capital, to cashcrops, where they could have been used for the production of foodcrops. Thus, we exclude from this paper cashcropping on contract-farming schemes taking place on land not allocated to the homestead. Contract-farming is regarded here as a special type of cashcropping, where farmers are bound by a contract, enjoy a secure market, receive extension advice and can purchase inputs on credit. Farmers in these schemes may therefore find it easier to secure an income from cashcropping, which may reflect positively on their food security status. On the other hand, they may find it harder to reach food self-sufficiency because they are bound by a contract out of which there is no escape, and they may very well be pushed into a next contract by the company.

### Contract-farming

Contract-farming is an institutional form whereby agricultural production is carried out according to an agreement between farmers and a buyer which specifies certain production and marketing arrangements (Jaffee, 1987 :1). In a preface to Jaffee's article (1987), Watts and Little mentioned the following three characteristics of contract-farming: (i) a futures or forward market in which a buyer or processor commits himself in advance to purchase a crop acreage or volume; (ii) the linkage of product and factor markets insofar as purchase rests on specific grower practices or production routines and input and/or service provision by buyer-processors; and (iii) the differential allocation of production and marketing risk embodied in the contract itself.

Contract-farming arrangements vary considerably. Falling under the generic term contract-farming include specific contractual arrangements such as satellite farming, nucleus estate, outgrower schemes, *etc.* Notwithstanding specific differences, the contract-farming arrangements have some common features. The grower supplies labour, some of the inputs and the funding, and transport facilities. The buyer (who could be a private firm, public agency or a joint venture of several types) may supply technical assistance, loans, inputs or marketing services. The arrangement often specifies the conditions of sale (price, quality, volume, *etc.*) and the division of risks and responsibilities between the partners. The buyer retains the right to reject substandard produce.

---

[3] In Swaziland, no contract-farming arrangements exist for edible cashcrops such as maize. A further reason is that it may be impossible in practice to identify edible (staple) cashcroppers, as there is no suitable sample frame.

Proponents of contract-farming argue that it has, among others, the following advantages for the farmer: the promise of secure access to inputs and technical advice that might not otherwise be available to peasant producers; deductions from delivery imply that the lack of cash to pay for these inputs upon delivery need no longer act as a barrier to peasant access to vital agricultural resources; the *skills and discipline acquired through adaptation to modern agronomic practices involving adherence to strict time-tables for planting and harvesting, for the application of specified quantities of fertilizers and insecticides, the need for keeping accounting records, etc., would spill over into other producers and for the economy as a whole* (Daddieh and Jonah, 1987 :8). Farmers are also assured a ready market for their crops, hence a regular source of income, and where the buyer offers no loan, generally banks will accept a contract as collateral.

On the other hand critics of contract-farming argue that it is an institution developed by powerful economic and political groups to increase agricultural productivity and specialisation, to appropriate the gains from these improvements, and to pass on the relevant costs and risks to farmers. It further creates and strengthens market imperfections so that private interests gain at the expense of social misallocations of resources. In addition, the buyer controls the more profitable sector, *i.e.* the marketing of the final product, and the buyer benefits by gaining greater control over a crop than possible under spot market conditions, yet he does not incur the costs and risks of actual investment in production. Often the buyer is in a monopsonistic position, thus he is not only able to dictate prices but also to manipulate standards to make adjustments for raw material and market imbalances. Furthermore, farmers tend to be locked into a dependent relationship with the buyer because of the increased crop specialisation and use of material inputs. The farmers tend to lose their autonomy, as the buyer controls many agronomic decisions.

Contract-farming tends to concentrate on the production of relatively high-value commodities for export rather than basic foods for local consumption. Some arrangements require settling farmers onto identified land (often owned by the buyer or the State) in order to take part in the scheme. On the other hand, some contractual arrangements involve farmers using their own land.

## GOVERNMENT POLICIES

The Swaziland Government has given priority and emphasis to cashcropping for a long time. In the Post Independence Development Plan, one of the objectives was to ... *convert the Swazi farmer from being a cultivator, eking out a subsistence existence supplemented by wage earning, to a full time profitable yeoman class of farmer.* (Swaziland Government, 1969 : 67). This objective is reiterated in the Second National Development Plan, 1973-1979, where the first aim of agricultural policy is listed as being ... *to assist Swazi farmers in making the transition from subsistence activity to semi-commercial and commercial farming.* (Swaziland Government, n.d. :45). The transition was expected to be attained by increasing the marketed production of key foodcrops and cashcrops (especially maize, cotton and tobacco) by Swazi farmers, primarily by raising crop yields per hectare and by introducing more farmers to cash farming. The Third and Fourth National Development Plans echo this policy on cashcropping.

Contract-farming, as explained above, is a special type of cashcropping. Its history in Swaziland goes as far back as the early 1960s when Vuvulane Irrigated Farms were established. Mention of productive contract-farming schemes first appeared in the Post Independence Development Plan (Swaziland Government, 1969 : 16,30). The Second and Third Plans are silent on contract-farming. But contract-farming is cited in the Fourth National Development Plan, 1983-84 to 1987-88 where ... *it is widely recognised that future agricultural development in the modern sector should concentrate on more labour-intensive irrigation schemes on the nucleus/smallholder model. The experience of Vuvulane is considered to provide a successful example in this respect.* (Swaziland Government, 1985 : 145).

The main programme to assist SNL farmers in making the transition from subsistence to commercial farming has been the Rural Development Areas Programme, initiated before independence in 1968  The programme, partly financed with British aid and World Bank loans, included physical reorganisation of land use patterns, provision of improved infrastructure, as well as the provision of extension services, input supplies and credit facilities. The results have not been very good though, and implementation of the programme *per se* was stopped after 1983, when external funding of the programme came to an end. No further large-scale rural development programmes have been mounted since then. Aided development now takes place through *ad hoc* funded projects, none of which are specifically directed towards cotton or tobacco production.

## COTTON AND TOBACCO PRODUCTION IN SWAZILAND

### National Level

The importance of cashcrops at the national level can be illustrated by listing a number of variables, such as the contribution to Gross Domestic Product, creation of employment opportunities, the number of farmers growing cashcrops, the area under these crops and the total output. We have made some attempts to calculate the contribution to the GDP, but because the figures provided by the Central Statistical Office on national accounts are so erratic and for most years so obviously wrong, we decided not to pursue the issue.

Data on employment in the cashcropping sector on SNL are not available. Some studies however give indications of labour hired by cashcroppers. An example is a survey of 140 cotton farmers in the southern part of the Lowveld, carried out in 1980, which shows that 62,9 percent of these surveyed cotton farmers hire labour for harvesting, with an average of 13,3 hired labourers (Sterkenburg and Testerink, 1982 : 33-34). It has also been argued that labour shortages, especially during the harvest period, form a constraint on the extension of cotton production (*e.g.,* FAO, 1981 : 37-38), thus indicating potential employment opportunities.

Figures on the number of cashcroppers over the years are also scarce. From the few available figures, it appears that the number of tobacco growers remains fairly constant at about 3,5 to 4 percent of all SNL homesteads (3,9 percent in 1971-72; 4 percent in 1978-79 and 3,5 percent in 1983-84; (Testerink, 1984 : 19). The now defunct Casalee contract-farming tobacco scheme contributed significantly to an increase in the number of tobacco farmers. In this scheme alone, the number went up from 25 in 1985 to an estimated 410 in 1987, thus representing 1,9 percent of all

SNL homesteads in the Middleveld (Levin, 1987 : 36). The number of cotton growers increased from 3,9 percent in 1971-72 to 13,5 percent in 1978-79 and then dropped to 8 percent in 1983-84 (Testerink, 1984 : 19).

The cotton growers are concentrated in the Lowveld, as is clearly shown in Table 1, probably because of favourable climatic conditions for growing cotton, and unfavourable growing conditions for growing the staple crop, maize. Two thirds of the cotton growers can be found in this agro-ecological zone, an additional quarter are located in the Middleveld. Furthermore, a high 22 percent of all SNL farmers in the Lowveld grow cotton. The majority of the tobacco growers are situated in the Highveld (42,6 percent) and the Middleveld (40,1 percent), but proportionally, the Lubombo and Highveld regions score highest: 4 percent and 5,4 percent of farmers here grow tobacco. In total, 11,1 percent of all SNL homesteads can be defined as cashcroppers.

## Table 1
### Regional distribution of cashcropping SNL, 1983-84

| | Cotton growers No. | % | Tobacco growers No. | % | All cash-croppers No. | % | All SNL homesteads No. | % |
|---|---|---|---|---|---|---|---|---|
| Highveld | 127 0.9% | 3,0 | 785 5.4% | 42,6 | 895 6.2% | 15,2 | 14 465 100% | 27,2 |
| Middleveld | 1 123 5,1% | 26,5 | 739 3,4% | 40,1 | 1 776 8,1% | 30,1 | 22 033 100% | 41,5 |
| Lowveld | 2 699 22,0% | 63,7 | 146 1,2% | 7,9 | 2 800 22,8% | 47,5 | 12 259 100% | 23,1 |
| Lubombo | 208 6,6% | 6,8 | 172 4,0% | 9,3 | 426 9,8% | 7,2 | 4 349 100% | 8,2 |
| Swaziland | 4 237 8,0% | 100 | 1 842 3,5% | 100 | 5 897 11,1% | 100 | 53 106 100% | 100 |

Source: Data from CSO Agricultural Census (1983-84).

The area under major crops on Swazi National Land is reported in the Annual Statistical Bulletins of the Central Statistical Office (Swaziland Government, 1980-1987). These are the only source used here, even though there are unexplained variations in figures published in different years but pertaining to the same growing season. It is the only source, however, that provides annual figures.

Table 2 gives an overview of the area under cotton, tobacco and maize. Maize is clearly the most important crop in terms of area: about three quarters of all cropped SNL land is under this crop in any given year. The area under tobacco is difficult to interpret, as the total area under this crop is small, and relatively small variations can change the overall picture dramatically. It is clear, however, that the area under tobacco as a percentage of total cropped SNL is extremely small: it never gets near the 1 percent mark. The area under cotton increased considerably between 1971-72 and 1978-79, from almost 4 000 hectares (4,9 percent of cropped SNL) to

17 709 hectares (18,0 percent). Thereafter, however, the hectarage dropped to 6 492 hectares in 1983-84 (8,6 percent). A possible explanation for this is stagnating cotton prices, accompanied by an increase in the cost of production, possibly resulting in a shift towards maize production. This argument is supported by a comparison of gross margins for maize and cotton, as presented in a recent World Bank report (1987: Table 7), reproduced here as Table 3, and by the increase in the area under maize from 72,3 percent in 1978-79 to 84 percent in 1983-84 (Table 2).

### Table 2
### Area under cotton, tobacco and maize, 1971-1987, SNL

| | Cotton | | Tobacco | | Maize | |
|---|---|---|---|---|---|---|
| | Total area (ha) | % of total cropped SNL | Total area (ha) | % of total cropped SNL | Total area (ha) | % of total cropped SNL |
| 1971-72 | 3 933 | 4,9 | 308 | 0,4 | 62 311 | 78,0 |
| 1972-73 | 3 493 | 4,1 | 319 | 0,4 | 70 555 | 81,9 |
| 1973-74 | 9 666 | 10,6 | 507 | 0,6 | 68 851 | 75,8 |
| 1974-75 | 11 336 | 13,1 | 260 | 0,3 | 60 999 | 70,4 |
| 1975-76 | 10 130 | 12,2 | 561 | 0,7 | 59 799 | 72,0 |
| 1976-77 | 7 925 | 11,2 | 582 | 0,8 | 53 902 | 76,3 |
| 1977-78 | 7 013 | 10,1 | 582 | 0,8 | 53 902 | 77,3 |
| 1978-79 | 17 709 | 18,0 | 254 | 0,3 | 71 145 | 72,3 |
| 1979-80[a] | 17 709 | 18,0 | 254 | 0,3 | 71 145 | 72,3 |
| 1980-81 | 13 035 | 16,9 | 524 | 0,7 | 55 654 | 72,4 |
| 1981-82 | 11 575 | 14,5 | 524 | 0,7 | 58 936 | 74,1 |
| 1982-83 | 7 536 | 13,2 | 419 | 0,7 | 44 143 | 77,1 |
| 1983-84 | 6 492 | 8,6 | 167 | 0,2 | 63 582 | 84,0 |
| 1984-85[a] | 6 492 | 8,6 | 167 | 0,2 | 63 582 | 84,0 |
| 1985-86[a] | 6 492 | 8,6 | 167 | 0,2 | 63 582 | 84,0 |
| 1986-87[a] | 6 492 | 8,6 | 167 | 0,2 | 63 582 | 84,0 |

[a] Estimates.
Source: CSO Annual Statistical Bulletins 1980-1987, Cotton Board Annual Reports.

Assuming that cotton farmers are capable of producing maize at a high level of efficiency, the higher gross margin for maize may induce cotton growers in the Middleveld, whose maize growing conditions are better than in the Lowveld, to shift to maize. The returns per man-day for maize (both intermediate and optimum) are substantially higher, thus warranting the shift for the Middleveld farmer (Table 3). An additional factor may be the Government's promotion of maize self-sufficiency around the early eighties, thus pushing (mainly Middleveld) farmers into maize production. A further explanation may be a shift to off-farm wage employment, with, on the one hand, higher returns per man-day than the E2,50 earned by producing cotton and, on the other hand, a more secure income source (especially in view of a drop in yields due to a severe drought during the period when the decline in hectarage under cotton started). Most probably, however, the decline in area under cotton can be ascribed to a combination of these factors. A recent decline in off-farm wage employment opportunities however, has probably resulted in a situation where cotton production is again a good way of earning a cash income,

Total cotton production and yield have fluctuated widely over the years, from a modest 2 282 tonnes in 1971-72 to a record 14 922 tonnes in 1980-81. Yields ranged from a low 540 kg/ha in 1978-79 to a high 1 692 kg/ha in 1977-78 (Figure 1), which is likely to be explained by variations in rainfall.

### Table 3
### SNL crop budgets, 1985 prices

| Crop | Yield[a] kg/ha | Total costs per ha | Total output value per ha | Man-days per ha | Gross margin[b] E/ha | Return per man-day E |
|---|---|---|---|---|---|---|
| Maize intermediate[c] | | | | | | |
| - Highveld | 2 550 | 333 | 791 | 78 | 458 | 6,1 |
| - Middleveld | 1 770 | 259 | 527 | 65 | 268 | 4,1 |
| - Lowveld | 850 | 178 | 264 | 60 | 86 | 1,4 |
| Maize optimum[d] | | | | | | |
| - Highveld | 4 250 | 563 | 1 318 | 50 | 755 | 15,1 |
| - Middleveld | 2 550 | 384 | 791 | 45 | 407 | 9,0 |
| - Lowveld | 1 275 | 270 | 395 | 40 | 125 | 3,1 |
| Cotton | 850 | 714 | 398 | 125 | 316 | 2,5 |
| Tobacco air-cured | 700 | 515 | 910 | 145 | 395 | 2,7 |

[a] Gross yield less 15 percent for harvest/storage losses.
[b] Including family labour.
[c] Tractor-ploughing, ox-harvesting and sowing, hybrid seed, medium fertilization, hired assistance for weeding; improved storage, active farmers.
[d] Commercial farmers on SNL (less than 10 percent of households), tractor cultivation, adequate fertilizer and weeding by herbicide.
Source: The World Bank (1987 : Table 7).

Studies have been carried out on contract-farming in Swaziland. Levin (1987) gives a detailed overview of production schemes, in which contract-farming arrangements are mentioned. Mkhabela (1985) studied the Vuvulane Irrigated Farms -- a sugar cane contract-farming scheme. Boeren and Sithole (1989) recently did research on Vuvulane and Mphetseni (a pineapple scheme). However, none of these studies mentioned above make reference to the contribution of contract-farming to food security. There is a need to investigate the contribution of contract-farming to food security. The two main buyers of cotton in Swaziland are Cotona and Clark Cotton. Both have contractual arrangements under which the buyers give individual farmers inputs on credit, in return for an obligation of the farmer to sell all his cotton to the buyer, who then deducts the loan from the sales.

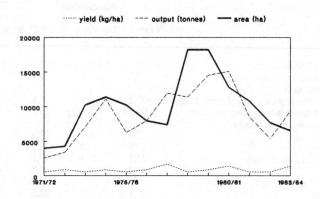

····· yield (kg/ha)   ––– output (tonnes)   ▬▬ area (ha)

**Figure 1: SNL cotton area, output and yield, 1971-72 to 1983-84**

### Household Level

#### *Socio-economic characteristics*

Further analysis of data from the Agricultural Census 1983-84 shows that cashcroppers have a significantly larger population residing on the homestead: 9,7 versus 7,7 for non-cashcroppers (Table 4), thus enabling them to draw upon a larger labour pool. Nevertheless, as was shown above, labour availability for the most labour consuming tasks has been regarded by some authors as a bottleneck in the further development of commercial production, especially cotton.

Cashcroppers (especially cotton growers) are generally "better off" than non-cashcroppers. Cattle ownership, often used as a wealth indicator, is significantly higher among cashcroppers, whose mean herdsize is 19,4 head of cattle compared with a herdsize of 14,8 for non-cashcroppers. About a fourth of the cashcroppers and a half the non-cashcroppers do not own cattle.

There is no significant difference in terms of the use of modern building materials, but other criteria relating to production do show significant differences. Tractor ownership, as well as oxen-span ownership is much higher among cashcroppers, and the use of tractors for ploughing is much more prevalent. Extension services are used more frequently by cashcroppers, which clearly indicates that this is a more progressive group of farmers, especially when we take into consideration that extension workers are often meeting with groups of farmers rather than visiting individual homesteads, which means that the farmer has to go out and collect the extension message. Where extension workers do visit individual farmers, however, they tend to focus their attention on the more progressive farmers.

## Table 4
### Some socio-economic characteristics of SNL cashcroppers 1983-84[a]

| | Cashcroppers | | | Non cash-croppers | All SNL home-steads |
|---|---|---|---|---|---|
| | Cotton | Tobacco | All | | |
| Total number of homesteads | 4 237 | 1 842 | 5 897 | 47 209 | 53 106 |
| Resident population (mean) | 9,7 | 9,7 | 9,7 | 7,7 | 8,0 |
| Number of cattle held | | | | | |
| (owned + kept for someone else)(mean herdsize) | 21,2 | 15,5 | 19,4 | 14,8 | 15,4 |
| Percentage of homesteads owning no cattle | 28,5 | 19,5 | 25,9 | 47,3 | 45,0 |
| Modern building materials used on: | | | | | |
| All dwellings | 12,5 | 6,7 | 10,9 | 9,5 | 9,7 |
| Most dwellings | 13,2 | 12,2 | 12,9 | 13,5 | 13,4 |
| Less than half of dwellings | 25,1 | 33,7 | 27,5 | 28,8 | 28,6 |
| None | 49,2 | 47,4 | 48,7 | 48,2 | 48,3 |
| Main method of ploughing: | | | | | |
| Tractors only | 27,4 | 9,9 | 22,3 | 14,5 | 15,4 |
| Oxen only | 51,1 | 60,2 | 53,9 | 60,7 | 59,9 |
| Tractors and oxen | 13,9 | 25,1 | 17,0 | 11,9 | 12,5 |
| Percentage of homesteads owning one or more tractors | 14,3 | 5,3 | 11,5 | 2,3 | 3,3 |
| Percentage of homesteads owning at least one span of oxen (6 or more) | 36,2 | 39,5 | 36,9 | 22,2 | 23,9 |
| Use of extension service: | | | | | |
| Six or more times per year | 10,1 | 11,7 | 10,6 | 4,8 | 5,4 |
| Three to five times per year | 8,7 | 8,8 | 8,8 | 4,3 | 4,8 |
| One or two times per year | 19,4 | 18,9 | 19,0 | 10,8 | 11,7 |
| No contact with extension workers | 61,7 | 60,6 | 61,6 | 80,1 | 78,1 |
| Commercial fertilizer usage: | | | | | |
| Every year on most crops | 26,5 | 45,4 | 32,2 | 31,0 | 31,1 |
| Most years on most crops | 12,8 | 13,0 | 12,6 | 7,6 | 8,1 |
| Less than half of the years on less than half of the crops | 18,4 | 19,5 | 18,6 | 15,4 | 15,7 |
| Not used | 42,3 | 22,1 | 36,5 | 46,0 | 45,0 |

[a] In percentages, unless stated otherwise.
Source: Data from CSO Agricultural Census (1983-84).

There is no significant difference in the use of commercial fertilizers, although tobacco growers use fertilizers significantly more often.

### Area under crops

As part of the Agricultural Census 1983-84, a sample survey was carried out and land was measured. Table 5 shows results from further analysis of this data, giving areas under various crops. The mean total area under crops is significantly larger for commercial farmers than for non-cashcroppers: 3,2 hectares versus 1,5 hectares per homestead. This is also reflected in the distribution over farm-size categories, where only 22,1 percent of the cashcroppers own less than one hectare of cropped land and more than half have more than two hectares. For the non-cashcroppers, these figures are 51 percent and 22 percent respectively.

Although commercial farmers keep less than half of their land under maize (48,8 percent), as opposed to 87,7 percent by non-cashcroppers, the mean area under maize is not significantly different for the two groups: 1,4 hectares and 1,3 hectares respectively. This may lead to the conclusion that the "surplus land" is used for the cashcrops. In other words, land has been set aside for maize production to satisfy home consumption. Conceivably, higher maize yields amongst cashcrop farmers will probably offset the larger families of these farmers, especially under Middleveld and the Highveld growing conditions.

## Table 5
### Areas under different crops, SNL, 1983-84

| | All cashcroppers | | | Non cashcroppers | All SNL homesteads |
|---|---|---|---|---|---|
| | Cotton growers | Tobacco growers | Total | | |
| Number of homesteads | 242 | 57¹ | 295 | 2 502 | 2 797 |
| **Total area under crops, excluding fallow:** | | | | | |
| < 0,5 ha | 5,8% | 12,3% | 6,8% | 27,1% | 24,9% |
| 0,5 - 1,0 | 14,5 | 19,3 | 15,3 | 23,9 | 23,0 |
| 1,0 - 2,0 | 28,1 | 26,3 | 27,8 | 27,1 | 27,1 |
| ≥ 2,0 | 51,7 | 42,1 | 50,2 | 22,0 | 25,0 |
| Mean (ha) | 3,2 | 2,0 | 3,0 | 1,5 | 1,6 |
| Mean area left fallow | 0,1 | 0,1 | 0,1 | 0,1 | 0,1 |
| **Area under maize:** | | | | | |
| 0 | 8,7 | - | 7,1 | 1,2 | 1,9 |
| < 0,5 | 28,5 | 19,3 | 26,4 | 31,0 | 30,5 |
| 0,5 - 1,0 | 20,2 | 22,8 | 20,3 | 25,0 | 24,5 |
| 1,0 - 2,0 | 21,1 | 38,6 | 24,7 | 24,9 | 24,9 |
| ≥ 2,0 | 21,5 | 19,3 | 21,4 | 17,9 | 18,2 |
| Mean % kept under maize | 42,9 | 73,4 | 48,8 | 87,7 | 83,6 |
| Mean (ha) | 1,3 | 1,4 | 1,4 | 1,3 | 1,3 |
| Mean for those growing maize (ha) | 1,4 | 1,4 | 1,5 | 1,3 | 1,3 |
| **Area under cotton** | | | | | |
| 0 | - | 93,0 | 18,0 | 100,0 | 91,3 |
| < 0,5 | 34,7 | 3,5 | 28,5 | - | 3,0 |
| 0,5 - 1,0 | 21,1 | 1,8 | 17,3 | - | 1,8 |
| 1,0 - 2,0 | 25,2 | 1,8 | 20,7 | - | 2,2 |
| ≥ 2,0 | 19,0 | - | 15,6 | - | 1,6 |
| Mean % kept under cotton | 49,3 | 3,8 | 40,4 | - | 4,3 |
| Mean (ha) | 1,6 | 0,05 | 1,3 | - | 0,1 |
| Mean for those growing cotton (ha) | 1,6 | 0,8 | 1,6 | - | 1,6 |
| **Area under tobacco:** | | | | | |
| 0 | 98,3 | - | 80,7 | 100,0 | 98,0 |
| < 0,5 | 1,7 | 93,0 | 18,0 | - | 1,9 |
| 0,5 - 1,0 | - | 7,0 | 1,4 | - | 0,1 |
| 1,0 - 2,0 | - | - | - | - | - |
| ≥ 2,0 | - | - | - | - | - |
| Mean % kept under tobacco | 0,1 | 9,0 | 1,8 | - | 0,2 |
| Mean (ha) | - | 0,2 | 0,03 | - | - |
| Mean for those growing tobacco (ha) | 0,03 | 0,2 | 0,2 | - | 0,2 |
| **Area under other foodcrops[a]:** | | | | | |
| 0 | 37,6 | 19,3 | 33,9 | 35,7 | 35,5 |
| < 0,5 | 44,6 | 57,9 | 47,1 | 53,4 | 52,8 |
| 0,5 - 1,0 | 10,3 | 12,3 | 10,8 | 7,2 | 7,5 |
| 1,0 - 2,0 | 6,2 | 8,8 | 6,8 | 2,6 | 3,1 |
| ≥ 2,0 | 1,2 | 1,8 | 1,4 | 1,1 | 1,1 |
| Mean % kept under other foodcrops | 7,8 | 13,8 | 9,0 | 12,3 | 11,9 |
| Mean (ha) | 0,3 | 0,3 | 0,3 | 0,2 | 0,2 |
| Mean for those growing (ha) | 0,4 | 0,4 | 0,4 | 0,3 | 0,3 |

[a] Includes: beans, groundnuts, pumpkins, cowpeas, sesame, mungbeans, sorghum, jugobeans, soyabeans, sunflower, rice, yams, sweet potatoes, melons, cabbages, tomatoes, onions, potatoes, garden, orchard, bananas, and "other crops".
Note that in the categories of areas, the upper boundaries are excluded.
Source: Data from CSO Agricultural Census, (1983-84).

Cotton farmers on average have 1,6 hectares under cotton, which clearly shows the importance of the crop. This is reiterated by the fact that these farmers keep, on average, almost half their land under this crop. Tobacco farmers keep an average of 9 percent of the land under tobacco, which means that this crop also is an important income source for these farmers.

As is the case with maize, there are no significant differences between the groups concerning the area under other foodcrops. Presumably, food production is thus secured before farmers embark on cashcrop production, although we should keep in mind that Lowveld conditions for growing maize are generally unfavourable, resulting in low yields.

Unfortunately, there are no figures available on production and yields, total income, or the contribution of cashcrop income to total homestead income. Further research in this area is clearly needed.

## CASHCROPPING AND FOOD SECURITY

In defining cashcropping, we have largely focussed on farm-level criteria, for the simple reason that we propose to test the hypothetical effect of cashcropping on household-level food security. The underlying, simplified, hypothesis here is that cash earned from cashcrop sales can be used for the purchase of food, thus stressing access to, rather than production of, food; the two aspects of food security.

Because the cashcrops under review are also export crops from a national point of view, food imports may have to compensate for food not produced locally because of cashcrop production.

Food availability and affordability is thus determined also by policies on food trade and pricing policies. Maxwell (1989 : 23) quotes cases where increasing agricultural exports were associated with rising food prices caused by declining food production and restricted imports (e.g. Brazil in the 1970s); thus endangering national food security. He then goes on to quote studies in Bangladesh and Ethiopia, where it was found that food imports fluctuated in direct proportion to foreign exchange earnings from export agriculture. He recognises that this evidence does not prove that food imports compensate fully for food required but not produced locally, but it does suggest that they are linked. As the country would thus be dependent on international food prices these examples may also be counted ... *as part of the case against export agriculture, by showing that national food security is a hostage to international commodity prices.* (Maxwell, 1989 : 24). Policies towards cashcropping can therefore not be held constant. State interventions in import regulations and price policies may be required.

Von Braun and Kennedy (quoted by Maxwell, 1989 : 24), based on a literature survey, found that there is no apparent trend in the effect of cashcropping on the level of household food security; in some case the effect was positive, in other cases it was negative. Two studies done by the FAO of ... *tea in Kenya and cotton in Zambia found that nutritional status was independent of cashcropping.* (Maxwell, 1989 : 24). The results of a study by Kennedy and Cogill (1988 : 1 079) suggest a positive impact of cashcropping (sugar in Kenya) on household incomes, as well as on househol' ~~l~rir intake; both effects, however, were found to be small. The extent to which such development can be replicated elsewhere however, they state, would depend on factors such as ... *effects of cashcropping on real income, sources and control of income, agricultural production strategies, expenditure pattern, household decision making, demand for land and labour, and allocation of food and other resources within the family.* (Kennedy and Cogill, 1988 : 1 080). They conclude by stating that *The conventional wisdom that an increased emphasis on commercial agricultural production necessarily results in a deterioration of household food security is not borne out by the data from the present study.* (Kennedy and Cogill, 1988, : 1 080).

Studies explicitly dealing with the relationship between cashcropping and food security in Swaziland are non-existent. Two studies, dealing with nutritional status, and touching upon this issue could, however, be identified. The first one is a study by Cappetta, who monitored dietary intake in approximately 100 households using a 24-hour recall and questionnaire method, during the period June 1978 to June 1979. She states that ... *overall, the Middleveld and Highveld diets were more adequate than the Lowveld diets, when excluding the cashcropping areas, Lavumisa and Vuvulane[4], from the sample.* (Cappetta, 1983 : 174), thus implicitly indicating that in these cashcropping areas the dietary intake was more adequate than in the rest of the Lowveld. She continues to observe that ... *nutrition appeared most favourable in Vuvulane, a full-time sugar producing and cashcropping area.* (ibid : 174). The sample from this area, however, is very small (six households) and when testing the effect of income from cashcropping on nutritional status of households, the relationship was not found to be significant (Cappetla, 1983 : 185).

The National Nutrition Survey (Swaziland Government, 1983 : 40) also did not find a significant relationship between the occurrence of stunting[5] and the type of crop grown on the homestead. Those homesteads growing cotton and tobacco had occurrences of 12,2 percent severe stunting, 16,4 percent moderate stunting and 71,4 percent none. The figures were not found to be significantly different from the total rural sample or from the Highveld agro-ecological zone where cashcropping is least prevalent (ibid : 62) (see also Table 6). But these results have to be treated with caution, however, as the study did not actually focus on the relationship between cashcropping and the nutritional status. The cashcroppers are all regarded as one group, thus neglecting the importance of the proportion of land under the crop and nutritional status to total homestead income. Such data is unfortunately not available, and the research proposed here seeks to fill this gap.

Other studies, dealing with the relationship between cashcrop production and foodcrop production on homestead level suffer from similar problems. In a recent study on land tenure (Marquardt, 1988), a group of commercial maize and cotton/tobacco producers was not found to be significantly different from non-commercial farmers where the ability of the homestead to produce enough maize

---

[4] Lavumisa is situated in the southern part of the Lowveld, which is characterised by a high prevalence of cotton production; Vuvulane is an irrigated contract-farming scheme in the north of the Lowveld, where major crops are sugar and vegetables.

[5] Stunting was expressed as severe; moderate; and none, based on height-for-age Z-scores of children younger than five years.

to feed itself was concerned. An earlier study by Testerink (1984) indicates that of the cotton/tobacco farmers, 78,6 percent suffer a calculated maize deficit[6], and in the year 1982-83 they bought an average of 215 kilograms of maize per consumption unit, which is roughly equal to the annual requirement (Testerink, 1984 : 26). Of this group of cashcroppers, 92,6 percent purchased some maize during the year, whereas for all other groups of farmers[7] this percentage varied around 75 percent. Although there are obvious problems with the translation from purchasing figures to the level of maize self-sufficiency (1982-83 was a dry year; farmers may sell maize just after harvest either because of immediate cash needs or because of lack of storage facilities, *etc.*), the study indicates that cashcroppers were not maize self-sufficient and therefore had to buy food.

**Table 6.**
**Percentage distribution of stunting, by agro-ecological zone.**
**Rural sample only, 1983**

|  | Severe stunting | Moderate stunting | No stunting | n |
|---|---|---|---|---|
| Highveld | 10,5 | 19,5 | 70,0 | 1 108 |
| Middleveld | 10,4 | 21,3 | 68,3 | 1 603 |
| Lowveld | 8,9 | 19,2 | 71,9 | 1 226 |
| Lubombo | 10,7 | 24,1 | 65,1 | 196 |
| Total | 10,0 | 20,3 | 69,7 | 4 133 |
|  |  |  |  |  |
| Cashcroppers (n) | 12,2 | 16,4 | 71,4 | 372 |

Source: Swaziland Government (1983).

This finding is contradicted by an analysis of recent Agricultural Census data where a statistically significant difference was found between cashcroppers (defined as cotton and/or tobacco growers) and non-cashcroppers where maize self-sufficiency was concerned: 23,3 percent of the cashcroppers claim to always produce enough maize for homestead consumption, versus 15,9 percent of the non-cashcroppers. On the other end of the scale, a quarter of the cashcroppers and 35,1 percent of the non-cashcroppers never produce enough (Table 7).

Each of the three studies mentioned here arrives at a different conclusion, ranging from a negative impact of cashcropping on maize self-sufficiency, via no impact, to a positive impact. Each of these studies has its own shortcomings and set of definitions, which may very well explain the differences in outcome. It is, however, clear that there is a definite need for further research, aimed at the relation between cashcropping and food security. Furthermore, none of the studies have touched upon the role contract-farming schemes (can) play in cashcropping *cum* food security.

---

[6] The calculation was based on potential production levels in a "normal" year, taking into consideration use of inputs, farm technology, area under crops, *etc.* for the individual homestead.

[7] A total of seven groups was identified, ranging from non-commercial farmers with insufficient land to various types of semi-commercial and commercial farmers.

### Table 7
### Cashcropping and maize self-sufficiency, 1983-84

|  | Cashcroppers |  | Non-cashcroppers |  | Total |  |
|---|---|---|---|---|---|---|
| Always enough[a] | 1 372 | 23,3 | 7 501 | 15,9 | 8 873 | 16,7 |
| Mostly | 1 218 | 20,7 | 8 716 | 18,5 | 9 934 | 18,7 |
| Sometimes | 1 818 | 30,8 | 14 445 | 30,6 | 16 263 | 30,6 |
| Never | 1 489 | 25,3 | 16 547 | 35,1 | 18 036 | 34,0 |
| Total | 5 897 | 100,0 | 47 209 | 100,0 | 53 106 | 100,0 |

[a] "Always" means 100 percent of the time; "Mostly" means greater than half of the time; "Sometimes" means less than half of the time; "Never" means zero percent of the time.
Source: Data from CSO Agricultural Census, 1983-84.

## PROPOSED RESEARCH

There is clearly a need to gain better insight into the way in which cashcropping influences food security in Swaziland. The main aim of the proposed research is to investigate the importance of cashcropping in terms of generating an income to sustain food security for which measurable nutritional status will be used as a proxy. Data pertaining to homestead-level variables is proposed to be collected from cashcroppers in contract-farming schemes, cashcroppers outside contract-farming schemes and non-cashcroppers. The following questions will have to be addressed:

o    What has the contribution of cotton and tobacco production been to export earnings and to what extent has cashcropping contributed to the creation of employment opportunities;

o    How are extension advice, marketing and credit facilities organised for cashcroppers and how can these be improved;

o    What role has contract-farming played, or can potentially play, in the further development of cashcropping, especially in the context of improvements in extension advice, marketing and credit facilities;

o    For contract-cashcroppers, what are the present contractual arrangements; do cashcroppers benefit; what are the shortcomings of the system, and how can it be improved;

o    What is the economic profitability of cashcropping, *i.e.*, how do gross margins and returns per labour-day compare with those for other crops;

o    What are the differences in production levels of food crops for contract-cashcroppers, cashcroppers and non-cashcroppers;

o    What is the contribution of cashcrop sales to the total income from crop sales and to the total homestead income for the three categories of farmers;

o    How is the income derived from cashcrop sales controlled and distributed within the homestead and, directly related to this;

o    How is the income from cashcrops used, *i.e.*, what proportion is spent on food purchases, what proportion is re-invested and what proportion is used for other purposes;

o    Is the nutritional status of cashcroppers, contract-cashcroppers and non-cashcroppers different in terms of caloric intake and anthropometric measurements.

# REFERENCES

Boeren, F.C.C.M. and V.M. Sithole. 1989. *Contract-farming and Outgrower Schemes in Swaziland: Lessons from Vuvulane Irrigated Farms and Mphetseni Pineapple Settlement Scheme.* Research Paper No. 25. Social Science Research Unit. University of Swaziland.

Cappetta, M. 1983. Population, Food and Nutrition: Swaziland, 1940-1982. In: de Vletter, F. (ed) *The Swazi Rural Homestead.* Social Science Research Unit. University of Swaziland.

Daddieh, C.K. and K. Jonah. 1987. *The Political Economy of Contract-farming and Smallholder Outgrower Schemes: A Case Study of the Ghanaian Oil Palm Industry.* Legon.

Dilon, J.L. 1984. *Technology versus Hunger: Problems and Prospects.* Paper presented at the National H. Grace Lectureship in Agriculture. University of Alberta. Edmonton.

FAO. 1981. *Cotton Development in Swaziland.* Rome.

Jaffee, S. 1987. *Case Studies of Contract-farming in the Horticultural Sector of Kenya.* Working Paper No. 7. Institute of Development Anthropology. New York.

Kennedy, E. and B. Cogill. 1988. The Commercialisation of Agriculture and Household-Level Food Security: The Case of Southwestern Kenya. In: *World Development.* Vol. 16 No. 9.

Levin, R.M. 1987. *Land Tenure Arrangements on Agricultural Production Schemes: A Research Report.* SSRU. University of Swaziland.

Maxwell, S. 1989. *In Defence of Cash Crops - An Unpopular View.* Paper presented at Research Seminars Series. Rural Development Studies. Institute of Social Studies. The Hague.

Sterkenburg, J.J. and J. Testerink. 1982. *Agricultural Commercialisation in Swaziland: Cotton Production on Swazi Nation Land.* Department of Geography of Developing Countries. University of Utrecht. The Netherlands.

Swaziland Government, Central Statistical Office. 1980-1987. *Annual Statistical Bulletins.* Mbabane.

Swaziland Government. 1969. *Post Independence Development Plan.* Mbabane.

Swaziland Government. undated. *Second National Development Plan.* 1973-1979. Mbabane.

Swaziland Government. undated. *Third National Development Plan.* 1978-79 to 1982-83. Mbabane.

Swaziland Government. 1983. *Swaziland National Nutrition Status Survey.* Nutritional Status Report. Mbabane.

Swaziland Government. 1985. *Fourth National Development Plan.* 1983-84 to 1987-88. Mbabane.

Testerink, J. 1984. *Agricultural Commercialisation in Swaziland : Farmers Compared.* SSRU Research Paper No. 11. University of Swaziland.

The World Bank. 1986a. *Poverty and Hunger: Issues and Options for Food Security in Developing Countries.* Washington D.C.

The World Bank. 1986b. *World Development Report, 1986.* Washington D.C.

The World Bank. 1987. *Swaziland Agricultural Sector Update.* Eastern and Southern Africa Projects.

# 19

# Horticultural Marketing In Zimbabwe: Experiences From The Mutoko-Uzumba Smallholder Farmer Project

*Albert Jaure*[1]

## INTRODUCTION

Horticultural produce in Zimbabwe is an uncontrolled commodity that is generally marketed on a daily auction basis. The prices are determined by supply and demand with Harare being the hub of horticultural marketing where prices are "quoted" on the Independent Market. Producers range from plotholders, peri-urban cooperatives, smallholder farmers, large-scale commercial farmers and state farms. Large scale producers generally channel their produce through the wholesale markets while the small producers normally handle their own marketing through the city auction floors. The main problem in the marketing of smallholder horticultural produce is that the major crops and varieties have a low market demand on the export and high income local market.

## COMMODITY MARKETS

### Export Markets

The export market for Zimbabwe is lucrative if targeted to high value/low volume horticultural products which include: yellow maize, sweet corn, cherry tomatoes, mange tout, strawberries, fine beans, baby carrots, purple passion fruit, citrus, flowers, spices.

The high value/low volume products can either be fresh produce, processed or semi-processed products like dried dehydrated vegetables and fruit juice concentrates. Fresh fruit and vegetable exports generally have to be tender, stringless, easy to peel and have an attractive and appetising colour. At the moment, these are mainly being produced by large-scale commercial farmers.

For export, producers normally supply export agents such as African Produce Marketing and Mazoe Valley Marketing, to do the packaging and exporting on their

---

[1]Agricultural and Rural Development Authority (ARDA), Harare, Zimbabwe.

behalf. They can also pack the produce, deliver to a local agent in the importing country, clear the goods and handle the distribution.

Zimbabwe, being landlocked, relies heavily on airfreight to transport the horticultural products to different overseas destinations. Based on 1987 exports, Zimbabwe's main trading partners on the overseas markets in order of importance are the United Kingdom, The United Arab Emirates, the Netherlands and France.

## Regional Markets

Zimbabwe's main regional trading partners in order of importance are: South Africa, Mozambique, Botswana, Gabon and Angola. Fruits and vegetables with an unfavourable volume-to-value ratio should ideally be confined to local and regional markets. This would include such produce as avocado, mango, guava, potato, lemon, grapefruit, tomato, vegetables, and so on.

## Domestic Markets

The existing domestic market channels for producers include the following:

o    cooperative wholesale markets like the Fruit and Vegetable Cooperative (FAVCO);

o    private wholesale markets, which include the Independent Market, P & P, and Harare Market Development Holdings;

o    small-scale individual wholesalers;

o    local authority daily auction floors for smallholder farmers;

o    export brokers, like the African Produce Marketing and Mazoe Valley Marketing;

o    producer middlemen and wholesale middlemen; and

o    processing companies.

Harare acts as the hub through which produce is then channelled to other towns. Volumes of produce handled by different channels are not readily available but for the purposes of this paper, emphasis will be placed on the smallholder marketing chain.

Based on the A.R.D.A. survey conducted in Harare in 1989, 68 percent of the vegetables passing through the Harare outlets are channelled through Mbare Musika, the major local market. The large-scale commercial farmers generally channel their produce through the wholesale markets.

o    On average, 75 tonnes of produce passes through Mbare Musika daily. Tomato is the single largest crop marketed through Mbare Musika, followed by mango and onion. Concerning leaf vegetables, rape is more prominent than cabbage.

o   The main consumer target for the Mbare Musika produce is the low income group, mainly in the high density suburbs.

o   About 5 percent of the produce channelled through Mbare Musika is supplied by commercial farmers, 10 percent by smallholder farmers from Mutoko and 5 percent by smallholder farmers from Uzumba. The rest of the produce is mainly supplied from Chinamora Communal area, and smaller volumes from Goromonzi, Seke, Chipinge, Kariba, Murewa, Bindura, Kwekwe and Marondera.

## MARKETING STRATEGIES

The commercial farmer cooperative wholesalers are generally developing into multi-purpose cooperatives, including fruit and vegetable marketing, input supply, agronomic back-up, market research, packaging and processing. The wholesalers target to supply institutions which buy in bulk (*e.g.*, hospitals, the army), whereas export produce is targeted to wholesalers in the importing countries. Potatoes, cabbage, bananas and oranges are the leading income-generating crops on the domestic market for the wholesalers.

Smaller farmer groups are also cooperating in sharing pack-house facilities and group marketing for export. These small groups tend to specialise in high value/low volume fruits and vegetables for export. The second grade produce is channelled through the supermarkets and hotels and the lowest grade is auctioned for stockfeed.

The smallholder farmers are responsible for marketing their own produce and commute to and from the market 1,3 to 1,8 times per week on average, depending on the season. Smallholder produce is generally channelled through the city daily produce auction floors. Nearly 49 percent of the smallholder produce is purchased by hawkers and 34 percent by stallholders. The remainder is channelled through the individual small scale wholesalers, restaurants, supermarkets and hotels.

### Smallholder Marketing

In order to investigate some of the factors affecting smallholder marketing, A.R.D.A. conducted a production survey in Mutoko and Uzumba in 1988, and again in 1989 to cover some of the Harare market outlets. The Uzumba survey was confined to the two main producing areas, *viz.* Karimbika and Chipfunde. The Mutoko survey was more extensive and covered 17 out of a total of 19 wards.

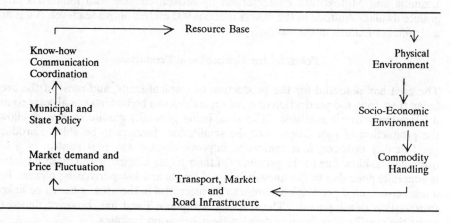

**Figure 1: Factors affecting smallholder marketing**

*Socio-economic and Physical Characteristics of Survey Areas*

The resource base of the survey areas was characterised by the following features:

The average family size in Mutoko Communal Area is 6,8 with a range of 15. There is no significant difference in the average numbers of males and females among the households. The average number of males per household is 3,39 compared to 3,42 for females. There is generally more female labour available than male labour with an average of 1,69 females per household compared to 1,07 males.

In Uzumba Communal Area the average family size is 7 with 3,45 males versus 3,56 females. There is no significant difference in the household profiles for Mutoko and Uzumba in the survey area. Labour is not in short supply.

The average farm size in Mutoko is about 2,3 hectares with a range of 11. The average area put under vegetable production is 0,6 hectares (26 percent of the land holding). Most farms consist of loamy soils which make up about 60 percent of the soils. The red soils occupy about 21 percent, and the black soils cover only about 19 percent of the soils.

In Uzumba, the average farm size is about 3,44 hectares with 1,25 hectares (36,34 percent) under vegetables. Beans, potatoes and cabbage, with a relatively high demand on the high-income market, occupy an insignificant hectarage on smallholder farms.

The climate of Mutoko is sub-tropical with cool dry winters and hot rainy summers. The mean annual rainfall for Mutoko is 696 millimetres. The mean monthly temperature is 14,9°C in July increasing to 22,3°C in October. Most of the lands are frost-free except for a few isolated pockets.

Soils are generally moderately shallow to moderately deep. Coarse grained sands and loamy sands over fersiallitic sandy loams.

Uzumba and Mutoko are characterised by broken country with numerous large granite dwalas. Altitude in the valleys is about 900 metres above sea level. Vleis are a significant feature in the valleys.

## Potential for Horticultural Production

The area has potential for the production of tropical fruits, and most of the area being frost-free, the production of most vegetables can be undertaken all year round if irrigation water is available. The area, being generally granite sand veld, allows the production of root crops. For the smallholder farmers to be able to produce good quality produce, it is critical to improve disease and pest control in a co-ordinated fashion, due to the proximity of their plots. Chemical and disease control is generally poor due to the unavailability of inputs and low purchasing power. For a market-oriented production system to be successful in the area, it has to be linked to irrigation development. The National Irrigation Fund has, however, failed to assist the smallholder farmers develop their irrigation facilities.

### Socio-Economic Environment

Most smallholder farmers in the area are involved in horticultural production either at subsistence or commercial level. The size of the local market is small, so most of the produce has to be transported to distant markets. The biggest market is in urban areas (Harare in this case) but unfortunately most of these rural areas are a long way from urban centres. The transport cost, in this case, is very high. Due to the low purchasing power of the rural communities, the sizeable local market is for leaf vegetables, rape, and tomatoes that are used as a relish.

In most rural areas there is hardly any horticultural market infrastructure to talk about; if anything, the local district councils will have provided retail stalls which only offer a roof shelter and a concrete table. It is rare to find market facilities, retail or wholesale, with storage and cooling facilities.

Collection and bulking-up of smallholder produce is very expensive because of the dispersion of the small volumes which is influenced by the scattered settlement pattern. Access roads to most of the homesteads off the main road, are either non-existent or impassable by truck. The collection loops in Mutoko, for instance, range from 40 to 150 kilometres -- to load an 8-tonne truck and 6-tonne trailer.

The smallholder farmers mainly produce and market on an individual (family) basis but what is required is group action on the part of the producers to give them collective bargaining power. The biggest challenge is in organising the smallholder farmers into self-sustaining and viable groups for production and marketing purposes.

## COMMODITY HANDLING AND MARKETING

Normally, smallholder horticultural marketing is characterised by:

o  poor post-harvest handling;

o  poor packaging;

o transport constraints;

o exploitation by the middlemen;

o poor market information;

o high market losses;

o poor farmer coordination and information exchange; and

o reduced farmer benefits.

The smallholder farmers have more than one outlet for their horticultural produce. Only 17 percent of the farmers in Uzumba and 23 percent in Mutoko use the local district outlets as their main markets; the rest rely on the Harare markets. The volume of produce, in crates, transported per trip per farmer, is very variable. On average the smallholder farmers market 25 crates of produce per trip.

August and September are the peak vegetable marketing periods, with no labour competition from the field crops.

A minimum of 48 hours lapse from time of picking (harvesting) to the time of marketing. The fruits and vegetables have to be harvested, graded, packed in wooden crates, tins or pockets and transported to the roadside. On average, one man-day is required to harvest, grade, pack and transport 20 to 30 crates of tomatoes to the roadside. Where family labour is inadequate, casual labourers are hired at a rate of $2,50 a day despite the stipulated government rate of $3,50 per day for agricultural workers. Wheelbarrows and ox-drawn carts are used to transport the produce from the gardens to the roadside. The rental rate for ox-drawn carts is $7,00 per load irrespective of distance.

The greater percentage of farmers (77 percent) now grade their produce but grading criteria are not standardised. Some of the grading criteria used include size, soundness of fruit (quality), ripeness, buyers' wants and freshness of produce.

Soon after harvesting and grading, the produce should be cooled down quickly to temperatures of 10° to 7°C at 98 percent relative humidity to prevent product dehydration and slow down the respiratory processes, thus increasing the product's shelf-life.

Due to a shortage of natural and motorised cooling facilities on the smallholder farms, produce tends to be over-exposed to the sun. This results in accelerated respiratory processes and rapid product deterioration. Transport shortage forces the farmer to harvest some of the crop when it is already overripe. Field losses, especially for tomatoes, can be as high as 18 percent of the gross yield.

The production of horticultural produce is carried out all year round. Summer production is slightly less than winter production because the farmers will also be concentrating on the field crops. In the study area, horticulture offers an all year round source of income. About 2,5 tonnes of vegetables are marketed annually per household. Bananas and mango are the leading fruits produced in the survey area.

A comparison of family fruit sales and fruit consumption shows that family consumption is only about 19 percent, and the rest of the fruit is targeted for the market. This reflects the importance of fruits and also vegetables as a source of cash income rather than food in the survey area.

The average family income from fruit sales is about $600 *per annum*, a figure which is comparable to the annual income from field crops in the survey area. Improvement of the smallholder horticultural marketing system would significantly improve household incomes in the survey area.

### Transport System

Most of the smallholder farmers transport their produce to the market by lorries. 61 percent use lorries, 33 percent use buses and 6 percent use vans to transport the produce. The transport fee per crate ranges from 70c to $1,00. For produce transported by bus, the farmers may have to pay an additional 30c to 50c for unloading the produce. Produce transported by bus has to be packed in tins, and produce transported by lorries has to be packed in wooden crates, or bags. Besides paying the produce transport fee, the farmers have to catch a bus to and from the market, which is about $12,00 from Mutoko to Harare.

It is usually difficult to synchronise the timetable for the buses with trucks collecting farmer produce, to enable the farmer to catch the bus to the market after loading his/her produce onto the truck. In some cases, there is no daily bus service and in some areas the buses start off very early in the morning -- 4 a.m., at which time the trucks will not have started collecting farmer produce. Some farmers catch the bus to the market, leaving friends and relatives to load their produce onto the truck, but in some cases the truck and produce never get to the market due to mechanical failure or other reasons, thus leaving the farmers stranded at the market place in Harare.

With the gravel roads, it is very difficult to provide reliable transport to the farmers during the wet season. The rough roads cause a lot of bruising and crushing of produce, especially overripe tomatoes. It is not uncommon to find boxes and tins of produce abandoned on the roadside for days, due to transport shortage. The shortage of passenger transport forces the farmers to illegally hitch-hike on the loaded trucks and, in the event of a fatal accident, the farmer's family receive no compensation.

To the private transporters, the transportation of smallholder horticultural produce is not very attractive because of the high repairs and maintenance cost caused by the rough roads, and the return trips with the empty crates are not chargeable. There is a small volume of chargeable goods on the return trips, *e.g.*, fertilizers and cement, etc.

### Market Demand and Price Fluctuations

There is need to undertake a product demand survey for the smallholder marketing channels. It has not been possible to estimate the demand for the different fruits and vegetables based on their price responses to different supply quantities. There is no systematic and continuous recording of smallholder produce prices.

It is crucial that a smallholder market information collection and dissemination system be designed and implemented. Generally the smallholder farmers sell at prices slightly below those published in the daily newspapers. The market supply and demand situation plays an important role in fixing prices.

## Market Facilities

In Harare, most smallholders channel their produce through the Mbare Musika producer section, where daily auctions are held from 4.00 a.m. to 10.00 a.m. The market facility provides an open air auction with no price determining system. The farmers pay $4,00 for a tarred area of nine square metres to display his/her produce for sale. The sales are purely by negotiation between the individual farmer and the buyers. The farmers complain of the poor lighting, distant toilets, rampant theft in the market, limited marketing time, poor accommodation facilities, and increased encroachment by commercial farmers in the smallholder market. The City Council has tried introducing smallholder decentralised wholesale markets in the high density suburbs like Mabvuku, Highfield, Glen Norah, *etc.*, but these all failed except in Mabvuku, which is still operational. Most of the hawkers and stallholders oppose the idea of setting up decentralised wholesale markets for fear of promoting retailing by the producers.

The market wastage varies with the crop and increases during the rainy season, and during the glut periods. The average market losses are as follows:

| | |
|---|---|
| Vegetables (rape) | 14,77% |
| Tomatoes | 10,77% |
| Cabbage | 9,22% |
| Onions | 4,68% |
| Potatoes | 1,94% |
| Lemons | 3,81% |

## Government and Municipal Policies

The Government has left the marketing of horticultural products to private enterprises, and continues to help the smallholder farmers establish their bulking, storage and distribution system. There is a serious shortage of trucks locally and Government assistance is required in making special allocations to groups with the money to be able to establish their transport fleet. The Government should strengthen the Central Statistical Department to enable it to collect and disseminate smallholder horticultural production and market information. The Municipality should provide better market facilities, preferably under roof to allow trading under all-weather conditions. Adequate sanitary facilities, lighting, secure accommodation, and more market time should be provided.

# ARDA/EEC PROJECT TO PROMOTE HORTICULTURAL MARKETING ASSOCIATIONS

Under the Mashonaland East Fruit and Vegetable Programme, being implemented by the Agricultural and Rural Development Authority and sponsored by the European Economic Community, the smallholder farmers are being organised to form horticultural marketing associations. Through collective marketing, the farmers will have more price bargaining power for their produce.

Through the association, the farmers are being trained to share and control their own transport system, thus reducing dependence on the middleman.

The associations are to be developed into wholesale marketing agencies to minimise the travelling to be done by the farmers and to market the produce on behalf of the farmers. The associations will be equipped with grading equipment, warehouses and cooling facilities where possible. The associations are aiming at diversifying the marketing channels for the produce from smallholder farmers.

The project is also providing specialised horticultural extension to improve farmer knowledge of the crops, to introduce new genetic material, and to diversify the range of crops produced. Under the project, it is also proposed to develop and implement a market oriented production strategy. To be able to implement the programme, the smallholder irrigation development components need to be accelerated. There is potential for gravity-feed irrigation schemes but in some cases the water source does not allow such a design. Diesel and solar pumping offer alternatives to gravity feed schemes, but the high capital costs are prohibitive to develop these schemes. More studies have to be done to establish the problems and ways of improving the implementation of smallholder irrigation schemes. The hydrological impact of establishing pump schemes in the vleis should be determined and suitable recommendations made.

## RECOMMENDATIONS

Any attempt to improve smallholder marketing has to assume an integrated approach covering the following areas:

o   market information system and coordination;

o   market infrastructure, grading and packaging;

o   road network and condition;

o   availability of vehicles and back-up facilities for repairs and maintenance;

o   farmer organisation framework;

o   agronomic back-up and farmer training;

o   irrigation development;

o   input supply and credit for horticulture;

o    devising and implementing a market oriented production strategy; and

o    distribution and accounting systems.

More research is required to determine how best to integrate the above factors in a smallholder marketing programme.  Ongoing research in the area includes an assessment of the impact of the Mashonaland East fruit and vegetable programme on the development of the smallholder horticultural production and marketing systems.

More research is required to determine the appropriate commodity handling procedures ideal for smallholder farmers, from the harvesting stage up to the retail outlet stage.

The potential for processing should be established and recommendations made on the cultivars suitable for both processing and the fresh market.  Already some work has been identified by the Intermediate Technology Development Group in this regard (Sandels, 1987).

## REFERENCES

Jones, D. 1989. *The Markets of Dubai and Jeddah for Fruit and Vegetables from Zimbabwe.* Adviser Market Study for Horticultural Exports. International Trade Centre.

Sandels, A. 1987. *The Potential for Food Processing Projects in the Rural Areas of Zimbabwe.* A Report to Intermediate Technology Development Group (ITDG), U.K.

# 20

# The Role Of Ruminants In Promoting Food Security In Farming Systems In The SADCC Region

*Lindela R. Ndlovu*[1]

## INTRODUCTION

Although livestock products do not generally form a substantial part of the diet of low-income people, ruminants play an indispensable role in the food security of rural households. They provide draught power and manure that are essential to cropping, cash income, meat, milk and they are an important store of wealth. In addition, the urban demand for livestock products (meat, milk and fibre) is increasing. Valuable resources (*e.g.*, money and human consumable grains) are sometimes diverted from supplying food to rural people in order to meet the urban demand for livestock products. This paper discusses the contribution of ruminant livestock to farming systems in rural areas and the ability of rural people to secure access to enough food. The paper also discusses constraints on improving the productivity of ruminant livestock and outlines needed research.

### Role of Cattle

Cattle are the most prominent livestock species in the SADCC countries (Table 1), outnumbering goats and sheep by at least a three to one margin in all countries except Lesotho, where goats and sheep are kept primarily for mohair and wool production (Molapo and Schact, 1988).

The number of cattle in Table 1 does not indicate the skewness of ownership. Ownership for the purposes of this paper also includes cattle "held" by households but not belonging to them (Scoones and Wilson, 1988). Data from Zimbabwe will be used to illustrate this unequal ownership; the author believes the situation is similar in other SADCC countries but data are not available.

Collinson (1982) showed that only 28 percent of households owned or managed more than four cattle in Zimbabwe. Later surveys in the same area showed ownership ranging from about three to nine cattle per household (Shumba, 1984; Mombeshora, Agyemang and Wilson, 1984; GFA, 1987 and van Eckert and

---

[1]Lecturer, Department of Animal Science, Faculty of Agriculture, University of Zimbabwe.

Mombeshora, 1988). Nationally, an average of six to seven cattle per household has been established (Zimbabwe Government, 1986; Chipika, 1988).

**Table 1**
**Ruminant livestock in SADCC, 1985, 1986 and 1987**
**('000)**

|  | Cattle | | | Goats | | | Sheep | | |
|---|---|---|---|---|---|---|---|---|---|
|  | 1985 | 1986 | 1987 | 1985 | 1986 | 1987 | 1985 | 1986 | 1987 |
| Angola | 3 360 | 3 338 | 3 390 | 960 | 965 | 970 | 250 | 255 | 260 |
| Botswana | 2 459 | 2 400 | 2 300 | 1 138 | 1 000 | 1 050 | 200 | 210 | 210 |
| Lesotho | 520 | 520 | 520 | 1 000 | 1 010 | 1 020 | 1 400 | 1 420 | 1 430 |
| Malawi | 1 020 | 1 050 | 940 | 799 | 810 | 700 | 185 | 186 | 185 |
| Mozambique | 1 330 | 1 340 | 1 350 | 360 | 365 | 370 | 106 | 115 | 116 |
| Swaziland | 648 | 650 | 655 | 268 | 270 | 275 | 30 | 32 | 35 |
| Tanzania | 14 000 | 14 300 | 14 500 | 6 450 | 6 500 | 6 550 | 4 100 | 4 300 | 4 500 |
| Zambia | 2 690 | 2 770 | 2 850 | 395 | 240 | 420 | 75 | 46 | 80 |
| Zimbabwe | 5 103 | 5 364 | 5 500 | 1 533 | 1 550 | 1 600 | 538 | 550 | 570 |

Source: FAO Production Yearbook (1989).

Avila (1985) reported that smallholders in Zimbabwe kept cattle for draught power manure security, milk and meat. The importance of draught is also borne out by surveys of herd composition which report a 1:1 ratio between oxen and cows (Mudimu 1983; Shumba, 1984; van Eckert and Mombeshora, 1988). Draught oxen make up about 30 percent of the herd (Shumba, 1984; van Eckert and Mombeshora, 1988). For a six animal herd this represents only two oxen. It has been estimated that adequate draught power for communal area cattle is obtained from a span of four oxen (Tembo and Elliot, 1987).

The use of four oxen has been questioned and it has been suggested that two oxen are adequate (Goe, 1985). However, at the start of the ploughing season rural area cattle are in very poor condition and two oxen would be unable to supply adequate draught power. Working animals utilise free fatty acids mainly from mobilisation of fat reserves as their main source of energy for skeletal muscle. Most traditionally-owned stock have very little fat reserves after a dry season.

The shortage of adequate draught power has been shown to be ... *the single most important explanatory factor to failure of communal agricultural production in Zimbabwe.* (Chipika, 1988). Shumba (1984) also showed that farmers who own cattle plough more land and achieve higher yields per unit area than non-cattle owners. Timely access to draught power to perform essential cropping activities has been identified as a possible cause for this difference (Shumba, 1984; Muchena, 1988). Thus inadequate draught power directly affects the food security of rural households. To overcome the shortage of oxen, some farmers utilise cows but cows are 20 to 30 percent less efficient than oxen (Howard, 1980).

Cattle manure is of great importance to smallholders. Its quality and value will vary with soil types (Mugwira and Mukurumbira, 1984); in wet areas, manure assumes great importance. Traditionally-owned cattle produce little manure because of low feed intake, slow digestibility of the diet and slow rates of removal of undigested matter from the gastro-intestinal tract of animals. Six adult cattle produce about five tonnes of manure per year but this is barely sufficient for a communal farmer. Households without cattle have little access to manure. In the poor sandy soils of communal areas, this lack of manure can result in low crop yields.

Indigenous cattle of the *bos indicus* type produce about 0,5 to 2 litres of milk per day depending on the season and stage of lactation. But animals have not been selected for milk yield, as most farmers do not see milk as a priority area, although it is very valuable in child nutrition. Crossbreeding may improve these yields but the cost of feed to support higher milk production may not be justified by the selling price of milk.

For a smallholder to progress, he needs replacement stock. But many calves do not survive until maturity. An important index that measures these parameters is the weaning rate which is defined as the number of calves weaned per cow exposed to the bull. This figure takes into account the fertility of the cows, the number of abortions/still births plus the survival of calves born live up to weaning. Traditionally-held cattle perform poorly in this index; weaning rates of 40 percent are not uncommon (Kategile, 1984). This means farmers must keep five cows to wean two calves! The causes for low reproductive performance are many but nutritional infertility and diseases are paramount. The improvement of weaning rates from traditional herds has often been overshadowed by the concern of policy-makers for overgrazing and overstocking. A popular view is to reduce cattle numbers in smallholder herds rather than to improve the feed resource base.

Finally, the supply of beef is an important foreign currency earner in such countries as Zimbabwe and Botswana. Beef is also an important component of urban diets. To supply both the external and internal demand, cattle fattening is encouraged. Unfortunately diets for fattening often consist of human edible cereals like maize. This puts cattle in direct competition for food with human beings. Ruminants have evolved a digestive system capable of utilising feed resources inedible to human beings.

## Role of Goats

Goats are the second most important livestock species in most SADCC countries (Table 1). Lesotho is an exception in this regard, mainly because of the unpopularity of goat meat in Lesotho (Leteka, personal communication). Over 90 percent of the goats in the SADCC region belong to smallholder/rural farmers (SACCAR 1988a). The popularity of goats in most traditional farming sectors is mainly due to cultural factors and the farmers preference for goats for family food and income generation (Avila, 1986). Hale (1986) reported that the cash goal was very important. Many children who go to school depend on goat sales for school fees. The choice of the goat for family meat could be related to its small carcass size so that it can be eaten without refrigeration. In Lesotho, goats are kept almost solely for their mohair which brings in cash income to the farmers (Makhooane, 1986).

The productivity of goats in the SADCC region is low (SACCAR, 1988b) but the breeds are hardy and prolific. In Lesotho, goats produce about one kilogram of mohair per head while goats of the same breed and genetic pool produce about four kilograms per head in South Africa. The reason for the low mohair production in Lesotho is poor nutrition (SACCAR, 1988b). Since goats are readily sold or slaughtered by smallholders in the other SADCC countries, reproductive performance of the female is a key production trait. Reproductive performance of the female is assessed by several indicators:

o   the fertility of the herd (*i.e.*, number of females exposed to the male that give birth to live progeny as a percentage of the total number of females exposed to the male);

o   weaning weight of the kids;

o   number of kids weaned as a percentage of the females exposed to the male; and

o   the kidding interval, which is days between two consecutive kiddings in the same animal.

The number of kids weaned is a function of the number of offspring born per female at each parturition and the number that die before weaning. Under station conditions, indigenous goats have been shown to have a 60 percent rate of twins and triplets (Sibanda, 1988; Phoya, 1986; McKinnon, 1986). Ndlovu and Royer (1988) and Karua (1988) reported twinning rates of about 30 percent in communal areas of Zimbabwe and Malawi respectively. Phoya (1986) reported twinning rates of only 15 percent in traditionally managed Malawi goats whilst in Lesotho twinning is selected against in Government stud farms (Leteka, personal communication).

Lebby and Matsapha (1985) reported a twinning rate of about 20 percent for goats in the middleveld of Swaziland. Thus we can see that the reproductive potential of the goat is not fully utilised at parturition in traditional flocks in the region. The situation is intensified by high kid mortalities prior to weaning (Hale, 1986; Ndlovu, and Royer, 1988; Molefe, 1986; Phoya, 1986; Makhooane, 1986). Long kidding intervals in the region have been reported by Phoya (1986) and Ndlovu and Royer (1988). A combination of the above factors means that the traditional farmer is losing substantial potential cash income and meat because of low productivity of his/her flock, even though the flock is biologically capable of performing better. The main causes have been identified as nutrition and disease (Hale, 1986; Lebbie and Matsapha, 1985; Mtenga, Sarwatt and Njombe, 1986; Ndlovu and Royer, 1988; SACCAR, 1988a). The goat offers fast returns because of its short (compared to cattle) life cycle. Increasing the productivity of goats would greatly improve the income-earning potential and nutritional status of rural households. Contrary to popular belief, the goat is much less destructive to the environment than cattle, if well managed. Thus increasing goat productivity is unlikely to result in environmental degradation.

## Role of Sheep

Sheep are not important in most SADCC countries except for Lesotho (Table 1) and Botswana. In Lesotho, the sheep are of the Wool Merino type but a few dual purpose Merinos are being introduced (Molapo and Schact, 1988). In Botswana, the desert sheep breed is the Karakul which is valued for its pelt. In the other SADCC countries, including Botswana, most of the sheep are indigenous meat breeds. The Merino sheep produce about 2,5 kilograms of wool per head in Lesotho, yet the same breed of sheep produces about four kilograms of wool per head in South Africa. Meat yield from indigenous sheep is low due to poor dressing percentages (Kusina, 1987). Reproductive performance is low (67 percent lambing rate and mortality rates of about 30 percent are common).

In summary, biological constraints on improved productivity include a number of diseases precipitated by poor nutrition and breed characteristics. Traditional farmers lack knowledge of breed characteristics and, as a result, selection to enhance productivity is non-existent.

## SOCIO-ECONOMIC CONSTRAINTS ON LIVESTOCK PRODUCTIVITY

### Marketing Policies

Even though the traditional farming sector readily sells goats to raise cash income, in most SADCC countries marketing policies are unclear. Often farmers have to rely on the informal market -- selling to neighbours or private traders. This situation is fraught with uncertainty as available cash in communal areas is limited and private traders are not always available when the cash is needed. Where government facilities have been provided (e.g., Cold Storage Commission goat sales in Zimbabwe) the price offered is often unattractive. In Zimbabwe this is mainly because of the inadequate grading system. Goats are sold per kilogram of live weight with little attention paid to the condition of the animal. For example a farmer who sells a well-fleshed goat of 28 kilograms gets no more than a farmer who sells an old goat of 28 kilograms! Such pricing does not encourage farmers to adopt technologies that improve the body condition of their animals.

### Farmer Objectives

Far too often researchers focus on developing an ideal animal producing an ideal product without considering the farmers' objectives. A classical case is beef production from traditional herds, where the owners are not primarily interested in slaughtering/selling their animals because cattle are a valuable source of inputs into the cropping system. The goal of research and action programmes should be to improve the productivity of products or services valued by farmers.

### Communal Ownership of Land

The problems of managing and improving communally-owned land have been discussed by several authors including Hardin (1968), Cousins (1988) and Scoones and Wilson (1988). Most of the land in SADCC countries is communally owned and this has tended to retard the more adventurous farmers as they cannot be allowed to fence and develop sections of the grazing land. There is need to review ownership of grazing land, as a means of improving the resource base.

## RESEARCH PRIORITIES

It is hypothesised that poor nutrition is the major constraint on improved productivity of ruminant livestock in the SADCC region. Improvement of the nutritional status of livestock would reduce incidences of disease, improve growth rates and draught power output and reduce reproductive wastage. It is also hypothesised that pricing policies that reward farmers for improving the condition of their stock would accelerate ruminant production in the region.

There is also a need to improve the feed resource base in terms of quality and quantity of feeds. Most ruminant livestock in the SADCC region, as in other parts of Africa, depend on naturally-occurring vegetation which the animals harvest. The quality and quantity of such vegetation is at the mercy of the vagaries of the weather. During the wet season, there is an over-abundance of good quality feed but quality and quantity quickly deteriorate as the vegetation matures and as the dry season approaches. In the dry season, the animals have to survive on sparse forage that is low in nitrogen and high in indigestible cell wall fractions which limit its utilisation. Research should be aimed at optimising the use of forage produced during the wet season. Production of forage that is tolerant to drought should be investigated. West African research on fodder banks could provide valuable leads and lessons on this. Biotechnology is another valuable tool worth pursuing for propagation of drought tolerant forages.

Despite a wealth of scientific literature on the potential of crop residues as animal feeds, their use in rural livestock systems is still very limited. It is time to move the research from stations to on-farm trials to test acceptability and sustainability utilising crop residues. The economics of harvesting, storing and transporting these forages need to be established.

## CONCLUSION

Ruminant livestock are important to food security in the SADCC region as sources of manure, draught power, cash income, food (milk and meat), and as long term investments. But current levels of production in the region are low. The major constraints are nutrition, disease, management, marketing policies and land tenure. Research is also needed to improve the feed resource base.

## REFERENCES

Avila, M. 1985. Intra- and Inter-household Decision-making in the Mangwende and Chivi Communal Areas: Preliminary results. *Farming Systems Research Unit Annual Report*. Department of Research and Specialist Services. Ministry of Lands Agriculture and Rural Resettlement. Harare. Zimbabwe.

Chipika, S. 1988. Livestock Ownership and Inequality with Particular Reference to Cattle: The case of some Communal Areas in Zimbabwe. In B. Cousins, C. Jackson and I. Scoones (eds) *Proceedings of Workshop on Socio-economic Dimensions of Livestock Production in the Communal Lands of Zimbabwe. 12-14 September. 1988.* Centre for Applied and Social Sciences. University of Zimbabwe. Harare. Zimbabwe.

Collinson, M. 1982. *A Diagnostic Survey of the South of Chibi District, Zimbabwe for Adaptive Research Planning.* CIMMYT Eastern Africa Economics Programme Occasional Papers Report No.5. CIMMYT. Nairobi. Kenya.

Cousins, B. 1988.  Community Class and Grazing Management in Zimbabwe's Communal Lands. In B. Cousins, C. Jackson and I. Scoones (eds) *Proceedings of Workshop on Socio-economic Dimensions of Livestock Production in the Communal Lands of Zimbabwe. 12-14 September. 1988.* Centre for Applied and Social Sciences. University of Zimbabwe. Harare. Zimbabwe.

GFA. 1987. *Study on the Economic and Social Determinants of Livestock Production in the Communal Areas.* Gesellschaff fun Agraprojecte Ubersee. Final report to the Ministry of Lands, Agriculture and Rural Resettlement. Government of Zimbabwe.

Goe, M.R. 1983.  Current Status of Research on Animal Traction. *World Animal Review.* Vol. 45 : 2-17.

Haidin, 1968.  The Tradegy of the Commons. *Science.* Vol. 162 : 1243-1248.

Hale, D.H. 1986.  Systems of Production in Three Communal Lands in Zimbabwe. In K.O. Adeniji and J.A. Kategile (eds) *Proceedings of the Workshop on Improvement of Small Ruminants in Eastern and Southern Africa, 18-22 August 1986.* OAU/IDRC. Nairobi. Kenya. : 181-193.

Howard, C.R. 1980.  The Draft Ox : Management and Uses. *Zimbabwe Agricultural Journal.* Vol. 71 No.1 : 89-97.

Karua, S.K. 1988.  Reproductive Performance and Growth of the Indigenous Malawi Goat under Traditional Systems of Management. In J. Harrison (ed) *Proceedings of Workshop on Goat Development, 11 -13 January, 1988.* French Embassy. Harare. Zimbabwe. : 69-78.

Kategile, J.A. 1984.  Need for More Milk Production in SADCC Countries: A Challenge to Animal Scientists. In P.J. Boyle (ed) *Proceedings of a SACCAR Workshop on Smallholder Dairy, Small Ruminants, Pig, Poultry and Rabbit Production in the SADCC Countries, 26-27 November 1986.* SACCAR Workshop Series No. 4, Gaborone, Botswana. : 3-5.

Kusina, N.T. 1987.  *Effect of Plane of Nutrition on Growth and Body Composition of Indigenous Growing Intact Lambs.* M.Phil thesis. University of Zimbabwe. Department of Animal Science.

Lebby, S.H. and P.R. Matsapha 1985.  Goat Production in the Middleveld of Swaziland. In R.T. Wilson and D. Bouzart (eds) *Small Ruminants in Africa Agriculture.* : 224-250. ILCA, Addis Ababa. Ethiopia.

Makhooane, M. 1986.  Sheep and Goat Production in Lesotho. In P.J. Boyle (ed) *Proceedings of a SACCAR Workshop on Smallholder Dairy, Small Ruminants, Pig, Poultry and Rabbit Production in the SADCC Countries, 26-27 November 1986.* SACCAR Workshop Series No. 4, Gaborone, Botswana. : 46-48.

McKinnon, D.S. 1986.  Some Aspects of Small Ruminant Production in Mozambique. In P.J. Boyle ed. *Proceedings of a SACCAR Workshop on Smallholder Dairy, Small Ruminants, Pig, Poultry and Rabbit Production in the SADCC Countries, 26-27 November 1986.* SACCAR Workshop Series No. 4, Gaborone, Botswana. : 52.

Molapo, M. and W. Schact. 1988.  *Livestock Research in Lesotho.* Paper presented at the SACCAR/ILCA Livestock Planning Workshop, 28 November to 2 December, 1988. Harare, Zimbabwe.

Mombeshora, B.G., K. Agyemang and R.T. Wilson. 1984.  Livestock Ownership and Management in the Chibi and Mangwende Communal Areas of Zimbabwe. *ILCA Small Ruminant and Camel Group Document No. SRC 2.* International Livestock Centre for Africa. Addis Ababa. Ethiopia.

Mtenga, L.A., S.V. Sarwatt and H.P. Njombe. 1986.  Goat and Sheep Production in Tanzania. In P.J. Boyle (ed) *Proceedings of a SACCAR Workshop on Smallholder Dairy, Small Ruminants, Pig, Poultry and Rabbit Production in the SADCC Countries, 26-27 November 1986.* SACCAR Workshop Series No. 4. Gaborone. Botswana.

Muchena, M.E. 1988. The Effect of Ox Sharing Arrangements on the Supply and Use of Draught Animals in the Communal Areas of Zimbabwe - Preliminary Findings. In B. Cousins, C. Jackson and I. Scoones (eds) *Proceedings of Workshop on Socio-economic Dimensions of Livestock Production in the Communal Lands of Zimbabwe. 12-14 September. 1988.* Centre for Applied and Social Sciences. University of Zimbabwe. Harare. Zimbabwe.

Mudimu, G.D. 1983. *The Draught Power Problem in Zimbabwe : An Extension View of the Causes, Effects and Solution.* Paper presented at the CIMMYT Technical Networking Workshop on the Draught Power Problem. 16-20 October 1983. Mbabane. Swaziland.

Mugwira, L.M. and L.M. Mukurumbira. 1984. Comparative Effectiveness of Manures from the Communal Areas and Commercial Feedlots as Plant Nutrient Sources. *Zimbabwe Agricultural Journal.* Vol 81 No.6. : 241-250.

Ndlovu, L.R. and V. Royer. 1988. A Comparative Study of Goat Productivity in Three Different Regions of Zimbabwe. In J. Harrison (ed) *Proceedings of Workshop on Goat Development, 11-13 January 1988.* French Embassy. Harare. Zimbabwe. : 55-61.

Phoya, R.K.D. 1986. Goat Production in Malawi. In P.J. Boyle (ed) *Proceedings of a SACCAR Workshop on Smallholder Dairy, Small Ruminants, Pig, Poultry and Rabbit Production in the SADCC Countries. 26-27 November 1986.* SACCAR Workshop Series No. 4. Gaborone. Botswana. : 49-51.

SACCAR. 1988a. *A Project on Wool and Mohair Production in SADCC.* Project proposal submitted to Winrock International. Arkansas. USA. by SACCAR.

SACCAR. 1988b. *Livestock Improvement in SADCC.* A project proposal for collaboration with International Livestock Centre for Africa (ILCA). Addis Ababa. Ethiopia.

Scoones, I. and K. Wilson. 1988. Households Lineage Groups and Ecological Dynamics. Issues for Livestock Research and Development in Zimbabwe's Communal Areas. In: B. Cousins, C. Jackson and I. Scoones (eds) *Proceedings of Workshop on Socio-economic Dimensions of Livestock Production in the Communal Lands of Zimbabwe. 12-14 September. 1988.* Centre for Applied and Social Sciences. University of Zimbabwe. Harare. Zimbabwe.

Senyatso, E.K. 1986. The Effect of Season of Lambing on Sheep Production in Botswana. In: P.J. Boyle ed. *Proceedings of a SACCAR Workshop on Smallholder Dairy, Small Ruminants, Pig, Poultry and Rabbit Production in the SADCC Countries. 26-27 November 1986.* SACCAR Workshop Series No. 4. Gaborone. Botswana. : 43-45.

Shumba, E.M. 1984. Reduced tillage in the communal areas. *Zimbabwe Agricultural Journal.* Vol. 81 No.6. : 235-240.

Sibanda, R. 1988. The Potential of the Indigenous Goat. In: J. Harrison (ed) *Proceedings of Workshop on Goat Development. 11-13 January 1988.* French Embassy. Harare. Zimbabwe. : 139-144.

Tembo, S. and K.M. Elliot. 1987. *The State of Use and On-going Research on Draught Animals Power (DAP) in Zimbabwe.* Paper presented at a workshop on Animal Traction and Agricultural Mechanisation Research in SADCC. 10-14 August 1987. SACCAR. Gaborone. Botswana.

Van Eckert, M. and B. Mombeshora. 1988. Livestock Production in Zimbabwe's Communal Lands. In: B. Cousins, C. Jackson and I. Scoones (eds) *Proceedings of Workshop on Socio-economic Dimensions of Livestock Production in the Communal Lands of Zimbabwe. 12-14 September 1988.* Centre for Applied and Social Sciences. University of Zimbabwe. Harare. Zimbabwe.

Zimbabwe Government. 1986. *Zimbabwe National Household Survey Capability Programme (1986)* Agriculture and Livestock Survey of Communal Lands. Prepared by Central Statistics Office. Harare. Zimbabwe.

# VI

## Access To Food: Nutrition Research, Feeding Refugees, And Coping With Drought

# 21

# Nutrition Strategies
# In Malawi

*Louis A.H. Msukwa*[1]

## INTRODUCTION

*We, the Principal Secretaries and Heads of Institutions directly
concerned and entrusted with the responsibility of administering,
managing and promoting a public service that ensures sound socio-
economic development that will provide for all Malawians the basic
necessities of life........ note with concern that malnutrition amongst
children is still a problem that can jeopardise the future well being
of our nation.* (Malawi, 1986).

Malnutrition is probably the biggest development problem the third world countries
are facing. A shorthand expression for the ultimate cause of malnutrition is
"poverty". In this context, poverty refers not only to inadequate household income
or purchasing power but also the lack of resources in general. These resources may
include access to suitable agriculture land or other forms of employment, the level
of education, knowledge or technology, access to the means for preventive and
curative health care, and the existence of adequate time or household labour supply
(CSR, 1988a). In short the malnutrition problem is a development problem and
can only be solved in a development context.

Several studies in Malawi have shown that chronic Protein Energy Malnutrition
(PEM) is widespread. In addition to PEM, anaemia, vitamin A deficiencies and
goitre, other nutritional problems are prevalent in Malawi. According to Ministry
of Health statistics, nutritional deficiencies rank third among the ten leading causes
of death in children accounting for 11,2 percent of all child deaths in hospitals and
are a contributing factor in most of the remaining causes. Anaemia affects 15 to 25
percent of pregnant women and poor maternal nutrition is a factor in the high
incidences of low birth weight (Malawi Government, Ministry of Health, 1986).

The purpose of this paper is to briefly describe the various major studies that have
led to our current understanding of the nature of the nutritional problems, followed

ocial Research, Zomba, Malawi.

by a discussion of the strategies Malawi has taken over the years to deal with the problem.[2]

## AN OVERVIEW OF NUTRITIONAL RESEARCH IN MALAWI

The first major nutritional research undertaken in Malawi was carried out in 1938-39 in Nkhotakota district and two urban centres of Zomba and Blantyre. This study included food intake measurements for each of the three rural villages and three socio-economic groups in the urban areas (Platt, 1940). In all the survey areas, it was found that consumption of protein was enough to meet the daily requirements while there was an overall shortfall of calorie intake, over the ten month period of the survey. the overall deficit was 8,2 percent for the rural villages and -1,4; -1,5 and -26,6 percent for the well-to-do, moderate means and poor urban household respectively. For the rural villages, it was found that highest calorie intake deficit (-28,5 percent) was in January and the highest surplus (+17,2 percent) was recorded in July, a period immediately after harvest. A final interesting finding was that women and infants recorded the highest calorie intake deficit (-27,8 percent) compared with +4,6 percent for adult males -1,3 percent for boys 16 to 20 years old and -0,8 percent for girls aged 16 to 20 years (Platt, 1940).

### Table 1
### Monthly fluctuations of calorie intake

| Month | Requirements | Intake | Difference |
|-------|-------------|--------|------------|
| December | 2 245 | 2 130 | - 5,1% |
| January | 2 208 | 1 580 | -28,5% |
| February | 2 022 | 2 006 | - 0,8% |
| March | 2 115 | 1 721 | -18,6% |
| April | 1 967 | 1 722 | -12,4% |
| May | 1 573 | 1 401 | -11,0% |
| June | 1 895 | 1 786 | - 5,8% |
| July | 1 966 | 2 304 | +17,2% |
| August | 1 620 | 1 617 | - 0,2% |
| September | 1 843 | 1 691 | - 8,2% |
| Average over ten months | 1 942 | 1 784 | - 8,2% |

Source: Platt (1940).

The general conclusion from this pioneering survey is that the greatest nutritional problem was inadequate calorie intake and that the problem was highest during the period just before harvest. Secondly, the urban poor had the highest overall deficit and finally, women and infants had the highest calorie intake deficit.

rition in Malawi see for example M
status as revealed throug

**Table 2**
**Comparison of calorie value of recorded dietaries and
allowances for energy expenditure**

| Age - Sex group | Requirements | Intake | Difference |
|---|---|---|---|
| Men | 2 483 | 2 597 | + 4,6% |
| Women and infants | 2 608 | 1 883 | -27,8% |
| Boys  16 - 20 years | 2 752 | 2 788 | + 1,3% |
| Girls 16 - 20 years | 2 551 | 2 531 | - 0,8% |
| Boys  10 - 16 years | 1 903 | 1 387 | -27,1% |
| Girls 10 - 16 years | 1 974 | 2 087 | - 5,7% |
| Children 2 - 10 years | 1 337 | 1 441 | - 7,8% |

Source: Platt, (1940).

In 1970 a survey was undertaken by the Ministry of Health in the Lower Shire region. This was a cross-sectional survey which included anthropometric measurements of 547 children under five and 543 adults. The study showed that 44 percent of the under fives were underweight -- ranging from 18 percent among the 0,5 month age group to 65 percent among the 12 to 17 month olds. In the same survey it was found that 12 percent males and 13 percent of females aged 5 to 19 years had a weight for height below 80 percent of standard. Among adults, 14 percent males and 8 percent females were underweight (Malawi Government, Ministry of Health, 1970).

The most comprehensive data on nutritional status in Malawi was collected in the 1981-82 National Sample Survey of Agriculture. The results of this nationwide survey were published in 1984 by the National Statistical Office in three volumes. The Centre of Social Research undertook a further analysis of the data, relating nutritional status to several other variables (CSR, 1988a). The findings of this survey are in several respects, similar to the findings of the 1938-39 study in Nkhotakota. The most important finding of the 1938-39 and 1981-82 studies is that the incidence of malnutrition is highest during the period just before harvest and that the major problem is inadequate calorie intake. During the pilot phase of the NSSA, nutrient intake was also measured and it was found that protein intake was generally adequate.

But the NSSA analysis undertaken by the Centre of Social Research has gone beyond previous surveys. An attempt was made to isolate the most important characteristics of the nutritionally vulnerable sub-groups within the smallholder sector. It is clear from the analysis that the underlying causes of malnutrition could be summed up in one word -- poverty. Small land holdings, low cash incomes, poor access to improved water and sanitary facilities, lack of access to extension services, low educational levels, inadequate labour, low meal frequency, morbidity, *etc.*, are all associated with malnutrition (CSR, 1988).

Apart from the three studies described above, the Centre for Social Research undertook several nutritional surveys between 1982 and 1988, including the three year (1986 to 1989) prospective study, the Malawi Maternal and Child Nutrition

Study (MMCN).[3] The results of these studies do confirm the major findings of the above: an incidence of low weight for age, ranging from 21 to 47 percent, depending on the area and season of the survey, and a prevalence of stunting of between 45 percent and 65 percent. The statistics collected through the Maternal and Child Health services also confirm these figures.

The major cause of malnutrition in Malawi could be described as lack of access to adequate food for the majority of households during certain parts of the year. This leads to low meal frequencies. In the NSSA pilot survey, it was revealed that average meal frequency was only 1,6. In a 1988-89 survey undertaken in Thyolo District, we found that, in the months immediately before harvest, only 2,1 percent of the households had one meal or less per day. This proportion increased to 40,7 percent just at the beginning of the rains (November/December) and to 56,8 percent just before harvest (February/March). The main reason for reduced meal frequency is early depletion of food in storage. As can be seen from Table 3 below, over 55 percent of households interviewed depleted their 1987-88 harvest after five months.

### Table 3
### After how many months was food crop depleted?
### (1987-88 season)

| Month | Number of households | % of households | Cum. % |
|---|---|---|---|
| <2 months | 67 | 11,1 | 11,1 |
| 2 - 3 months | 149 | 24,7 | 35,8 |
| 4 - 5 months | 118 | 19,5 | 55,3 |
| 6 - 8 months | 107 | 17,7 | 73,0 |
| After 8 months | 91 | 15,1 | 88,1 |
| Did not deplete | 72 | 11,9 | 100,0 |
| Total | 604 | 100,0 | |

Source: Msukwa (1989 : Table 4.10).

As we have pointed out elsewhere (Msukwa, 1984), the main reason for the inability to produce enough food is the lack of access to adequate land coupled with poor access to agricultural inputs, including agricultural extension. Coping strategies for those unable to produce enough include sharing with other relatives, incurring debts, seeking casual labour, *etc*. However, because these strategies do not give them adequate food, the majority resort to changing the composition and frequency of meals (Peters and Herrera, 1989).

## STRATEGIES FOR DEALING WITH MALNUTRITION

Over the years, the Malawi Government has developed a number of programmes aimed at improving nutrition. These programmes are carried out by various

---

[3]For details on these studies see Msukwa (1983); Ettema and Msukwa (1985); CSR (1988b) and Peters and Herrera (1989).

ministries, departments and voluntary organisations. One such programme which can directly affect nutrition is the Maternal and Child Health Programme (MCH). One of the objectives of MCH services is to improve the nutritional status of children by reducing the incidence of underweight children through regular growth monitoring, nutrition education, food supplementation and rehabilitation of the severely malnourished children.

Clinic coverage in Malawi is, by African standards, impressive. During the NSSA survey, it was found that 50 percent of all under five and 75 percent of all under two had a growth monitoring card. In a recent survey in Thyolo Highlands, nearly 68 percent of all under five had a growth monitoring card. It is through the under fives' clinic programme that the clinic feeding programme (CFP) is implemented. This programme aims at giving supplementary food to children judged to be at risk according to their weight for age, their recent pattern of growth and clinical judgement.

Our analysis of NSSA shows that out of 1 382 underweight children (weight for age under 80 percent of normal), only 230 or 17 percent were on a supplementary feeding programme. However, a total of 478 children were on supplementary feeding which means that only 48 percent of children on supplementary feeding were below 80 percent weight for age. But the CFP is aimed at treating malnutrition rather than preventing it. The most important programme aimed at preventing malnutrition is nutrition education which is carried out by the Ministry of Health and the Private Hospital Association through clinics; the Ministry of Community Services through the Home Economics Programme in conjunction with the Ministry of Local Government, the Ministry of Agriculture, Ministry of Education and Culture, and various church organisations and voluntary agencies.

In the CSR evaluation of these programmes, we found that apart from MCH clinics, coverage by other ministries and organisations was very low. In fact, only 23 percent of women included in the surveys had ever attended a nutritional class other than talks given at MCH clinics, which was 77 percent (Muskwa, 1983 and 1984).

Apart from the low coverage, nutrition education has been ineffective. In spite of the results of the various studies given below, until recently nutrition education has been based on an assumption that households had access to adequate food but lacked the knowledge to prepare balanced diets to ensure good nutrition. The nutrition education offered in the country has also been based on a wrong assumption that "the main food deficiency in the country is protein deficiency and that animal protein was better than vegetable protein". Yet the results from surveys have shown that protein intake in the normal Malawian diet was adequate. The source of the error on the adequacy of food arose out of the notion that Malawi as a nation was self-sufficient in maize production even though nutrition research findings as early as 1940 had demonstrated that many families went hungry a good part of the year. These families did not seem to have been taken into account when developing nutrition education programmes. There is some evidence that this has been due to poor dissemination of nutrition research findings and the lack of a strong lead institution. For example, the Interministerial Food and Nutrition Committee that was established in the 1970s to coordinate nutritional activities was ineffective due to inadequate resources. Malnutrition has been everybody's business but nobody's main responsibility. The political sensitivity of malnutrition and the

whole question of food security is another factor that has prevented the earl
incorporation of research findings into nutritional programmes.

Low coverage and inappropriate messages are two of the factors that have rendered
conventional nutritional interventions ineffective in the past. With wide coverage
appropriate targeting and relevant messages, the traditional areas for nutritiona
intervention can have considerable direct impact on the nutritional status of the
population. However, Malawi has now come to the conclusion that in order to solve
the nutritional problem, more has to be done than just traditional interventions. I
is now recognised that improved nutrition is a central goal of development and tha
it is affected by the overall development process. Therefore, apart from devising
mechanisms for dealing with short-term acute nutritional problems caused by natura
disasters, short- and long-term strategies have to be adopted to tackle chronic foo
insecurity especially among the lowest income groups. Such long term solutions are
to be found, in part, through rapid and sustained economic development.

Thus significant advancements have been made in recent years in elevating the
importance of nutrition in national development planning. This has stemmed from
advocacy initiatives which have been supported by better information (Quinn and
Chiligo, 1988). A number of events have taken place in Malawi that have led to the
current importance now given to nutritional problems. These include the holding
of a nutrition workshop organised by the Interministerial Food and Nutrition
Committee which, among other things, recommended an evaluation of the Nutrition
Education Programmes. A second workshop was held in 1984 at which the result
of the Nutrition Education Evaluation were presented. The publication of the
National Sample Survey of Agriculture and Nutritional maps, based on NSSA data
in 1984 and 1986 respectively, helped to call attention to malnutrition in Malawi
The climax of activities to promote public policy debate on nutrition was the
convening of an Interministerial Symposium on Nutrition and Development for
Principal Secretaries in August of 1986. As a result of all these important polic
statements, strategies for dealing with the problem have been outlined. A review o
these is provided below.

## RECENT POLICY STATEMENTS AND STRATEGIES
## FOR DEALING WITH MALNUTRITION

A number of resolutions were made at the 1986 Principal Secretaries Symposium on
Nutrition and Development. The following are relevant to the topic under
discussion:

o   review of existing land tenure systems as they relate to agricultura
     productivity and nutrition;

o   impact of removal of government subsidies on smallholder production

o   after reaching a consensus that Malawi is experiencing rapid population
     growth vis-a-vis the general level of national income, the socio-economi
     infrastructure that Government is able to provide and availability of foo
     to the rural and urban population, it was resolved to intensify the chil
     spacing programme and to have the Economic Planning and

Development Department coordinate the formulation of a population policy;

o   technical ministries responsible for development activities should devise deliberate policies and programmes that will alleviate the burden shouldered by women;

o   steps be undertaken to review frequently conditions of service (of those employed) in line with changing economic factors and devise agricultural programmes that will focus on a number of alternative cash and food crops for both large and small holdings so as to improve the levels and distribution of income;

o   emphasis in production and extension programmes should be made on the importance of other food items (apart from maize) and to intensify production of food crops related to ecological zones of Malawi;

o   a nutrition section responsible for planning, coordinating and evaluating nutritional programmes be located in the Economic Planning and Development Department in the Office of the President and Cabinet (as opposed to the Ministry of Agriculture);

o   research results on crop storage technologies be disseminated to the entrepreneurs who can develop and market the technologies to farmers;

o   due to low coverage of existing nutrition extension services, existing facilities should be strengthened and the primary health care programme be implemented expeditiously;

o   to increase nutritional awareness, a specific week during the year termed "Nutrition Week", be identified. Such a period can be used to increase the nation's knowledge of the steps and actions necessary to prevent malnutrition.

These resolutions have been given in full so as to show how serious the Principal Secretaries took the problem of malnutrition and their recognition of the fact that the problem was not only for the Ministry of Health but for every ministry and organisation concerned with development. This is clearly shown in the diversity of the resolutions. A number of strategies were proposed for dealing with the concern of each of the resolutions. Some of these strategies have been or are being implemented. The most important strategy is the establishment of the Food Security and Nutrition Unit in the Office of the President and Cabinet. The second is the agricultural and rural development strategies being proposed to increase the productivity of the smallest of smallholders and to increase their income.

The Food Security and Nutrition Unit was created in the Economic Planning and Development Department in 1987. Part of the Unit's mandate is to review the food and nutritional implications of current and planned policies, as well as to develop a surveillance system to monitor the food and nutrition situation at both the national and household levels. Recently, the Unit produced its first "Food and Nutrition Bulletin". The bulletin was presented to the top development policy-making body, the National Development Council.  Apart from presenting an analysis of the national food situation, the Bulletin goes on to state:

> Even during years of relatively good harvest, a significant number of urban and rural households are faced with chronic food insecurity as they are neither able to procure nor purchase enough food to satisfy their families' minimum food requirements ...... Close to one third of all children born do not survive to reach their fifth birthday, and of those who do survive, 55 percent suffer from chronic malnutrition .... To ensure the good nutrition of all the population, planners must also work towards ensuring that households have sufficient access to adequate quantities of maize in order to satisfy their nutritional requirements.  Without enhancement of incomes of the poor, or some alternative entitlement scheme, reaching higher production targets could generate large and expensive national maize surpluses ..... Increasing the ability of the poor to buy food is equally as important as producing these higher quantities.

On the general development front, the Government undertook a review of the National Rural Development Programme in July 1988.  The review concluded:

> ..... if methods could be found to create more modest increases in the production of the majority of smallholder farmers, this would better serve the dual objectives of increasing national production levels as well as household incomes.

Following this review, there is a proposal for a pilot project aimed at improving food security and the nutritional situation of food-deficit households -- mostly those with small landholdings.  The objectives of this pilot scheme are:

a)    Improved productivity of food crops by expanding smallholder credit to give poorer food-deficit families better access to small amounts of credit for fertilizer; and

b)    Assisting families to gain access to additional sources of income, through work programmes in which participants are remunerated in kind, wage employment, and self-employment.

Although these initiatives and similar ones like the Pilot Credit Scheme for the landless (Malawi Mudzi Fund) and the Social Dimensions of Adjustment Project are somewhat late, they are a tangible demonstration that Malawi has come to recognise the malnutrition problem as primarily a development problem whose solution lay in sustained development.  A start has been made and everyone realises it will not be an easy path to the goal of good nutrition for everyone.  The short-, medium- and long-term goals spelt out in various government policy documents, including the Statement of Development Policy 1987-1996, and the National Health Plan of Malawi 1986-1995 will require the efforts of everyone concerned, the government local development agencies, international organisations and research community.

## The Role of Research

Apart from the Food Security and Nutrition Unit documents, none of the documents give adequate emphasis to the importance of research in solving the malnutrition problem. Unless research becomes an integral part of strategies for solving the nutritional problem, these new initiatives might not fare any better than the NRDP. Rukuni and Eicher (1987) posed an important overall research question *how to assure adequate consumption of food for the entire population throughout the year at the least possible cost?* This question needs to be asked continuously because circumstances do change with time and a relevant reply to the question today may not be so tomorrow. Specific research questions which will need to be constantly asked if the strategies are to succeed include:

o  what are the characteristics of the vulnerable groups and why are they vulnerable?

o  how do these individuals, families or groups survive. In other words, what are their survival mechanisms?

o  what can be done to reduce their vulnerability and how should it be done?

o  how do existing social, economic and health policies affect these groups?

o  how do the programmes specifically designed for the vulnerable groups affect them (monitoring and evaluation)?

Social scientists, agriculturalists, technologists, *etc.*, will all have to participate because the problem of malnutrition is multi-faceted. It has to do with technology, economics, as well as people's behaviour. The contribution of every discipline in the research programme would be necessary. Not only will the various disciplines have to work together but researchers will have to work closely with the policy makers and implementers. This is the only way we can avoid the past mistakes -- preaching to people to eat more meat when they have no access to meat. Research as far back as 1938 has shown that the problem was not protein but calorie deficiency.

## REFERENCES

Ayoade, R.B. 1987. *Child Health and Nutrition.* A Ministry of Agriculture and Health paper presented at a Workshop on Child Raising Practices. 22-27 November. Highlands Hotel. Blantyre.

Blantyre, A.D.D. 1987. *Preliminary Assessment of the Food Situation and the Impact of Agricultural (General Purpose) Act.* Working Paper 5/87. Blantyre.

Centre for Social Research (CSR). 1986. *Nutrition Problems in Malawi.* Paper presented at the Nutrition Symposium. 31 July to 2 August. University of Malawi. Zomba.

Centre for Social Research (CSR). 1988a. *The Characteristics of Nutritionally Vulnerable Sub-groups within the Smallholder Sector of Malawi.* A report from the 1980-81 NSSA. University of Malawi. Zomba.

Centre for Social Researoh (CSR). 1988b. *Report of Workshop on Household Food Security and Nutrition.* Zomba 28 - 31 August. Centre for Social Research. Zomba.

Ettema, W. and L.A.H. Msukwa. 1985. *Food Production and Malnutrition in Malawi*. Centre for Social Research. Zomba.

Greenberg, C.J. 1978. *Nutrition Problems and Programmes in Malawi*. Paper prepared for Primary Health Care Seminar, Lilongwe.

Malawi Government, Ministry of Health. 1986. *The National Health Plan 1986 - 1995*. Ministry of Health. Lilongwe.

Malawi Government, Ministry of Health. 1986. *Interministerial Symposium on Nutrition and Development for Principal Secretaries*. 31 July to 2 August. 1986. Vol. I. Resolution and Minutes. Ministry of Health. Lilongwe.

Malawi Government, 1987. *Statement of Development Policies 1987-1996*. Economic Planning and Development. Lilongwe.

Malawi Government, Food Security Unit. 1989. *Food Security and Nutrition Bulletin*. Vol. 1, No.1. Office of the President and Cabinet. Lilongwe.

Msukwa, L.A.H. 1983. *Nutrition Education in Malawi*. A preliminary report on the Evaluation of Nutrition Education. Centre for Social Research. Zomba.

Msukwa, L.A.H. 1984. Agriculture and Nutrition. In: Centre for African Studies (ed) *Proceedings of Conference Malawi: An Alternative Pattern of Development*. University of Edinburgh.

Msukwa, L.A.H. 1989. *The Work of Malamulo Hospital : An Evaluation Report*. Centre for Social Research. Zomba.

Mtimuni, B.M. (undated) *Nutrition Problems and Programmes in Malawi*. Presented at Workshop on Design and Implementation of Rural development Strategies and Programmes. Bunda College of Agriculture. Lilongwe.

Ounpuu, S. 1988. *Seasonality, Child Nutrition and Women's Activity Patterns*. A case study in Chilunga Village, Malawi. MSc. Thesis, University of Guelph.

Peters, E.P. and Herrera, G. 1989. *Cash Cropping, Food Security and Nutrition : The Effects of Agricultural Commercialisation among Smallholders in Malawi*. Final Report to USAID. Harvard Institute for International Development. Cambridge. USA.

Platt, B.S. 1940. Report of a Nutrition Survey in Nyasaland. (unpublished).

Quinn, V. and M. Chiligo. 1988. *Food and Nutritional Surveillance in Malawi : Past Experiences and Future Directions*. Presented at the Third African Food and Nutrition Congress, 5-8 September. Harare.

Rukuni, M. and C.K. Eicher (eds) 1987. *Food Security for Southern Africa*. UZ/ MSU Food Security Project. University of Zimbabwe. Harare.

# 22

# Regional Experience In Food Supplies For Refugees And Drought Situations

*P.L. Simkin[1]*

In the short space available, it will only be possible to deal superficially with some of the issues which the World Food Programme and other donor agencies have been involved with in the procurement and distribution of food supplies to refugees, displaced populations and drought victims in the past year.

In 1987-88 there were large-scale movements of maize from Zimbabwe for drought relief and the market deficits in Zambia, Malawi and Mozambique. Most of this was provided in the form of food aid purchased by Western donor countries and aid agencies. The World Food Programme helped to coordinate the purchase and road transportation of almost 200 000 tonnes to these countries.

There have been two successive years of good rains in the region and, as a result, Zambia moved into a export surplus situation with between an estimated four to six hundred thousand metric tonnes of maize available for export in 1989. In addition Zambia national reserve stocks are reported to have been restored to the quarter of a million tonne level. Some 30 000 tonnes of maize have been purchased from Zambia by international agencies for Malawi, but there are severe shortages of storage and internal transport in Zambia and this has resulted in significant storage losses. There could be serious effects on future production if the producers' cooperatives are unable to sell their surplus stocks. In the meantime efforts are being made to implement a programme to store maize under tarpaulins on concrete plinths.

In Malawi the 1987 crop deficit was brought about by a combination of factors including drought, mealie-bug infestation of the cassava crop in the lake shore areas, reduction in the fertilizer subsidies and a massive influx of refugees from Mozambique. The national strategic grain reserve dropped from 220 000 tonnes in April 1987 to 12 000 tonnes in 1988 in spite of the fact that over 120 000 metric tonnes of maize were imported in the same period.

The recovery of the food supply situation in Malawi has been more gradual. The Mozambican refugee population has continued to grow at an alarming rate and by mid-1989 had reached over 730 000. The 1988 cropping season was characterised

[1]World Food Programme, Area Director, Southern Africa.

by heavy rains which produced water-logging and severe flooding in the lower Shire Valley. Many areas still suffer from mealy-bug infestation of the cassava crop although in a much less severe form than the 1987 infestation. Nevertheless it has been possible for the Government to purchase over 70 000 tonnes of the 1988-89 maize crop and use this to start to rebuild the strategic grain reserve in the Lilongwe silos.

Maize supplies for refugees are, however, still being imported into Malawi and this will probably continue into 1990 until the strategic reserve has been rebuilt to quarter of a million tonnes. It could then probably be considered safe for donors to restart purchases of refugee maize requirements in Malawi. Malawi has allowed the 730 000 refugees to inter-settle with existing Malawian communities living along its border with Mozambique. In view of the population pressures on land in Malawi, there is no possibility of allocating agricultural or grazing land to refugees. However, in some parts of the border in the Dedza and Ntcheu districts refugees cultivate crops in Mozambique, but return to Malawi at night. This enables about 10 000 families to supplement their food aid rations with their own produce.

Only in Zambia has it been possible to implement successful agricultural settlements for refugees at Maheba and Ukwimi, where the majority are rapidly achieving self-sufficiency. Elsewhere refugees in Malawi, Zimbabwe and Swaziland are almost entirely dependent on food aid provided by the international community. This aid is coordinated jointly by UNHCR and WFP, but there have been gaps in deliveries of certain commodities. The risk of these occurring would be reduced if all donors made their food aid pledges for refugee feeding to one agency. In Zimbabwe, where there are 80 000 Mozambican refugees in four strictly controlled camps, the daily ration for each refugee is 400 grams maize meal; 20 grams vegetable oil, 30 grams beans, 30 grams dried fish, with supplementary feeding for vulnerable groups of 20 grams sugar and 40 grams of DSM. Because of difficulties in obtaining beans for local purchase in the region, WFP imported 320 metric tonnes sultani PYE beans from Burma. There are, however, acceptability problems with this commodity. The refugees consider that these beans have a bitter flavour and cause stomach upsets. Consequently, no beans or pulses were issued for several months before substitute pulses could be purchased and distributed to the refugee camps.

In Malawi refugees are given either 450 grams whole maize or 400 grams maize meal, 40 grams beans, 40 grams groundnuts and supplementary feeding for vulnerable groups. This ration does not include dried fish because there are insufficient resources to provide this. Moreover, it has proved impossible to buy the full requirements of groundnuts in Malawi and there have been gaps in supply while shipments were procured from other countries. The resource situation for both purchasing and shipping food for refugees has been and continues to be precarious. Without timely pledges from donors it is simply not possible to build up the reserve stocks which would provide a fall-back position when gaps in supply occur. If refugees are not given land to produce their own crops, they are entirely dependent on international food aid with all the uncertainties in supply. Recently, the World Food Programme's governing body, the Committee on Food Aid Policies and Programmes (CFA) recognised that it is no longer appropriate to provide food assistance to refugees from emergency resources. Protracted refugee situations need to be supported with development activities to improve the skills, education, health and food production of refugees. As more and more demands compete for limited donor resources, Government requests for assistance to refugees will be expected to address the need for such development aspects.

The general scarcity of international donor resources is even more pronounced in the case of Mozambique. It is estimated that Mozambique has food aid importation requirements for the 1989-90 marketing year of 597 000 metric tonnes maize 147 000 metric tonnes wheat and 64 000 metric tonnes rice.

In contrast, four of Mozambique's neighbours -- South Africa, Tanzania, Zambia and Zimbabwe -- are embarrassed by the sheer size of their maize surpluses. Some maize is being purchased in Zimbabwe and sent by truck via Malawi to Niassa, Zambezia and Tete provinces of Mozambique, but the limitations of the railways to move significant quantities to the coastal cities of Beira (approximately 7 000 metric tonnes per month) and Maputo indicate that unless more locomotives and trucks are made available, the bulk of Mozambique's maize requirements will have to be brought in by ship. Zimbabwe's maize export price has been reduced from US$190 to US$150 per tonne for the past 12 months and although this is well above the current export price of South African maize, it is considered to be a competitive price for northern and central Mozambique.

To conclude, it is clear that given the necessary credit for buying fertilizer and hybrid maize seed, access to markets and fair producer prices, small scale farmers have demonstrated that they can produce large maize surpluses in average rainfall years. There also seems to be no doubt that this would also apply to Mozambique and Angola if peace is restored. However, the vulnerability of small-scale farmers to drought also requires safety nets and these can best be provided by on-going food for work programmes which could be rapidly expanded in times of crop failure and so avoid all the disincentives which free drought relief food hand-outs have in chronic deficit areas. Population pressures on land in some areas like the south of Malawi mean that there will be always large numbers of families who need to supplement their production by seeking work and this can best be provided by organised labour-intensive programmes on such activities as soil conservation, reforestation, trench agriculture, dam and access road building. The international community should assist countries that produce surpluses to store and export these. The danger which Tanzania, Zambia and Zimbabwe now face is that they will be unable to sell their current surpluses. This could depress next season's producer prices and set another deficit cycle in motion.

Lastly, it is obvious that future crisis management will not only depend upon adequate grain stocks in the region, but also on improving the regional transportation capacity to rapidly move maize to affected areas.